Praise for Sinclair McKay:

'One of my favourite historians'
Dan Snow, *History Hit*

'I loved this book, apposite and wise'
David Aaronovitch, *The Times*, on *Berlin*

'Powerful, grips by its passion and originality'
Max Hastings, *Sunday Times*, on *Dresden*

'Fascinating, riveting, unsettling and wonderfully
rich in period detail'
Craig Brown, *Mail on Sunday*, on *The Mile End Murder*

'Lucid, well-researched and rich in detail'
John Preston, *Daily Mail*, on *The Spies of Winter*

'A truly breathtaking, eye-opening book'
A. N. Wilson, *Reader's Digest*, on *The Secret Life of
Bletchley Park*

T0332091

Meeting Churchill

A Life in 90 Encounters

SINCLAIR McKAY

PENGUIN BOOKS

PENGUIN BOOKS

UK | USA | Canada | Ireland | Australia
India | New Zealand | South Africa

Penguin Books is part of the Penguin Random House group of companies
whose addresses can be found at global.penguinrandomhouse.com

Penguin Random House UK,
One Embassy Gardens, 8 Viaduct Gardens, London SW11 7BW

penguin.co.uk
global.penguinrandomhouse.com

Penguin
Random House
UK

First published by Viking 2023
Published in Penguin Books 2024
001

Typeset by Jouve (UK), Milton Keynes
Printed and bound in Great Britain by Clays Ltd, Elcograf S.p.A.

The authorized representative in the EEA is Penguin Random House Ireland,
Morrison Chambers, 32 Nassau Street, Dublin D02 YH68

A CIP catalogue record for this book is available from the British Library

ISBN: 978-1-405-96255-1

To my brilliant mother Helen

Contents

Introduction

Winston Leonard Spencer Churchill was a reality star. His long life – constantly intense and extraordinarily full – was also a lifelong performance. This is not intended as criticism. From his defining turn-of-the-century experiences on the heat-hazed battlefields of Empire and in the freezing trenches of World War One, to his inspirational leadership throughout World War Two and the quite extraordinary body of writing – Nobel Prize-winning – that he produced before and after, here was a man who was consciously constructing the narrative of his own life even as he lived it.

At every step, he stopped to see who was looking. And if not enough people were looking, he worked to draw yet more attention to himself.

None of this is necessarily bad; it is undeniably the case that, in the days of darkest crisis, the starry lustre of his language and his bullish good humour brought infusions of optimism that genuinely drove the nation on, and conjured the deepest confidence that the evil of Nazism would be vanquished.

Churchill wove himself into the tapestry of history by immersing himself in the study of it. History was the frame for his understanding of the world and its ancient cycles of life and death and war. A compulsive reader, Churchill discovered for himself the classic eighteenth- and nineteenth-century works of Edward Gibbon and

Thomas Babington Macaulay – he 'devoured' and 'rode triumphantly through' *Decline and Fall of the Roman Empire* at the age of twenty and Macaulay's twelve-volume *The History of England* aged twenty-two, though he was taken aback at Macaulay's treatment of his famous forebear the Duke of Marlborough. Churchill used his own powerful prose to impress upon our own times a vast and extraordinarily detailed account of the war through which he led the nation. In his own eyes, he was – as his acquaintance Albert Einstein might have said – the point of singularity.

Nor does the term 'reality star' here indicate any kind of hollowness: Churchill was intensely human, brimming not only with vigour and vanity and wit, but also with the most acute sensitivity to romance and loss. His intemperate rages – especially those directed at other cultures – shocked those around him. Yet he could also be moved to tears by the cheapest black-and-white B-movie. He cried openly, and very frequently.

So how might the span of such a vast life, lived at such a level of intensity and observation, be encompassed in a short book? It is revealing to see that life through the eyes of others. The accounts from those whom Churchill met throughout his ninety years reveal an extraordinary range of impressions. Some were saucer-eyed with adoration; others were thrilled with his attentiveness; others still were more ambiguous, or indeed repulsed. This is true whether those meeting him were famous or perfectly ordinary. From Victorian school friends to fellow soldiers on bloody battlefields; from kings (and the Queen) to millworkers; from US presidents to 1960s show-business figures: every encounter reveals a facet of Churchill – a glint as though caught in a mirror – as well as an element of the person meeting him.

And as well as the better-known historic turning points, it is instructive to look at encounters in more everyday circumstances: the moments that formed the warp and weft of his personal life. For instance, his compulsion to stand out could sometimes be a shade eccentric. It might be said that he even designed costumes for himself; he had a fascination for unusual, very wide-brimmed hats for wear at leisure, and for square-rimmed bowlers in town. In the early 1900s, it was reported that one such hat – so unique in style – had so amazed his political opponents at a Manchester meeting that the city's gentlemen's hatters were thereafter besieged with requests for the same model. His overcoats had luxuriant astrakhan collars, the fur derived from lambskin. One female critic observed that he had to be dissuaded from designing his own military uniforms. He devised the first 'onesie' – a jumpsuit of his own invention, later termed a 'siren suit' because he wore it under the bombardment of the Blitz. Sometimes these siren suits were in khaki, sometimes in plush green velvet. In deeper repose, he favoured vast silk dressing gowns splashed with oriental designs and coloured richest emerald and ruby. Many who met him were mesmerized by this stage-like attire.

Image – and the cultivation of image – was of fantastic importance to Churchill. He did not just give speeches; he then had them re-recorded. His most famous oration, following the retreat from Dunkirk – 'we shall fight on the beaches' – was originally delivered to Parliament on 4 June 1940. Churchill himself then delivered the speech once more – four years after the war had ended – in 1949, as a recording that might be listened to by future generations. It was imperative to him that it was understood how he had shaped events. He was not leaving posterity to chance.

In this sense, Churchill – born in 1874, the early autumn of the Victorian era, and living right through to the apotheosis of the Rolling Stones in 1965 – was a pioneer modernist.

He was also the rare kind of politician that people could imagine themselves in the pub with. For this reason, people assumed that they knew his character. Even now, there is a sort of shorthand – darkest hour, V-signs, growling, sharp snappy comebacks – that is understood to form his essence. And yet look again: the people who did know him were seeing other qualities too.

In many contemporary accounts – from memoirs, diaries, letters – first impressions are captured, extraordinary tics revealed. In these, we see sometimes unexpected depths of self-doubt in Churchill; occasional moments of drink-fuelled malice; flashes of love, of loyal friendship, of burning intellectual curiosity. There are glimpses of the ugliest racism; but elsewhere, there are more human outbreaks of compassion.

In addition to all of this, there came a point in Churchill's life when – impossibly famous and toweringly powerful – he himself became a form of mirror, in which colleagues and friends and other leaders and celebrities, thinking they were gazing upon his neuroses and vanities, were in fact looking at their own.

His own modernist self-absorption did not necessarily make him a narcissist. It was genuinely to do with a sense of history, and the place that one man might take in that history. Nor did this of itself make him either a bad man or a good man. He could be both; sometimes simultaneously. But the point was about gripping the steering wheel of history, for good or for ill.

Through the years since his death in 1965, his historic reputation has frequently changed with the political tides. Currently, as a younger generation focuses fresh academic attention on hitherto unfamiliar angles of research, we are learning much more of Churchill the irredeemable and cold imperialist: the unapologetic racist and eugenicist who openly voiced the view that white Anglo-Saxon people were naturally superior to all other races.

We always knew that that Churchill was there; but such is this amazingly well-documented life – and such is the new digitized world of archives – that certain more elusive aspects of it can now be brought out in greater clarity, and at greater volume, as though on a mixing desk.

In today's world, Churchill is, to some, a vicious dinosaur: a man who wished to keep Empire alive because he sincerely believed that only he – and others like him – were fit to rule over distant regions of the earth. This Churchill is an adaptation of a previous model, in vogue throughout the 1980s: then, he was seen as an irresponsible blood-soaked warmonger, who ordered the aerial bombardment of helpless civilian populations and who – upon seeing the atomic horror unleashed upon Japan – wondered if the same might be inflicted on the lands behind the Iron Curtain, the image of which he had coined.

We would really have to go back to the Second World War – and the early 1950s, when he was returned to power as prime minister – to find the more benevolent Churchill, the 'grand old man ... wearing his famous bull-dog grin and smoking a big cigar' as the risqué music-hall comedian Max Miller sang.

But before that war, he was known among large working-class communities as the heartless aristocrat who sent in the troops to terrorize strikers. To this day, Churchill's actions at Tonypandy in 1910, and throughout the General Strike of 1926, have made him a byword for Tory callousness.

So for all the claims that Churchill has been subject to unhealthy hero worship across the decades, it is worth remembering that the opposite view was always there. And – like with any other complex, intricately patterned life – all these facets, as we shall see, are true.

Overture

4 August 1914 – When the Lamps Went Out

'Winston's vanity is septic,' wrote Margot Asquith of Churchill. 'He would die of blood poisoning if it were not for a great deal of red blood which circulates freely through his heart and stomach.'

Margot was the wife of Prime Minister H. H. [Herbert] Asquith. And she observed Churchill with a cold eye because he appeared to her to be electrified with excitement by war. This impression, shared by others, would come to define him in the years and decades to come.

Yet it is more than possible that, in her distaste, Mrs Asquith had fundamentally mistaken his grand-standing nature. In 1914, Churchill knew better than most the industrial-scale horrors that lay ahead. He was not blithe.

As a young man he had studied the craft of conflict as a subaltern at Sandhurst College, in the closing years of the nineteenth century. By that time, it was already apparent that an era of grand, chivalrous war, consisting of glitteringly decorated uniforms and flashing sabres and fine horses, had passed. More: it appeared that this was a new era of peace. Churchill and his fellow teenage trainee warriors at Sandhurst in 1893 were asking one another: How could there ever be a European war again?

'It did seem such a pity that it all had to be make-believe,' Churchill once said of his soldiering education, 'and that the age of wars between civilised nations had come to an end for ever. If it had only been 100 years earlier what splendid times we should have had! Fancy being nineteen in 1793 with more than twenty years of war against Napoleon in front of one! However, all that was finished. The British Army had never fired upon white troops since the Crimea [1853–6], and now that the world was growing so sensible and pacific – and so democratic too – the great days were over.'

This blend of teasing irony and quite genuine romanticism, written years later, was lightly deployed; yet it underlined his sense of the darkness to come.

On 4 August 1914, war was about to acquire a whole new meaning. In the wake of the German invasion of Belgium, there was continent-wide heart-pounding apprehension; the Foreign Office Rolls-Royce was drawing up outside the German embassy, and over in Berlin, a shouting, shrieking crowd outside the British embassy were aiming stones and bricks at its windows. Ultimatums were delivered, and without wider consultation, Churchill – now First Lord of the Admiralty with responsibility for the Royal Navy – had readied fleets of British warships making their way to the anchorage at Scapa Flow in the Orkneys.

Margot Asquith was present with her family in Downing Street on the night as the clock ticked closer to war. It had been a day of telegrams and dread. She, her husband, and all those gathered in the Cabinet Rooms were now awaiting the outbreak of war.

Aside from the distant muffled horns and bells of the river traffic on the Thames, the quiet of the evening was punctuated by the iron clangour of Big Ben. This was a night in which the waiting assumed its own terrible gravity. She was to record this moment in her memoir:

The clock on the mantelpiece hammered out the hour. I looked at the children asleep after dinner before joining Henry in the Cabinet room. Lord Crewe and Sir Edward Grey were already there and we sat smoking cigarettes in silence; some went out; others came in; nothing was said.

The clock on the mantelpiece hammered out the hour, and when the last beat of midnight struck it was as silent as dawn.

We were at War.

I left to go to bed, and, as I was pausing at the foot of the staircase, I saw Winston Churchill with a happy face striding towards the double doors of the Cabinet room.

Just months later, as the grotesque reality of that war had started to become apparent, Margot Asquith and Churchill were seated next to each other at a dinner. 'My God, this is living history,' he exclaimed to her. 'It will be read by a thousand generations . . . Why, I would not be out of this glorious, delicious war for anything the world could give me.' But then he added: 'I say, don't repeat that I said the word "delicious" – you know what I mean.' She clearly did not.

On that occasion, he did not express himself well. It is possible that after months and years of foreboding, the certainty of conflict had supercharged him with adrenaline. Certainly, like forest animals that sense the mighty forces clashing and trembling deep beneath the earth, and which accordingly become restive and agitated, Churchill had for some time detected the geopolitical tremors across Europe.

In 1912, he had warned in a letter to his cousin that 'it only needs a little ill will or bad faith' to precipitate terrible conflict between the great powers. On 28 June 1914, with the assassination of the chilly Archduke Franz Ferdinand and his wife in Sarajevo, that tectonic shift had finally occurred.

Churchill was among those who watched with a terrible fascination as the great powers assumed their positions: Austria–Hungary against Serbia, Germany with Austria–Hungary, Russia with Serbia. For some years beforehand, the ever-growing strength of Germany had inspired a vein of paranoid popular fiction in Britain, most notably in the spy thrillers of William Le Queux, which frequently featured villages and small towns being infiltrated by sinister Prussian agents intent on sabotage and mayhem. The Kaiser's realm was portrayed as uniquely, brutally intent upon stealing power and land, using low subterfuge as well as psychopathic violence.

In real life, the fear now focused upon Germany's intentions towards France. There were those in Britain who counselled neutrality. Because Churchill was not among them, he was accounted by some even at the time as a bloodthirsty warmonger.

On 28 July 1914, Churchill confessed in a letter to his wife, Clementine, that 'Everything trends towards catastrophe and collapse. I am interested, geared-up and happy. Is it not horrible to be built like that? The preparations have a hideous fascination for me. I pray to God to forgive me for such fearful moods of levity. Yet I would do my best for peace, and nothing would induce me wrongfully to strike the blow – I cannot feel that we in this island are in any serious degree responsible for the wave of madness which has swept the mind of Christendom . . .'

In terms of weird, terrible exultation, Churchill's

embarrassed admission was curiously echoed and reflected by a writer who might be thought in some ways to be his polar opposite. As the declarations of war echoed back and forth across borders, Stefan Zweig – a peace-loving Viennese essayist; in some senses the most perfect exemplar of the unified European sensibility – had initially watched with incredulity in Belgium as his friends started demonizing Germans. In Vienna, he observed 'the wild intoxication that mingled alcohol with the joy of self-sacrifice, a desire for adventure . . . the old magic of the banners and the patriotic speeches . . . To be perfectly honest, I must confess there was something fine, inspiring, even seductive in the first mass outburst of feeling.'

In this sense, the prelude to war feels not shadowed, but rather brightened with the current of revolution. All is about to be reordered; it is impossible not to feel excited.

Back in England, on what seemed to some like the periphery of this coming earthquake, Churchill could not disguise that jumpy, frenetic energy. Here was an imperialist who had already fought in India and Africa, and who appeared on the surface to have retained that youthful zeal for conflict. His alertness and readiness and apparent enthusiasm must have seemed a vulgar contrast to the sepulchral vision of Foreign Secretary Sir Edward Grey, who saw the lamps going out all over Europe.

Churchill's 'happy face', as described by Mrs Asquith, was frequently to be taken by many other people in the years to come – colleagues, enemies, friends – as an indication of his fundamental bellicosity. There would be others throughout the years, however – including his Labour opponent and World War Two deputy, Clement Attlee – who would see a more nuanced reality. And there were many women, too, to whom Churchill occasionally displayed his more vulnerable side. Margot Asquith clearly imagined that she had detected a broken moral compass. But this was not the case; in fact, the stark lessons of life and death and loss had been taught sternly to Churchill as a child.

Woom

Elizabeth Everest, 1879–89

Winston Churchill was born – reportedly some days prematurely – at Blenheim Palace on 30 November 1874, after his mother unexpectedly went into labour in the midst of a shooting party. It is sometimes said he was delivered in one of the palace's ten residential bathrooms. His father was politician and diplomat Lord Randolph Churchill, the third son of the Duke of Marlborough; his mother, Jennie Jerome, a one-time magazine editor, was from a family of American financiers. As was the case with upper-class families, a nanny was employed immediately. When Winston was a toddler, the family moved to Dublin; there Lord Randolph was to become secretary to his own father, the Duke of Marlborough, Viceroy of Ireland.

'You are not wise about money matters, my dear boy,' Churchill was told by his nanny, Mrs Elizabeth Everest, when he was still a dear boy.

He was considering swapping a bicycle repair kit for a more alarming purchase. She was having none of it. 'What on earth is the good of you having a bull-dog,' she demanded of him, 'unless it is to keep us all in fear of our lives?'

Yet this rebuke was the reverse of the fundamental truth of their relationship: that Elizabeth Everest was always fretful about little Winston's life and well-being. From the start, she was protective, and would remain so until her death twenty years later. She showed him a wider world than the one he knew. It was her world towards which his younger self cleaved.

She told him of her own home in Kent, and of how Kent was the finest of all counties. She told him 'its capital was Maidstone', and that around that town grew an abundance of 'strawberries, cherries, raspberries and plums'. Those words imprinted themselves indelibly; in the years to come, he would settle in his own dream home – Chartwell – amid the gentle orchard valleys of that Edenically conjured county.

In common with every child ever born, the infant Winston Churchill fiercely craved the nourishment of love. It was denied to him. His father seemed repulsed by him; at the very least, Lord Randolph's indifference was chillingly cold. According to the wildest rumours, possibly all human feeling had been extinguished by the liquid silver poison of mercury, which Randolph had been ingesting for his syphilis.

The apparent grandeur of Churchill's background could never quite make up for that absence of succour. His mother, Jennie, while warmer, was also abstracted and absent; the hunt balls and dinners of society consumed most of her attention. 'My mother always seemed to me a fairy princess,' wrote Churchill in his autobiography. 'She shone for me like the Evening Star. I loved her dearly – but at a distance.'

Before he was five, Churchill was adrift in a world of big, dark, draughty houses and harsh contemptuous words. His sanctuary was a large nursery; among his treasured toys was a model steam-engine set, and a magic lantern with a variety of slides. The rich colours in the darkness filled his imagination.

Elizabeth Everest was his one focal point of human

warmth; she had been taken on by the family a little after Churchill's birth in 1874. It was to her that the little boy Churchill would 'pour out [his] many troubles'. Mrs Everest was in her mid-forties (in that old-fashioned way, she was given the term of address 'Mrs' despite never having married). She was photographed in black, very much in the style of Queen Victoria: plump, with the shadow of a smile.

And she and the infant Churchill had adventures; but as the boy absorbed what seemed to him the vast world of Dublin's Phoenix Park his nanny could not disguise her own fears. Young Winston was, after all, the grandson of an essentially colonial administrator. 'Mrs Everest was nervous about the Fenians,' he later recalled. 'I gathered these were wicked people and there was no end to what they would do if they had their way. On one occasion when I was out riding on my donkey, we thought we saw a long dark procession of Fenians approaching. I am sure now it must have been the Rifle Brigade out for a route march. But we were all very much alarmed, particularly the donkey, who expressed his anxiety by kicking. I was thrown off and had concussion of the brain. This was my introduction to Irish politics!'

Throughout it all, Mrs Everest was always there, by his side through injury and fever. In this sense, she might be compared to the brilliant Peggotty in Dickens's *David Copperfield* – an unwavering moral compass point, not uneccentric, but also overflowing with love.

She told little Churchill how she had been with him as a baby on a trip to Paris, and how she had wheeled him up and down the 'Shams Elizzie'. Mrs Everest's nickname was 'Woom'; that was the closest baby Churchill could get to saying 'woman'.

But she did not just give the boy a sense of being loved; she tried to instil basic moral values too. On one occasion, as he wrote in a letter to his father (did he ever pay any heed to it?), little Churchill was out walking across a heath with Mrs Everest when they both spotted a snake moving through the grass. The boy Churchill's immediate instinct was to kill it, and it was Mrs Everest who stayed his hand. She told him that he should simply let the snake carry on with its business.

As Churchill reached the age of seven – with the shadows of an abusive boarding school and a sadistic head teacher addicted to flogging boys until 'they bled freely', as their fellows sat 'listening to their screams', creeping over his young life – Mrs Everest became the sole point of comfort in this new disorientating world of pain. It was she who rescued Churchill from the vicious establishment of St George's when, while on a few days' break at home, she glimpsed his lacerated flesh. Churchill's mother removed him from that school, sending him instead to the Misses Thomson's Preparatory School, by the sea in Hove, next to Brighton.

When Churchill wrote to Mrs Everest, he would offer 'one hundred thousand kisses'. On one occasion, aged around eleven and suffering from serious pneumonia, he wrote: 'I am feeling very weak. I feel as though I could cry at everything.'

Yet, despite her kindness, Mrs Everest was never shy of keeping young Churchill on what she considered the correct path; a more influential guide and teacher than either of his parents ever were. When it came to handing the young boy funds for what she saw as extravagances, Mrs Everest protested to Churchill's mother, insisting that she should not allow him to have money that he would simply throw away.

He repaid her steadfast affection with his own unabashed love; as a teenage pupil at Harrow, he invited her to Speech Day, and walked around the pretty hilltop village with her, arm in arm.

Winston's younger brother, Jack, was also her charge; but it was Winston who would retain his overwhelming love for her beyond childhood. As both boys reached a certain age, Mrs Everest was made redundant, with nothing in the way of care or solicitude from Churchill's parents. She found employment with one other family, and subsequently went to live with her sister in the realm of Mr Pooter: the north London suburb of Finsbury Park.

In 1895, word came to Churchill – by that time studying the art of war at Sandhurst – that she was ill. 'I travelled up to London to see her,' he recalled. 'She knew she was in danger, but her only anxiety was for me. There had been a heavy shower of rain. My jacket was wet. When she felt it with her hands she was greatly alarmed for fear I should catch cold. The jacket had to be taken off and thoroughly dried before she was calm again.'

It was Churchill who called in specialist doctors; that night, he had to return to Camberley by the midnight train from Waterloo, in order to be present for early morning parade. 'As soon as it was over, I returned to her bedside. She still knew me, but she gradually became unconscious. Death came very easily to her. She had lived such an innocent and loving life of service to others, and held such a simple faith, that she had no fears at all, and did not seem to mind very much.'

Churchill's father died the same year; both losses would haunt him dreadfully in different ways. He later dreamed that his father – who had throughout his life dismissed him – at last spoke to him properly as a ghost. Mrs Everest, though, represented the proper warmth of humanity. Churchill wrote of her: 'She had been my dearest and most intimate friend during the whole of the twenty years I had lived.' He naturally attended her funeral at the City of London Cemetery, Wanstead Flats, and thereafter paid for the upkeep of her headstone and burial plot.

Perhaps Mrs Everest, and her unbounded fine influence, gave him another virtue which – for the time – was relatively unusual. He was very much at ease in female company. For many men of his generation (and generations to come), what we might now term the patriarchal flavour of society was beyond question. Women did not have the vote. Indeed, Churchill himself was a latecomer to the idea of women's suffrage. Yet, unlike many of his peers, he was able to form warm, intellectually sparky friendships with a wide range of women throughout his life.

First, though, there was the matter of school.

Boy's Own

Leo Amery, 1886

After his preparatory education, Churchill – by his own admission not a natural academic – was sent to Harrow School, a village-like establishment on a hill overlooking distant London. And although he would later claim that Latin verb conjugations and calculus were horrors that he could not overcome, he nonetheless thrived under the benign headmaster Dr Welldon, finding fresh confidence and also forming surprisingly progressive views about education – including the use of magic lantern projection slides and films as lesson aids – which he would continue to promulgate throughout his life.

'There was one of my junior contemporaries of whom I saw comparatively little at Harrow, though a good deal more since, and (to quote his inscription in a volume of *The World Crisis*) "in ever varying relationship, but continual good will", namely Winston Churchill,' wrote Leo Amery, lifelong friend who would grant the world an insight into the young thug he first met at school.

'[Churchill] has, in his *Early Days*, described very amusingly our first encounter,' Amery recalled in his memoirs. 'I was standing at the edge of "Ducker", the school swimming pool, when I suddenly found myself propelled into the water by a foot in my back. I emerged spluttering to find that the perpetrator of this outrage upon my dignity as a sixth former was a red-haired, freckled urchin whom I had never seen before.'

Leo Amery – later Churchill's cabinet colleague, and like his friend a stout opponent of appeasement – described this first meeting with genuine warmth, though in terms of his immediate vengeance in the swimming pool he omitted one or two key facts. The first was that Churchill had yanked his towel off him before kicking him, naked, into the water. 'I had my immediate and thorough revenge on the purely physical plane when I caught him and made him accompany me into the water to learn respect for age and authority.' But by Churchill's recollection, the second omitted fact rather more pertinently involved Amery grabbing hold of Churchill and hurling him bodily into the deep end.

The lives of the two men would intertwine closely; both would be journalists at the time of the Second Boer War in 1899–1902 (where British and white Afrikaans fought bitterly in southern Africa, partly over gold deposits). Both would be in government (Churchill as Chancellor, Amery as Colonial Secretary) in the 1920s, and both would stand shoulder to shoulder in the shadowed 1930s, urging with all their might that Britain should be rearming urgently. By the 1940s, and World War Two, Amery would be the Secretary of State for India, and record with some repulsion his old friend's vehement views on the subcontinent and its people.

Amery had a most distinguished journalistic career with *The Times*. It began, in a sense, at Harrow, where he commissioned a new blood-and-thunder columnist for the school newspaper. As he later recalled:

> It is amusing to reflect that I was [Churchill's] first editor and press censor. He came to me one day – I was then schoolboy editor of the *Harrovian* – with an article on the recent assault-at-arms in the gymnasium. The article was highly critical, not to say scurrilous. I had to blue-pencil several of the choicest witticisms in spite of the writer's impassioned and almost tearful protests. Even what I passed in this and one or two subsequent articles went rather beyond the conventionally restrained tone of the *Harrovian*. Accordingly the Head Master, Dr Welldon, summoned the young author to his study and addressed him in the following terms: 'I have observed certain articles in the *Harrovian* newspaper lately, not calculated to

increase the respect of the boys for the constituted authorities of the School. As articles in the *Harrovian* are anonymous, I shall not dream of enquiring who wrote them. But if any more of the same character appear it may be my painful duty to swish [flog] *you*.

Army Dreamers

Ian Hamilton, 1896

Many of Churchill's young contemporaries from Harrow took the expected next step: they went up to either Oxford or Cambridge to study. Churchill's parents realized that his path would be different. He himself would wonder for decades afterwards how his life might have developed if he had been taught by dons – rather than teaching himself – the core of Classics and the habits of intellectual rigour. Nonetheless, he was naturally impelled towards the military. He applied – and after sitting several rounds of exams – was accepted by the Royal Military College at Sandhurst. He lacked the maths for Artillery or Engineers. But he had the physical fearlessness – and skill on horseback – for the cavalry. By 1895 he was photographed in the elaborate dress uniform – florid, frogged, Ruritanian – of the 4th Queen's Own Hussars; his red hair slicked, his expression precociously grave. Victoria's Empire awaited.

'Setting the fair sex aside tenderly but firmly on the mantelpiece,' wrote General Sir Ian Hamilton arrestingly in the 1930s, 'nobody . . . has touched my life at so many points as Winston Churchill. So much indeed has he done so that were my pages to give no glimpses of his strange voyage through the years, showing him sometimes as the Flying Dutchman, scudding along under bare poles; sometimes as the Ancient Mariner under flapping canvas in a flat calm; sometimes as a small boy playing with goldfish; my story would not be complete.'

General Sir Ian Hamilton was perhaps the most Victorian of Churchill's friends: a lavishly decorated soldier who saw action from India to the Boer Wars to (in that more industrialized age of war) Gallipoli. Thin, Scottish and terrier-browed, Hamilton first saw his own name displayed in a thousand railway-station bookstalls when Churchill the war correspondent published *Ian Hamilton's March* (his account of the campaign in Africa) in 1900.

Hamilton exulted in Churchill's friendship. And that story began under what he would have perceived as the golden light of the height of Empire; when, as a soldier, vast proportions of the world were his to wander.

'In 1897, Winston had got leave from his Regiment the 4th Hussars and had managed to get himself attached to the 35th Sikhs taking part in the Malakand Campaign among the hill tribes of the NW Frontier where he did very well,' wrote Hamilton, in a style that now seems close to the breathless fictions of Victorian boys' journals. That style also rather obscures the violent reality.

The Malakand campaign involved a besieged British garrison in a region of what is now Pakistan. At the time the area lay upon an arbitrarily imposed border between British-held India and Afghanistan, and was intended to forestall Russian predations. The result was boiling tension among the Pashtun locals. When British camps along the

Malakand Pass came under attack, reinforcements were summoned. Among them was young Churchill.

The steep valleys of the region were to echo with the cacophony of violent death; and the conflict would convulse that entire north-west frontier, most famously around the Khyber Pass. For Hamilton, though, writing in a manner that conjures old men in Pall Mall clubs talking over cigars and port, it was a bracing adventure.

'By the time I got command of a Brigade in the Bara Valley of the Tirah country,' Hamilton continued, 'the famous action on the Dargai Heights in which the Gordons had so distinguished themselves had taken place and we were involved in what was politely termed an evacuation, but was really a "get away" of the worst type . . . Characteristically, Winston had set his heart on sampling this, the most dangerous, disagreeable and thankless task in the whole military box of tricks . . . Really it was enough to make a cat laugh.'

But this was one of the repercussions of the frontier skirmishes – a further wave of violence, drawing in Pathan locals. 'Meanwhile I myself was standing literally as well as metaphorically on the edge of a precipice,' recalled Hamilton. 'I was commanding the only formed force left in the Valley – for a long line of some 20,000 troops marching with bag and baggage and thousands of camp followers along a narrow road through a series of deep ravines could hardly be considered a tactical unit.'

There was 'a secret fortified camp'. The 'spot was called Gudda Kalai which in the Pushtoo language means "the Den of Thieves". Thence we had to cover the getaway of our troops.' As Hamilton described it, this was in the face of 'cut-throats' whose aim was to 'slaughter as many infidels as possible'.

And in the middle of it all was young Churchill. It is almost possible to hear Hamilton's dry chuckle through the thickets of his vintage prose style.

'Winston . . . was not only a real help, but learnt a great deal more about soldiering and the strenuous and dangerous side of war; about dodging bullets, taking up rear-guard positions, and laying ambuscades; that he would not have learnt by years of parades and polo matches with his regiment.'

These frontier battles were all naturally rather more harrowing than General Hamilton's bluff account suggests. In one earlier battle that Churchill had joined, there was first the trek into a deep, silent, uncannily beautiful valley; he was accompanying a small imperial task force intent on a vicious 'punitive' raid against Pathan villagers which would involve destroying wells and towers. Those villagers were understandably intent upon resistance, concealing themselves on the hillsides, and then their ambush was sprung, with an explosion of wrenching violence. In Churchill's words: 'One man was shot through the breast and pouring with blood; another lay on his back kicking and twisting. The British officer was spinning round just behind me, his face a mass of blood, his right eye cut out.' He then added, with quiet irony: 'Yes, it was certainly an adventure.'

Hamilton was later offered the position of Commandant of Musketry at Hythe – rather than an Indian post, which would have prevented him taking part in the Second Boer War. Churchill, meanwhile, was 'now burning to see active service in Egypt'. And he had just published his first book, *The Story of the Malakand Field Force*.

A little later, Churchill wrote to Hamilton, addressing him as 'my dear General': 'I am anxious to get something at home after Egypt as I do not want to leave the army until I am fixed in politics,' declared the young warrior. 'But what. The only thing I can think of is the IB [Intelligence Branch]. I have some qualifications. But perhaps you would know whether this was in any way possible. It would interest me, and I believe I might be of use, as my pen is mightier than my sword . . .'

He added: 'Please say nice things about me to everyone at home. If you would call on my mother – 35A, Great Cumberland Place – she would be very grateful for news of me and to meet one who has shown me much kindness.'

A year later, both men were in North Africa and Winston was giving his friend 'a vivid account of his personal experiences fighting the Dervish host', of which we shall hear more in a later chapter.

In civilian life, and by the 1920s, the old soldier would be bemused by his friend's escapist enthusiasms:

On learning that the Council of the London Zoo were seeking to economise over tigers and lions by getting good citizens to adopt them, he offered to adopt a goldfish. A very fine specimen was sent him and the Council were so pleased with the patriotic spirit thus displayed that they followed up the donation with a consignment of several thousand freshly hatched specks of gold now safely domiciled at Chartwell.

He adores these animals. The hours glide blissfully by as he nourishes them with pinches of ants' eggs taken from what looks like a snuff box; or, in manipulating a miniature ram whereby the overflow from the pond is automatically pumped up and reintroduced to his unsuspecting children by adoption as fresh from the bowels of

Mother Earth; thus, as some may think, playing it rather low down on the little fishes.

Churchill was a child of Empire; it would have been unusual if he had questioned and objected to all the precepts of imperialism. In those days, few around him did. To Churchill, the ascendancy of Great Britain was as natural and as scientific as gravity; this was how the world worked. It was also natural in this world that young officers should seek marriage with society beauties. But for Churchill, the course of love was intriguingly unstraightforward.

Churchill in Love, Part One

Pamela Plowden, 1896

In its earliest days, Churchill's soldiering life in India with the 4th Hussars seemed to largely revolve around pleasure. He lived in a shared house with two other officers and an array of silent, ever-present servants; there were dawn drills, lunchtime rests, polo in the late afternoon and cooling spirits every evening. There was also the colonial social whirl: the lavish dinners with various British officials in sumptuous houses. It was at one such occasion — a polo tournament followed by dinner with the British Resident of Hyderabad — where the first documented instance of Churchill falling for a woman took place.

*

She was the dark-haired daughter of diplomat Sir Trevor Chichele Plowden, and renowned as a society beauty. Churchill's love for her seemed ardent from the very start. According to his later colleague, friend and biographer Jock Colville, the young subaltern was 'head over heels'.

Some of Churchill's correspondence to Pamela Plowden survives, though her own replies remain private. On the day after he met her, 3 November 1896, he wrote to his mother: 'I was introduced yesterday to Miss Pamela Plowden – who lives here. I must say that she is the most beautiful girl that I have ever seen – "Bar none" as the Duchess [of Marlborough] Lily says. We are going to try and do the City of Hyderabad together – on an elephant. You dare not walk or the natives spit at Europeans – which provokes retaliation leading to riots.'

There was some form of expedition, which thankfully involved neither resentful oppressed people nor riots. Again, Churchill's mother was informed via letter that Pamela was 'v beautiful and clever'. He continued to press his suit. Yet romance in an imperial age also meant separations of colossal distances and vast chasms of time. He was drawn away on military campaigns of dust and skirmish and blood; Pamela, in the meantime, returned to Britain.

Were this a Jane Austen novel, the heroine might have been alert to a curious note of hyperbole in some of the correspondence. In 1898, Churchill wrote to Pamela: 'One thing I take exception to in your letter. Why do you say I am incapable of affection? Perish the thought. I love one above all others. And I shall be constant. I am no fickle gallant capriciously following the fancy of the hour. My love is deep and strong. Nothing will ever change it . . .'

These are lines that, had they been uttered on the Victorian stage in a melodrama, would have drawn cynical jeers. The language is high yet the note is jarringly adrift.

As we shall see presently, Churchill was to hurl himself bodily into battle in Egypt and South Africa. In the case of the latter, taken prisoner by the Boers and effecting an extraordinary escape – thereby attaining great fame – he subsequently wrote to his mother that 'I propose to come home. Politics, Pamela, finances and books all need my attention.'

But, as it transpired, she did not require his attention; not romantically in any case. According to Colville, the two of them were staying as guests at Warwick Castle in the autumn of 1900 when Churchill proposed to her in a punt on the river. She turned him down.

By 1902, Pamela Plowden was engaged to Lord Lytton. She was to become – and would remain – the Countess of Lytton. Churchill congratulated her and hoped they would always remain friends. They did. This is a recurring motif in his story: strong friendships with strong women.

'He Detests Me!'

Herbert Kitchener, 1898

Churchill was already worried about money; his faltering, sputtering romance with Pamela Plowden was partly to do with his sense of financial insecurity, for the money bequeathed by his father was not prodigious, and in any case Churchill's mother had the more pressing need for it. Although it was pointed out by amused associates that Churchill always had enough money for Champagne and tailors, the inheritance was not bottomless and a sense of financial crisis would hover over him for the span of his life. In those early years, he found a way of combining his love for soldiering with his love for vivid writing and vastly multiplying his pay packet: he fought for Britain, and also wrote about it for the newspapers every step of the way.

Churchill 'was only making a convenience of it', declared General Herbert Kitchener in 1898. He had no intention of staying in the army and therefore should not take the place of 'others whose professions were at stake'.

Under the ancient skies of Egypt and Sudan, a thunderous military campaign against 'Dervishes' – local insurgents – was underway. General Kitchener, later to achieve a macabre immortality for his glaring image on the 'Your Country Needs You' World War One posters – was fixing his cold eye on wiping these insurgents out with the most modern weaponry. In this, he was being portrayed in the 'jingo' newspapers as the stern and unyielding totem of Britain's imperial strength.

Churchill was desperate to be in the action amid those antique sands – as part of the cavalry, but also as the vivid correspondent for the *Morning Post*, which would be paying him very handsomely for dispatches.

But Kitchener bitterly resented the very idea of young Churchill; he smelled his opportunism. Nor could he quite place him – was this aristocratic young upstart a soldier or a journalist? The general would have understood that the two roles commanded completely different loyalties. This appears not to have occurred to Churchill, however. 'It was a case of dislike before first sight,' the young man observed.

Perhaps if Churchill had not been the beneficiary of a campaign of nagging – including discreet prompts from as high up as the prime minister, Lord Salisbury, who had admired Churchill's writings on India and was also loosely a family friend – there might not have been so much froideur. This shameless sleeve-tugging involved Churchill's mother, and her titled friends. Lady Jeune wrote directly to Kitchener: 'Hope you will take Churchill. Guarantee he won't write.' It was a staggeringly empty guarantee; whether she was aware or not, Churchill had already signed a contract with the *Morning Post*.

And was General Kitchener wholly wrong to feel uneasy about having this plumpening, publicity-addicted prose stylist in the middle of his campaign? The British Army had censorship, but there were a hundred ways it might be circumvented. Why would a general wish to submit to the journalistic judgement of a twenty-three-year-old junior officer?

This was the high summer of exultant imperial adventure, with the British Army vowing to avenge the murder, some thirteen years beforehand, of General Gordon in Khartoum at the hands of the Mahdi (meaning 'Chosen One'). That had been tragedy, rather than adventure. The Mahdi was Muhammad Ahmad, and in 1885 he and his soldiers were fighting against Egyptian rule in Sudan (when Egypt was allied to the British Empire). General Gordon and his forces were besieged in Khartoum; by the time relief came, he and his garrison had been slain.

The incident had burned its way into the British consciousness. Even after the death of Muhammad Ahmad, who succumbed to typhus just months after the killing of Gordon, his forces – the Mahdists – had continued to fight in Sudan, and by 1898 there was a growing public appetite for a reckoning, fuelled by the press.

For this was also the new age of mass newspaper influence: the Elementary Education Act of 1870 had brought literacy and the purple delights of a popular press to vast numbers of new readers. It was also an age of literature for boys: weekly magazines such as *Boys of England* were filled with sword-flashing imperial adventure stories set in every corner of the earth. And the drumbeat of the Sudan campaign was being amplified to the most extraordinary degree by a press now aided by widespread telegraphy.

The 'special correspondents' – journalists who travelled with the army, and who wrote up eyewitness accounts of battles – gave their accounts a daily cliffhanging quality that were as addictive to the public as any blood-and-thunder fiction serial. They were a new breed of journalist – named, writing not dispassionately but instead with eyewitness adrenaline – and Churchill was an early master of this new form.

Popular culture was suffused with Sudan. There was even a remarkable advertisement in the popular *Daily Graphic*: 'The Soudan Campaign 1898 – Pimm's Number 1 well to the Front!' This was indeed referring to the well-known summer refreshment – now primarily associated with Wimbledon and English summers, but back in 1898 allying itself with colonial triumph. 'Pimm's Number 1 arrives at the Front,' ran the advert. 'Note what the gallant major said – vide London Morning Paper of 2nd August: "The Major swore he would preserve it to drink to the memory of Gordon when Khartoum was captured."'

It might be pointed out that General Kitchener was not opposed to Churchill alone; he did not want any popular journalists anywhere near the expedition, and did everything he could to deny them facilities. (In his novel *The Light that Failed*, Rudyard Kipling had this to say of special correspondents: 'You're sent out when a war begins, to minister to the blind, brutal, British public's bestial thirst for blood.')

Yet although Churchill is now widely viewed as one of the chief 'jingoes', his account of the Battle of Omdurman of 2 September 1898 – and its terrible, blood-slicked aftermath – would prove rather more morally considered than those of many of his journalistic contemporaries.

His reports from North Africa had begun as poetic dispatches from the Nile, contemplating historic ancient battles. Yet as serious action against the 'Dervishes' at Omdurman loomed, Churchill's articles suggested a sense of shifting gravity. This was still an adventure for the Boys of England – but he was also aware that the British military hardware involved made it a grimly uneven proposition for the lightly armed Mahdists.

'I was but three hundred yards away,' he reported, 'and with excellent glasses could almost see the faces of the Dervishes who met the fearful fire. About twenty shells struck them in the first minute. Some burst high in the air, others exactly in their faces. Others, again, plunged into the sand and, exploding, dashed clouds of red dust, splinters and bullets amid their ranks.'

For Churchill the soldier, there was a chance of what he would have understood as a cleaner fight, of doing battle the old way: he was there, on horseback, with his company the 21st Lancers, riding into a more evenly matched confrontation with their insurgent opponents. This was a cavalry charge that might have taken place 100 years beforehand. It was harrowing and bloody, but perhaps to Churchill seemed a shade more honest.

'The Dervishes stood their ground manfully,' he wrote in his journalistic account for the *Morning Post*. 'They tried to hamstring the horses. They fired their rifles pressing their muzzles into the very bodies of their opponents . . . They stabbed and hacked with savage pertinacity . . . Men, clinging on to their saddles, lurched hopelessly about, covered with blood from perhaps a dozen wounds . . . The whole scene flickered exactly like a cinematograph picture; and besides, I remember no sound. The event seemed to pass in absolute silence.'

In the wake of battle, Kitchener – referred to as the Sirdar, a term denoting his supreme commanding rank in the British-controlled Egyptian army – was not magnanimous towards the insurgents, and this Churchill could not forgive. The general ordered a round of vengeful executions. He also decreed the destruction of the tomb of the Mahdi – an act Churchill regarded as the purest, coldest sacrilege. He later wrote to his cousin the Duke of Marlborough, known as Sunny:

I try to be fair and not to allow my personal feelings to bias my judgment – but my dear Sunny, the Sirdar's utter indifference to the sufferings of his own wounded – his brutal orders & treatment with regard to the Dervish wounded – the shameless executions after the victory and the general callousness which he has repeatedly exhibited – have disgusted me. I have seen more war than most boys my age – probably more than any. I am not squeamish, but I have seen acts of great barbarity perpetrated at Omdurman and have been thoroughly sickened of human blood.

I shall always be glad that I was one of those who took these brave men on with weapons little better than theirs and with only our discipline to back against their numbers. All the rest of the army merely fed out death by machinery.

I wonder whether you will distrust the value of my opinion when I tell you that [Kitchener] detests me and has expressed himself freely on the subject – that he refused to have me with his Egyptian Army at any price – that he was furious with Sir Evelyn Wood for sending me out in spite of him – that my remarks on the condition & treatment of our wounded officers & men were reported to him and that every petty annoyance that ingenuity could suggest was obtruded on me in return.

Our Friends in the North

John Robert Clynes, 1900

In 1899, Churchill was a few months away from the adventure that would grant him cheering crowds: his experiences in the Boer War. Before that, there was his first tilt at a parliamentary seat – in Oldham, Lancashire. That tilt was unsuccessful. Following his South African exploits, however, suddenly Churchill was literally an icon, his image deployed for political posters. His efforts to begin a parliamentary career

began again, this time more fruitfully, the following year. There were
those in the newly formed Labour Party who watched this ascent
closely. One such — J. R. Clynes — is little remembered outside hardcore
Labour historians today. And yet he was a remarkable and prodigious
figure who shared Churchill's enormous capacity for self-education, and
whose rise from the cacophony of the mill floor to Home Secretary was
more astonishing than that of the man whose rise he observed.

The grinding roar of the African armoured train crash in
1899 – the line damaged by Boer saboteurs in the 'broad
undulation of the Natal landscape' – saw Churchill fuelled
by the adrenaline of both soldiering and journalism. Under
Boer gunfire, he and his associates scrambled to help the
injured, and also to right the engine upon the rails. 'Two
soft kisses sucked in the air,' he wrote in *My Early Life* of
the bullets that whistled past his head. Did he somehow
believe himself to be impervious to gunfire?

Some troops escaped; Churchill consciously stayed
behind with the others and faced capture. What then followed
was a short period of imprisonment in the Staats Model
School building in Pretoria – the 'barren ashes of wasted
life' he experienced in that captivity inspiring Churchill, as
he later claimed, to envisage domestic prison reforms.

But then came his brilliant escape (a matter of calculating,
in the deep of night, the radius of pools of electric light
shining on open courtyards, the depths of the shadows
around, and the heights of walls surrounding the compound),
and a quite extraordinary period of days as a hunted fugitive,
trekking across scrubby country, affecting insouciance, and
being taken in by English farmers. Thence to salvation – and
to journalistic glory, as the story was relayed back to Britain.

By 1900, now back home, he wanted – at least in his

own mind – to improve the lives of the working people via the mother of parliaments. But he had tried the year before, and some of those working people had been intensely sceptical from the start. 'Churchill was, and has always remained, a soldier in mufti,' said Lancashire mill hand turned Labour deputy leader turned Lord Privy Seal J. R. Clynes. 'A hundred years ago he might profoundly have affected the shaping of our country's history.'

In fairness to Clynes, he wrote this in his own memoirs in 1937, when Churchill's voice was echoing from the Essex wilderness, and a new war – to many – seemed unthinkable. But it was also based on a lifetime of careful observation: Clynes first met Churchill under industrial skies as the young man was first launching himself upon a parliamentary career.

For a man who loathed socialism to the depths of his soul and would come to be ardently loathed by many socialists in return – from workers in the north-east to the mining communities of South Wales – Winston Churchill had some fascinating encounters with a number of totemic Labour figures throughout his long political life. These interactions were not always marked by direct hostility; sometimes, on the part of those he met, there was a sort of wary fascination.

That first political battleground of Oldham was unlikely territory for a finely plumed aristocrat. Photographic records of the period always portray a stark world of heavy dark architecture and gasworks, hazy in the murk of polluted air. They convey something of the cold, of the damp; the noise and heat of the mills and mines can be imagined thereafter. Nonetheless, there were points of colour and light: a reel of recently colourized film taken in turn-of-the-century Halifax, on the other side of the Pennines – horses, trams, curious women, men and children – suggests that the world was dense brown rather than black.

Oldham, not far from Manchester, had long echoed with furious, driving industry. It was into this world that, in 1899, the twenty-four-year-old Winston Churchill – already bow-tied and stiff-suited – proposed to introduce himself to a class of people of which he had no experience at all. (A friend observed some years later that when Churchill first enquired about how and where working-class people took their holidays, he was puzzled by the term 'lodgings'; he had simply never come across the concept before of holiday rented rooms.)

'One day,' Churchill wrote of his early political ascendency, 'I was asked to go to the House of Commons by a Mr Robert Ascroft, Conservative member for Oldham.' Oldham was represented at the time by two MPs, a so-called 'double seat'; Ascroft wanted a junior partner. But Mr Ascroft soon passed away and the main candidacy now became Churchill's – that place in the House would be his as long as he could win electoral success. He was immediately plunged into a world in which matters such as the 'Tithes bill' – a form of welfare for the clergy – was arousing serious passion among the non-conformists of Lancashire. 'Neither my education nor my military experiences had given me the slightest inkling of the passions which such a question could arouse.'

Churchill's running mate for that double seat in his ultimately unsuccessful first campaign in 1899 was James Mawdsley, who was apparently both a socialist and a Conservative – and secretary of the Amalgamated Association of the Operative Cotton Spinners. 'I am a Tory Democrat,' Churchill declared at one point in the campaign.

'I regard the improvement of the condition of the British people as the main end of modern government.'

Yet at best he was addressing a semi-democracy: this was a point at which not only women did not have the vote, large numbers of working-class men were still disenfranchised. The Second Reform Act of 1867 had partly loosened the restrictions, so that men in urban boroughs who either owned property or paid over £10 a year rent as lodgers could vote. Still, this left millions without any sort of say about who represented them in Parliament.

Oldham was distinguished not only by its industry – the extraordinary capacity of its ceaseless cotton mills, plus a subterranean labyrinth of coal seams – but also by its collection of 'friendly societies' and the determined efforts to improve literacy, culture and education. Most people in this town would have left school at fourteen; yet many yearned for the realms of the Classics, and mathematics, and geology, and the other pursuits that the middle and upper classes filled their lives with at university.

It was also especially active in the field of trade unionism – at that stage the only voice that many workers could ever hope to have. Mawdsley, that anomalous socialist Tory, attracted mockery and hostility from various trade unions. 'They accused poor Mr Mawdsley of having deserted his class,' wrote Churchill. And what must they have thought of him – the aristocratic scion, the privileged gilded youth, who declared in Oldham meeting halls that 'never before were there so many people in England, and never before had they had so much to eat'? The sentiment may have been received with some astonishment; in any event, the Liberals triumphed.

But there was to be another election the following year.

And Churchill, returned from South Africa, decided once more to tilt at Oldham. All of this was being watched with particular interest by Clynes, who was in some ways the embodiment of that self-educated Lancashire society. Here was a socialist who dealt with management by means of quoting lines from Shakespeare, including bamboozling them with snatches of *Twelfth Night* – 'Be not afraid of greatness' – and *Julius Caesar*.

'I met Churchill during his Election campaign, having been chosen to lead a group of local Labour supporters to interview him, and obtain from him an exposition of his views of certain Labour topics,' recalled Clynes in his memoirs. 'I found him a man of extraordinarily independent mind and great courage. He absolutely refused to yield to our persuasions, and said bluntly that he would rather lose votes than abandon his convictions.'

He added, however, that Churchill 'possesses inborn militaristic qualities, and is intensely proud of his descent from Marlborough. He cannot visualise Britain without an Empire, or the Empire without wars of acquisition or defence . . . Now, the impulses of peace and international-ism, and the education and equality of the working classes, leave him unmoved.'

Clynes was writing that in 1937; the references to peace and internationalism suggest that he considered Stalin's Soviet Union to be a model of future society. It is also clear he never stopped regarding Churchill as delivering empty promises to the poor.

Nonetheless, in the 1900 general election Churchill was victorious in Oldham, partly because of his Boer War adventures, and the political triumph deepened his already glittering celebrity. Of the night of the count, he wrote:

'Our carriage was jammed tight for some minutes in an immense hostile crowd, all groaning and booing at the tops of their voices, and grinning with the excitement of seeing a famous fellow-citizen whom it was their right and duty to oppose.'

There Is a Better World

Sidney and Beatrice Webb, 1903–1908

Churchill was to prove as mercurial in Parliament as he had been out on the battlefield. He had stood as a Tory, but increasingly found himself chafing against the party's narrow bounds – and against the conventional discipline of Parliament. He undertook hugely profitable speaking tours, both at home and in the US; MPs then were unpaid, and his justification was that he had to ensure his financial security. But he also joined a loose affiliation of Tory rebels nicknamed the 'Hughligans' after their leader Lord Hugh Cecil. Then in 1904, in one of the many famous shock developments of his career, Churchill – a free trade enthusiast who opposed Tory protectionism – crossed the floor of the House, joining the Liberal Party. The Liberals came to power the following year under Henry Campbell-Bannerman; and Churchill came to government for the first time, as Under-Secretary for the Colonies.

Throughout these tumultuous days, Churchill's path crossed with that of a couple who ought in some ways to have been his dearest enemies.

*

She thought him 'egotistical, bumptious, shallow-minded'. But Beatrice Webb – the formidable campaigner, activist and intellect who can be credited with having laid the foundation stones of the welfare state – would scarcely have been expected to embrace Winston Churchill upon first meeting. Nonetheless, appalled though she was, their orbits continued to cross; and Churchill would come to insist that, in some senses, their passions were the same.

Was this true? Beatrice Webb's long and indefatigable career as a light of the Fabian Society – together with her husband, Sidney – gave her a measure of influence. It was she who wrote in 1909 of the need to 'secure a national minimum of civilised life ... open to all alike, of both sexes and all classes, by which we mean sufficient nourishment and training when young, a living wage when able-bodied, treatment when sick, and modest but secure livelihood when disabled or aged'.

Although a grave enemy of socialism, and seemingly frequently more concerned with his lucrative book deals and international book tours, Churchill did sometimes give voice to a desire to make life better for the working man.

Churchill and Beatrice first met at a dinner party in 1903. It was on that occasion that she found him unbearably full of himself. The following year, they met again, and she rounded on him in her diary: 'he drinks too much, talks too much, and does no thinking worthy of the name'. Four years after that, with Churchill now ensconced in government, a more promising encounter came. Sidney and Beatrice had been thinking – among other ideas – of a new system of labour exchanges. Churchill proclaimed himself keen on the concept and told them he hoped it might come within the purview of his department.

'Now let me say', he told Sidney, 'that you will always find the door of my room open whenever you care to come, and I hope you will feed me generously from your store of information and ideas.' He had already expressed sympathy and enthusiasm for other proposals to eradicate the evils of sweated labour.

It was around this time that David Lloyd George, then Chancellor, was exploring Germany and its Bismarckian system of social insurance. Upon Lloyd George's return, Churchill saw a grand opportunity for a breakfast meeting with the Chancellor and Mr and Mrs Webb, to see if the idea might be adapted in Britain. No sooner had the breakfast things been laid, however, than the brittle accord broke down. The very idea of social insurance – the workers paying into schemes – was almost the opposite of what the Webbs were hoping to achieve. As related by Webb's biographer Carole Seymour-Jones: 'Mr and Mrs Webb, singly and in pairs, leapt down his throat: "That's absurd; that will never do," they told the Chancellor. "It's criminal to take poor people's money and use it to insure them; if you take it you should give it to the Public Health Authority to prevent their being ill again."' It was reported that 'Sidney was too excited to eat his breakfast, and Lloyd George . . . was highly amused'.

In fairness to Beatrice Webb, her view of Churchill was not entirely devoid of redemption. 'I dare say he has a better side,' she noted, 'which the ordinary cheap cynicism of his position and career covers up to a casual dinner acquaintance. No notion of scientific research, philosophy, literature or art, still less of religion. But his pluck, courage, resourcefulness and great traditions may carry him far, unless he knocks himself to pieces like his father.'

And Churchill and the devoutly socialist Webbs were at least united in one belief, whether they knew it or not: a profoundly ill-judged adherence to the growing (and grotesque) Edwardian enthusiasm for eugenics. In 1906, Churchill declared: 'The existing organisation of society is driven by one mainspring – competitive selection. It may be a very imperfect organisation of society, but it is all we have got between us and barbarism.'

But in other ways, Churchill was struggling against a turning intellectual tide: his youthful and unshaped political vision was that of a benign aristocracy continuing to preside over a benign and patrician democracy, which in turn policed a vigorous and compliant workforce. This was not how increasing numbers of that workforce saw it. The contrast between the smog-slippened pavements of Oldham and the dazzling salons and chandeliers of his London social life could not have been greater. But was there an emptiness at the heart of those richly lit balls and dinners?

Churchill in Love, Part Two

Violet Asquith, 1906

By the standards of most men, Churchill was, by the age of thirty-two, startlingly successful. Famous in both Britain and America for his cliffhanging exploits, he was a Liberal MP (for Manchester North West) and a cabinet minister. By 1906, he was President of the Board of Trade, and his pinstriped trousers, made by tailor

Henry Poole, were striding the corridors of power. But in matters of the human heart, true love continued, somehow, to elude him. It was almost as though — for all his protestations — romance and settled family life were not in fact his true priorities. In this new Edwardian age, the smarter salons of London society were his to move through. But could romance ever be found within them too?

Violet Asquith (later Bonham Carter), daughter of prime-minister-to-be H. H. Asquith and later a magnetically charismatic writer, was a lightning-bright debutante with interestingly vertical features, a perpendicular face and nose, and an expression that could seem almost mournful in repose, even when garlanded in a tiara of flowers to be photographed for the society pages.

To be a debutante at that time meant to be dressed in white and presented before the King as a quasi-ceremonial means of entering society. Violet's aims extended rather further. She would later become a politician, a governor of the BBC and an enthusiastic proponent of European integration. The thread of her life was closely interwoven with that of Churchill's; their friendship was intense.

It has been rumoured that she nurtured an unrequited love for him. Might 'amused fascination' be a more accurate reading? Born in 1887, Violet was already vehemently aware of Churchill at the age of eighteen. In 1905, she recorded in her diary that she had spotted him at a particularly radical and fashionable night at the theatre:

I went to *The Enemy of the People* done by [actor/director Sir Herbert Beerbohm] Tree. Father and I had good places sent us – the theatre was packed with all sorts and conditions of men; many socialist ladies in scarlet dresses and an incongruous medley in the stalls ... Winston Churchill in the Trees' box shocked by [Ibsen's outspoken protagonist] Stockmann's bungling tactics with the crowd and Cicely [Horner] beside him looking beautiful – a box is her element – a large dark frame which seems to get her into focus. Tree didn't act Stockmann very well I didn't think; it is too subtle and complex a play for him – he does rather crude melodrama best.

Violet could not help but notice Churchill at this left-leaning extravaganza; incongruous among the progressive socialists in the audience, radiant in the golden glamour of his imperial military adventures. But their first proper encounter was the one that appeared to set the tone for a friendship that would endure across the decades.

'I first met Winston Churchill in the early summer of 1906 at a dinner party to which I went as a very young girl,' Asquith would write in her memoirs. 'Our hostess was Lady Wemyss and I remember that Arthur Balfour, George Wyndham, Hilaire Belloc and Charles Whibley were among the guests.' At that stage, Churchill was still Under-Secretary for the Colonies.

I found myself sitting next to this young man who seemed to me quite different from any other young man I had met. For a long time he remained sunk in abstraction. Then he appeared to become suddenly aware of my existence. He turned on me a lowering gaze and asked me abruptly how old I was. I replied that I was nineteen. 'And I,' he said almost despairingly, 'am thirty-two already. Younger than anyone else who *counts*, though,' he added, as if to comfort himself. Then savagely: 'Curse ruthless time! Curse our mortality! How cruelly short is the allotted span for all we must cram into it!'

Churchill's theatrics eventually subsided (he famously told her that 'We are all worms. But I do believe I am a glow-worm'), and he began to engage a little more fruitfully with the teenage girl beside him.

'Later on he asked me whether I thought words had a magic and music quite independent of their meaning,' Asquith recalled. 'I said I certainly thought so, and I quoted as a classic though familiar instance the first lines that came into my head: *Charm'd magic casements, opening on the foam / Of perilous seas, in faery lands forlorn . . .* His eyes blazed with excitement. "Say that again," he said. "Say it again – it is marvellous!"'

The young woman was puzzled – surely he knew Keats's 'Ode to a Nightingale'? But he didn't – he had neither read nor heard of it before.

There was a similar reaction when Asquith recited some scraps of Blake, naming the poet. Churchill comically imagined she meant the admiral of the same name, and wondered how he had found the time to write. 'I was astounded that he, with his acute susceptibility to words and power of using them, should have left such tracts of English literature entirely unexplored.' (Not unexplored for long – after this encounter, Churchill not only read but memorized all of Keats's odes. His capacity for self-education – he ploughed through Gibbon, Macaulay and the ancient Greeks while in India – verged on the demoniac.)

In this respect, Churchill was a little like Conan Doyle's Holmes – a brilliant mind, yet so abstracted that he had never learned or been taught that the earth revolves around the sun. Yet he could learn any new idea at quantum speed, and applied himself with intense focus to the most intractable of problems.

To this end, Churchill's initial encounter with a man whom he would come to despise saw them both – for the only time in their lives – on the same side.

Swelling to the Imperial Theme

Mahatma Gandhi, 1906

The man whom many working-class people regarded as their enemy would pull some surprisingly socialist-seeming reforms out of his government hat. In 1908, for instance, Churchill, as President of the Board of Trade, would enact a change in the law that meant that trade unions would for the first time not be held financially accountable for damages caused by strikes. In some matters, it did seem as though he genuinely wanted to improve the common lot of the people. Yet he still had intensely reactionary reflexes on some subjects: India and Empire being prime among them. Over the next forty years, through the gradual dissolution of the British Empire, Churchill's voice would growl louder and louder at the dismantling of what he considered the perfect system. He himself had spent his halcyon youth on those polo fields, and sipping Champagne in roseate Indian sunsets; it was certainly his perfect world. But even in his most violently bellicose moments, there were still outbreaks of insight.

*

It was not, strictly speaking, an encounter; more a near-encounter, but one freighted with its own historical ironies. There was a day when Mahatma Gandhi and Winston Churchill – the most dedicated of opponents – were in perfect accord.

'The Royal Assent to the Asiatic Ordinance in the Transvaal was withheld temporarily before the arrival of the Indian deputation in England,' ran a bone-dry news report on the only occasion that these two men ever appeared to be on the same side. The year was 1906; the issue was South African discrimination against the Indian population. Mohandas Gandhi, a young lawyer who had trained in London – and dressed not as he is best remembered, but rather in the western garb of frock coat and tie – had had a moment of radicalization when he was violently thrown off a train at Pietermaritzburg for refusing to obey the strict racial segregation rules in the carriages.

In South Africa, Indians were second class, and that apartheid was intensifying. With Indians being denied the right to vote, the matter had to be brought to England, and the Colonial Secretary. And in Parliament, Winston Churchill had his own view: that Mohandas Gandhi had a strong case.

'Though the reported version of Lord Elgin's reply did not commit him to anything definite,' ran the newspaper report, 'Mr Winston Churchill's announcement in the House of Commons shows that the ministers have been impressed with the justice of the complaints made by Messrs Gandhi and [close associate and political activist Hadji] Ally.'

But this moral support changed nothing and was not enough: what followed was Gandhi's first use of widespread civil disobedience against the South African government and his subsequent arrest: the peaceful protest was a technique that he would later deploy to Churchill's fury. Gandhi termed it *satyagraha*, meaning 'devotion to truth', and it took the form of industrial strikes and mass marches. After several years, the Boer government in part relented, backing down on a registration law that required all Indian citizens to be fingerprinted for police registers.

In 1915, Gandhi returned to India. The country was still regarded in Britain as the most glittering of the colonial jewels. Churchill himself was always inspired to new heights of gaudy romanticism when it came to India's place in Britain's empire and Britain's position as the keystone of world civilization. Gandhi conversely understood that empire as an abomination. His manner and tactics were mild but his will was greater than Churchill's.

That initial – unknowing – accord in 1906 would turn into a lifetime of mutual enmity, with Churchill stirred towards some of his most intemperate attacks. The most famous, cited so often today, is his 1931 comment to the Viceroy of India (how antique that title now sounds), when he described Gandhi thus: 'It is alarming and nauseating to see Mr Gandhi, a seditious Middle Temple lawyer, now posing as a fakir of a type well known in the East, striding half-naked up the steps of the Viceregal palace while he is still organising and conducting a campaign of civil disobedience, to parlay on equal terms with the representative of the Emperor King.'

In fact, Churchill's venom towards Gandhi – and the Indian independence movement in the 1930s – led various colleagues to wonder if he had lost all judgement. His vehemence drove many away, and once again, he drew apart from his own party.

Of all the seams of bitterness that the name Churchill evokes in many communities around the world, his imperialist attitude towards India and his apparent supreme indifference to the welfare of its people continue to inspire everything from academic monographs to entire books. There was his chilly and insulting dismissal of Gandhi's World War Two hunger strike as fake; then there was the vast and terrible catastrophe of the 1943 Bengal famine, for which many blame Churchill for deliberately making sure that the starving population were deprived of the grain supplies they desperately needed – a fiery controversy that continues to burn.

Further evidence of Churchill's imperial contempt can be found in the madly offensive comments made in 1943 to his old Harrow school friend – then Secretary of State for India – Leo Amery. He averred that '[they] breed like rabbits' and were a 'beastly people with a beastly religion'. This led to Amery regretfully voicing the view that, when it came to India, Churchill was 'not quite sane' and that he could not see much difference 'between [Churchill's] outlook and Hitler's'.

Yet, as with all these matters, there were occasional flashing anomalies in Churchill's apparently diamond-hard imperialism. One early instance concerned the shocking and barbaric Amritsar massacre in April 1919, when General Dyer opened fire upon huge numbers of defenceless Indians. Some 400 people were killed outright, and another thousand or so were horribly wounded. There were those in Parliament on the Tory benches who thought that Dyer should not be condemned; that he had acted correctly; and that the massacre had been provoked.

With his own salty views on 'natives', it might have been

expected for Churchill to also rally to Dyer's defence. However, he did not. 'However we may dwell upon the difficulties of General Dyer . . . one tremendous fact stands out,' Churchill declared to the House. 'I mean the slaughter of nearly 400 persons and the wounding of probably three or four times as many . . . That is an episode which appears to me to be without precedent or parallel in the modern history of the British Empire. It is an event of an entirely different order from any of those tragical occurrences which take place when troops are brought into collision with the civil population. It is an extraordinary event, a monstrous event, an event which stands in singular and sinister isolation.'

His speech in Parliament astonished many. But it is also instructive about his true views on the role of Empire and the use of force, and in some ways harks back to his condemnation of General Kitchener after the Battle of Omdurman.

'Men who take up arms against the State must expect at any moment to be fired upon,' Churchill said. But 'an unarmed crowd stands in a totally different position from an armed crowd. At Amritsar the crowd was neither armed nor attacking.'

Dyer claimed to have been confronted 'by a revolutionary army'. But what distinguished an army? 'Surely it is that it is armed. This crowd was *unarmed*. These are simple tests which it is not too much to expect officers in these difficult situations to apply . . . No more force should be used than is necessary to secure compliance with the law.'

True, it was easy enough talk like this 'in safe and comfortable England', Churchill continued. It was quite different from being confronted on the spot with a 'howling mob . . . quivering all around with excitement . . . Still these are good guides and sound, simple tests, and I believe it is not too much to ask of our officers to observe and to consider them. After all, they are accustomed to accomplish more difficult tasks than that.'

This view was intensely paternalistic, but under the imperialist hide lay the flesh of humanity. 'There is surely one general prohibition which we can make. I mean a prohibition against what is called "frightfulness". What I mean by frightfulness is the inflicting of great slaughter or massacre upon a particular crowd of people, with the intention of terrorising not merely the rest of the crowd, but the whole district or the whole country. We cannot admit this doctrine in any form. Frightfulness is not a remedy known to the British pharmacopoeia.'

As MPs around him in the House sought to make occasional harrumphing interruptions, Churchill pressed on. 'Governments who have seized upon power by violence and by usurpation have often resorted to terrorism in their desperate efforts to keep what they have stolen, but the august and venerable structure of the British Empire where lawful authority descends from hand to hand and generation after generation, does not need such aid.' Amritsar, he said, should remind us of the words of Macaulay, about 'the most frightful of all spectacles, the strength of civilisation without its mercy'.

Britain's 'reign in India or anywhere else has never stood on the basis of physical force alone, and it would be fatal to the British Empire if we were to try to base ourselves only upon it', Churchill concluded. 'The British way of doing things . . . has always meant and implied close and effectual cooperation with the people of the country. In every part of the British Empire that has been our aim, and in no part have we arrived at such success as in India, whose princes spent their treasure in our cause, whose brave soldiers fought side by side with our own men, whose intelligent and gifted people are cooperating at the present moment with us in every sphere of government and of industry.'

Gandhi might have pointed to the central flaw in this romantic vision: the fact that occupation and Empire were of themselves inherently violent.

Churchill, conversely, never stopped believing that he and his fellow officers had succeeded in making that part of the world a better place. Yet for all Churchill's growling words of animosity, there were meteor flashes of respect between the two men.

According to historian Richard Langworth, Gandhi in 1935 remarked: 'I have got a good recollection of Mr Churchill when he was in the Colonial Office, and somehow or other since then I have held the opinion that I can always rely on his sympathy and goodwill.'

Gandhi said this to his chief lieutenant, Ghanshyam Das Birla, who had lunch with Churchill at Chartwell following the August 1935 passage of the Government of India Act – a step towards independence. Churchill had opposed this bill 'and had said some pretty rough things'. But at the lunch with Birla, Churchill was magnanimous. 'Mr. Gandhi has gone very high in my esteem since he stood up for the Untouchables [the lowest of the Indian castes]. I do not like the Bill but it is now on the Statute Book . . . So make it a success.'

Birla then asked him: 'What is your test of success?' To which Churchill replied: 'Improvement in the lot of the masses . . . I do not care whether you are more or less loyal to Great Britain. I do not mind about education, but give the masses more butter . . . Make every tiller of the soil his own landlord. Provide a good bull for every village . . . Tell Mr Gandhi to use the powers that are offered and make the thing a success.'

Churchill in Love, Part Three

Ethel Barrymore, 1906

He might have been a political meteor, but she had lustrous dynastic claims: the actress Ethel Barrymore – sister to actors John and Lionel – was the glowing centre of a stage family that had conquered both the US and Britain. It was when she was treading the boards in London that Churchill found himself impelled towards that stage door . . .

Ethel Barrymore was one of the theatrical sensations of the age: beautiful, hypnotic, with the power to command audiences. And it was in Claridge's restaurant following these performances that, for a short time, Churchill was said to have besieged her with nightly flowers.

In this enthusiasm for theatre, he had form: there were rumours that in his more youthful days he had ardently courted a 'Gaiety Girl' – that is, one of the dancing show-girls who featured at the Empire Theatre. (She had thereafter told friends that he spent the night 'talking into the small hours on the subject of himself'.) Ethel Barrymore, by contrast, was an aristocrat – the queen – of her craft at that time.

54

During those heady evenings at Claridge's, Churchill is said to have proposed to Barrymore. However, she was more than aware of his own fame, and this – in part – was the sticking point. She could not, she said, 'cope with the great world of politics'. The theatricality might have been too intense even for her.

His Gay Best Friend

Edward Marsh, 1907 onwards

One of the great skills any top politician must possess as they move through those echoing Whitehall corridors and vast stately offices is the ability to inspire all the public and civil servants around them; not only to devise new laws and reforms, but to infuse every breast with enthusiasm, so that these might be carried through Parliament and into law. As a young cabinet minister, Churchill was said to have this power.

Equally, though, every top politician would find themselves immobilized in the blancmange of technicalities if they did not have the finest minds working by their sides. Churchill was very fortunate to alight on such a mind – a formidable polymath – who was to serve by his side for a number of years, and also to introduce him to a slightly more bohemian side of life.

'I pique myself on my immunity from the lust of blood,' wrote Edward Marsh lightly. 'But Winston wouldn't hear of my having a rifle: I might shoot *him*, and that would never do.'

Although homosexuality was illegal throughout Churchill's lifetime, there were 'confirmed bachelors' and women who lived together 'as sisters'. And if Churchill was ever homophobic, he apparently never gave any outward sign of it. One of his most trusted civil servants — a gay man who would become a great friend and a frequent guest at Chartwell — would later look back on his time with Churchill, from the Edwardian era and through the Great War and beyond, with clear-eyed amusement and terrific affection.

Edward Marsh was the sponsor and the fountainhead of the so-called Georgian poets; it was he who engineered the first and only meeting between Siegfried Sassoon and Rupert Brooke. He was a formidable literary translator, and had a keen eye for the best in avant-garde art. He was also great friends with the gay composer Ivor Novello, and brought him within Churchill's social radius.

Marsh juggled this intense aesthetic life with a role at the administrative and intellectual heart of government, working for Asquith as well as Churchill. But in the case of Winston, a friendship had sparked beforehand, in the fragrant ballrooms of London society. 'Beware of the Smart Set!' the philosopher Bertrand Russell had implored Marsh. To no avail.

According to Marsh's biographer Christopher Hassall:

There were occasions when Mr Churchill and he would meet at the same soirée, and they devised a pastime for the intervals when they happened to be standing together within sight of the ballroom door, watching the ladies make their entrance. On the basis of Marlowe's line 'Was this the face that launched a thousand ships?' they would assess the beauty of each newcomer as she appeared.

'Two hundred ships, or perhaps two hundred and fifty?' the one might remark tentatively, gazing ahead as he made his reckoning. 'By no means,' the other might reply. 'A covered sampan, or small gunboat at most.'

Among the very few who scored the full thousand in the opinion of both assessors were Lady Diana Manners and Miss Clementine Hozier, whom Mr Churchill was to marry.

Marsh was also intrepid enough to follow young Churchill out to Africa, set on bloodsport pursuits which at that time never merited a second glance. 'Before I started with Winston Churchill, towards the end of 1907, on the African journey,' he later recalled, 'I asked Mrs Patrick Campbell what she would do if she heard I had been eaten by a lion; and she admitted that she would laugh first, and then be very very sorry.'

Marsh wrote that he 'took to Africa at once. "The moment we arrived," as Winston picturesquely put it, "Eddie stripped himself naked and retired to the Bush, from which he could only be lured three times a day by promises of food." This was no more than a slight exaggeration . . .'

Soon the two men, hiking across a vast plain within sight of the heights of Kilimanjaro, happened upon one of the more awesome specimens of local wildlife, 'a female rhinoceros asleep under a solitary tree'. As Marsh described it: 'After hasty consultations and suitable manoeuvres for getting right with the wind, Winston fired. The rhinoceros leapt to her feet and rushed towards us, or rather as I felt towards *me*, pounding along like a runaway railway engine. "What should [I] do?" I stood my ground, with my finger on the trigger of my umbrella, planning as a Happy

Thought to jump aside at the last moment and open it upon her with a bang . . .'

But Winston's shot had been true; the poor beast could not charge any further. It collapsed.

At this, Churchill made an amused assessment of Marsh's reaction to extreme peril. 'Winston's attitude towards any chance display of sang-froid on my part had been expressed in a proverb he had learnt from his nurse [Mrs Everest]: "Where there's no sense, there's no feeling."'

Marsh was to follow Churchill through various cabinet postings, through to 1915 (we shall soon hear of the catastrophes of that year) and thence beyond.

It has been suggested that a series of childhood diseases rendered Marsh impotent in later life, and that his discreet homosexuality took the form of intense platonic bonds with men. Churchill, in any case, never appeared to be bothered by the sexual orientations of others – which perhaps lends some context to the apocryphal later story of an MP being caught *in flagrante* with a guardsman in the darkness of St James's Park. ('On the coldest night of the year?' said Churchill. 'Makes you proud to be British!')

Churchill in Love, Part Four

Clementine Hozier, 1908

'Have you read my book?' was the first thing that Churchill asked the woman who was to be his wife. The book in question was his biography of his father. Clementine told him that she had not, to which he replied that he would send it round to her the next day in a hansom cab.

It was Edward Marsh who was instrumental in forging Churchill's marriage: the genesis of the romance was a rather stiff lunch at the home of Lady St Helier, a friend of Churchill's mother. Also invited was Clementine Hozier, the twenty-three-year-old daughter of Lady Blanche Hozier – and a young woman who very much knew her own mind when it came to proposals, advantageous or otherwise. She had been engaged twice to the son of Viscount Peel; and a matchmaking effort that left her stranded in the middle of an elaborate hedge maze with Lord Bessborough – a scheme devised by her mother – had come to naught.

The invitation to lunch was superstitious; Clementine had been asked to prevent the number around the table being thirteen. Churchill, meanwhile, in his Whitehall office, was reluctant to attend. But Marsh told him sternly that it would be rude to pull out. And as soon as Churchill was seated next to Clementine, an instant flash of attraction set the course of his life thereafter.

Writing later of what would be the start of a most enduring and touching relationship, another of Churchill's lady friends considered Clementine's terrific strengths. 'I never thought of her in a political context but always as a Queen of Beauty on the ballroom floor,' recalled Violet Asquith. 'Until she married Winston I did not know that she had had a Liberal family background and tradition and – what mattered more – possessed strong Liberal instincts of her own. I soon discovered that she was in fact a better natural Liberal than Winston, and this discovery brought me much relief on her behalf. For in their early married life she shared the rough of his political fortunes to the full.'

That roughness was akin to the recent venomous Brexit debates; in matters such as House of Lords reform, for instance (the Liberal Churchill was now bracingly rude about hereditary Dukes inheriting political power), the newly married Mr and Mrs Churchill were exiled from some of the smartest dinner parties because their views were deemed unacceptable. Churchill was placed by many society hostesses on a list of 'untouchables'. Clementine was asked years later: was all of this a strain? 'I didn't mind a bit,' she said. 'It was so exciting – it made me feel heroic and proud!'

Friends such as Violet Asquith stayed loyal and true, and wrote through the rosy lenses of hindsight. But what were their immediate reactions when they first learned that Churchill had proposed to Clementine?

Letters from Slains Castle

Violet Asquith, August 1908

There was a rumour that Churchill's announcement that he was to marry Clementine, made to Violet and her family while she was holiday-ing in Scotland in 1908, led to the curious episode where Asquith went missing for several hours around the cliffs and dunes of the Aberdeen-shire coast. She was found unconscious, and later claimed she had been looking for a book. It has been latterly suggested that this was a self-destructive cry for help. The letters exchanged between Violet and her great friend Venetia Stanley (who also happened to be Violet's father's lover) might suggest otherwise.

Violet Writing to Venetia Stanley, August 1908

Life here is gloriously strenuous and healthy. I do 3 hours Greek a day . . . & golf with father on far the longest and most tempestuous links in Scotland – & sit . . . on the very edge of slimey barnacley rocks hauling up shimmering 'sathe' out of green deeps . . .

The news of the clinching of Winston's engagement to the Hozier has just reached me from him, I must say I am much gladder for her sake than I am sorry for his. His wife could never be more to him than an ornamental sideboard as I have often said & she is unexacting enough not to mind not being more. Whether he will ultimately mind her being as stupid as an owl I don't know – it is a danger no doubt – but for the moment she will have rest at least from making her own clothes & I think he must be a little in love. Father thinks it spells disaster for them both (unberufen). I don't know that it does that. He did not wish for – though he needs it badly – a critical, reformatory wife who would stop up the lacunas in his taste etc & hold him back from blunders . . . I have wired begging them both to come here (as he was going to) on the 17th – won't it be amusing if they do? Father is a little chilly about it – & W[inston] generally, & Margot has an odd theory that Clementine is mad! which she clings to with tenacity in spite of my assurances that she is sane to the point of dreariness.

Venetia Stanley to Violet in Reply

My darling, Aren't you thrilled about Winston. How I wonder whether Clementine will become as much of a Cabinet bore as Pamela [McKenna, wife of politician Reginald]. I don't expect she will as she is too humble . . . I had a very ecstatic letter from Clemmy saying all the suitable things. I wonder how stupid Winston thinks her . . .

Blood and Bullets

The Siege of Sidney Street, 1911

He was now Home Secretary, aged just thirty-five: the red hair receding, the face filling out, and the eyes staring into the lens with undiminished challenge. It was 1910–11 and the industrial dispute at the coal mine in Tonypandy, South Wales, damned Churchill irrevocably as the sworn enemy of the working classes – the events that are now still (misremembered) as Churchill sending in the troops to open fire on the strikers. This was not quite so; he had the troops in readiness, but the battles (without bullets) were fought with the police. However, there were troops present at a later battle in Llanelli.

The Tonypandy accusation – try uttering Churchill's name out loud in many parts of South Wales even now – also swings the light away from one of his most progressive achievements at the Home Office: serious prison reform, not only reducing the amount of time that offenders spent in solitary confinement, but also succeeding in reducing the size of the prison population overall.

Meanwhile, in parts of London's East End, Churchill's name is still associated with another outbreak of gunfire that has acquired folkloric status: the Siege of Sidney Street, at which Churchill's compulsive grab for the spotlight so enraged one Whitehall colleague that Churchill was compelled to make a teasing joke of it, imploring with a lisp: 'Oh, pleath don't be croth with me!' His encounter with the coroner at the inquest the week after seemed further criticism of this flamboyant grandstanding.

Churchill and Stalin missed first meeting each other in the squalid slums of east London; Stalin lived briefly in a vast dosshouse in Whitechapel in 1907. The area – dank with dark tenements and close, filthy alleys – was in part a sanctuary for numbers of radical displaced Russians and eastern Europeans; anarchy for some (though not for Stalin) was the creed.

In north London, the Tottenham Outrage of 1909 had involved two Russian revolutionaries trying to rob a payroll van; the result was carnage, with two people killed and twenty others injured. In December 1910, three anarchists – two of whom were George Gardstein and a man known enigmatically as 'Peter the Painter' – were holed up in a house just streets away from Whitechapel, having committed a jewellery robbery and the murder of three policemen. They were still armed, and only too willing to fire upon anybody who came close. Churchill was one of the men who decided to come close.

The crisis, later known as the Siege of Sidney Street, seemed to set Churchill off into a caper. Here was an encounter with the popular press – and thus, a wide and eager readership – who wanted to hear more of his exploits and devil-may-care antics. Especially, perhaps, in the wake of the 1905 Aliens Act, which was the first to swing the focus on to immigration in Britain, concomitantly pointing a hostile light on to recent arrivals.

But Churchill's business at Sidney Street was not to do with immigration; rather it was a hatred of communism and anarchism. His own personal appearance on that day, skirting the borders of the absurd, might have been a calculated aristocratic answer to such ideologies. The carefully tailored and faintly exotic clothes – the top hat, the vast overcoat with astrakhan collar – seemed more of a costume than the sort of attire one would normally expect to see a Home Secretary wearing.

There was a breathless report in *Reynold's Newspaper*:

Acting on secret information, a party of detectives, armed with revolvers, proceeded in the small hours to a house in Sidney Street, off the Mile End Road, where some men 'wanted' for the murder of the three city policemen on Dec. 16 were said to be in hiding.

Clearing the house of its other inmates, the officers were proceeding to arrest the miscreants when they were met by a heavy fire from the same terribly effective automatic pistols that shot down the police in Houndsditch. A sergeant was wounded severely, and the attack changed into a deliberate siege . . .

At last the police knew that by a quick, concerted movement their prey could be run to earth. They knew that the criminals would sell their lives dearly, and undue precipitation would only mean useless slaughter. Hundreds of unmarried constables were held in readiness while a picked forced of armed officers, all in mufti, was despatched around midnight to the scene of operations under the command of Chief Inspector Willis, Inspectors Collinson, Wensley and Hallam . . .

The anarchists' house had the horrible fascination of a house of death. Bullets were raining upon it. They spat at the walls, they ripped splinters from the door, they made neat grooves as they burrowed into the red bricks, or chipped off corners of them. Not a window was left intact.

The noise of battle was tremendous and almost continuous . . . some of the weapons had a shrill singing noise, and others were like children's pop-guns . . .

At this moment Mr Winston Churchill, Sir Melville Macnaghten, the newly-knighted chief of the City Police, Sir Nott Bower, and Mr Harry Lawson, MP for Mile End, came on the scene. The Home Secretary sauntered unconcernedly down Sidney Street and strolled up and down two or three times in front of the beleaguered house before it was suggested to him that the position was unsafe.

With a smile, Mr Churchill sought a less exposed post, but soon he was back again in the street directing operations, heedless of flying bullets. He took four or five Scots Guards a few yards nearer the house and directed their fire . . .

At this time smoke had begun to come out of the second floor window of the house, and the officers tightened their hold on their revolvers. 'The house is on fire, they will bolt now.' Seeing this, Mr Churchill sent two of the policemen with shotguns to join in the frontal attack from the shoeing forge . . . then to get a closer view, Mr Churchill went into the shoeing forge. The guardsman who was there knelt to fire and Mr Churchill stooped down and directed his aim. 'Fire at the door,' he said, and the bullet crashed across the street at point-blank range ... 'Let us make a rush,' said one of the plain-clothes men. 'No,' said the Home Secretary. 'We want no more loss of life.'

Other, that was, than those anarchist lives being choked and burned in the rising flames.

A week later, Churchill was facing the questions of Mr Godfrey at the inquest of the men then known as 'Joseph' and 'Fritz', about quite why it had been necessary for the Home Secretary to be physically present at the crisis. Had he in effect 'taken charge of the police'?

In the witness box, Churchill was anxious to impress upon the court that he had simply been there to lend them his 'support'. He cited – by example – a firefighter whom he recalled was 'a little man with a black moustache', who had asked him if it was right that the house fire should not be immediately extinguished. On this – and other questions from the police – Churchill had assured everyone present at the Sidney Street scene that they had 'the highest covering authority'.

'May I ask you what you mean by the highest covering authority?' asked Mr Godfrey. 'You did not mean your authority? You were not speaking of yourself?'

At this, Churchill reportedly smiled. 'I think I am the highest police authority,' he replied.

Colleagues and figures within the Metropolitan Police were levitating with resentment at the way that Churchill appeared to have utilized the violent, bloody, fiery crisis as a stage upon which he could somehow direct the limelight on to himself. There was little sense among them that Churchill's first-hand knowledge and experience of weaponry and close-quarters fighting was actually of practical assistance. The top hat and the silver-topped cane did not help his case. Yet this innate theatricality also made him an object of reluctant fascination to those who were ordinarily repelled by old-school jingoism.

Dining with the Bloomsbury Set

Ottoline Morrell, 1911

In 1911, Churchill and his friend F. E. Smith established The Other Club, a dining society inspired by The Club – an institution founded by Samuel Johnson and Joshua Reynolds in the late eighteenth century. The Other Club's executive committee was, declared its founders, to be wrapped in 'impenetrable mystery'; and the guest diners were politicians from both Houses and from all political parties and wings. To this end, evenings at The Other Club – hosted in the Pinafore Room at the Savoy – frequently featured Churchill's direst political enemies, including Andrew Bonar Law. This was central to his idea of how public life should be lived: principles and ideas debated with fury; personal relationships conducted with cordiality, and over a great many courses, and sluiced down with extraordinary quantities of wine and brandy. As The Other Club established itself, regulars came to include Lord Kitchener (another Churchill foe) and H. G. Wells (friend and, in print, occasional foe). But there were other, more fragrant dining societies in London, including the nascent Bloomsbury Group . . .

*

'He is very rhetorical,' noted Lady Ottoline Morrell of Churchill. Yet it was quite remarkable that the two of them had ever met in the first place: what business did he have at the bohemian dinner tables of the Bloomsbury Group?

Lady Ottoline (née Cavendish-Bentinck) was an aristocrat in an open marriage, rumoured to have been the inspiration for D. H. Lawrence's *Lady Chatterley's Lover* by dint of her affair with a young stonemason nicknamed 'Tiger'. But she was rather more fascinating for being the nucleus around which so much of Edwardian society rotated. Her passion for politics, history and economics, as well as art, resulted in a social whirlpool that included T. S. Eliot, Dora Carrington (a rumoured lover), John Maynard Keynes, Bertrand Russell (another rumoured lover) and Winston Churchill (emphatically not a rumoured lover).

She was married to Philip Morrell, a Liberal MP whose own extramarital affairs resulted in several children that Lady Ottoline would come to take in and look after. By 1911, the gaudy fame of Churchill – on the point of being made First Lord of the Admiralty – was a source of fascination to people like the Morrells. In addition to this, after periods of ostracism in previous years, there were now few society dining tables at which he was not present.

Lady Ottoline's first meeting with Churchill was not wholly favourable, according to her biographer Miranda Seymour:

The guests for 18 May included Virginia Stephen [later better known as novelist Virginia Woolf] and Roger Fry, both of whom had recently returned from the task of nursing Vanessa [Bell] in the Turkish village where she had collapsed; the centre of attention and guest of honour was Winston Churchill who neither of the Morrells knew well but who they felt would be a useful ally to acquire for Philip's career.

Churchill looked very fine in his full-dress uniform – he was going on to a ball at Buckingham Palace – and he expressed a gratifying admiration for two of their Picasso etchings, but Ottoline was irritated to find that he wanted to talk of nothing but politics: '[He] has a volcanic, complicated way of talking,' she noted, 'which is difficult to listen to, or to gather what he really thinks.' She might have been amused to learn that this was precisely the complaint which Churchill had lodged against her friend Henry James.

Yet it is more than possible that it was through Lady Ottoline that Churchill was first introduced to the pioneering economist John Maynard Keynes, of whom we will be hearing a little more later.

The Weaver of Tales

W. Somerset Maugham, 1912

As one of the nation's most formidable writers – yet the author of an early novel that he could not commend to anyone – Churchill always maintained a deep respect for those who could write brilliant, successful fiction. This had been an early enthusiasm; as a boy, he wrote fan letters to H. Rider Haggard, author of such glowing imperial adventures as King Solomon's Mines *and* She, *which blended jeopardy and orientalist exoticism. One of Churchill's more intriguing literary friendships was formed with the hugely popular novelist and playwright W. Somerset Maugham, whose best-known work now is* Of Human Bondage.

'I once said to Winston Churchill, "If I had not stammered, I might have gone into politics and with my knack for speaking languages I might have become our foreign minister." He looked at me and grunted. So I became a writer.'

Somerset Maugham did rather more than that; he also briefly became a spy. As a general rule, Churchill thrilled to all matters espionage – he was ever a sucker for a cipher. But in the course of their long friendship, spying led to their one episode of cross-purposes.

Maugham was born the same year as Churchill, and became a hugely successful novelist and playwright at around the same time as Churchill was rising in politics. He also invented the modern fictional spy genre as we know it – and it was all through first-hand experience.

He had been recruited by the recently formed Secret Intelligence Service during World War One, in 1915; and in 1917 was sent to Russia as the earthquake of the revolution was beginning. That 'knack for speaking languages' saw him travel from Vladivostok to St Petersburg on various small-scale espionage missions. It is not clear whether his friend Churchill (they met long before the outbreak of the Great War) knew the precise details of these forays as they were undertaken; by 1917, Churchill was out of the war cabinet and the inner circles of intelligence.

A few years after the war, however (when Churchill had returned to government, as Chancellor of the Exchequer), Maugham wrote a series of stories involving a spy called Ashenden. The very few in the know would have understood that these fictions were in fact ruthlessly autobiographical – that Ashenden was Maugham. Churchill certainly understood, and the perceived breach of security appeared to horrify him.

As Maugham's biographer Ted Morgan writes: 'The Ashenden collection, "a very truthful account of my experiences during the war when I was in the secret service", was not to appear for another ten years, held up by "[Maugham's] mysterious bosses in the Foreign Office", as his publishers explained it. According to a report there were originally thirty-one stories, but when Maugham showed them to Winston Churchill in draft, Churchill insisted that fourteen be destroyed as he considered them in breach of the Official Secrets Act.'

When the two men had first met just before the outbreak of war, there had instantly been a sense of friendly wariness on the part of Churchill, who recognized Maugham's intelligence and wit. According to Morgan:

It was at Stoke Court that Maugham first met Winston Churchill . . . there was a golf course nearby and the two men often played together in the afternoon, returning to the house for a substantial tea followed by a glittering formal dinner. It was late one night when the ladies had retired to bed and the men, changed into smoking jackets, were talking over their brandy and cigars that Churchill was startled by an intervention of Maugham's: a young man, very full of himself, had been holding forth at length, in the writer's view talking complete nonsense, when suddenly Maugham broke in and with one sentence, witty but devastating, silenced him. Everyone burst out laughing but the next morning Churchill came up to Maugham as he was peacefully reading the Sunday papers. 'I want to make a compact with you,' he said. 'If you will promise never to be funny at my expense, I will promise never to be funny at yours.'

Did Churchill ever know or sense Maugham's closeted homosexuality? Like Eddie Marsh, he was discreetly homosexual – though possibly a shade less discreet than Marsh. Either way, it made no difference to the depth and longevity of Churchill's friendship with him, at a time when other public figures would have recoiled from the possibility of being associated with scandal.

Maugham had a villa in the south of France, where his male lover – termed 'secretary' – resided (Mrs Somerset Maugham remained in England), and at which Churchill would frequently stay. There is a wonderful photograph of them both in the garden in 1937, together with their mutual friend H. G. Wells. In the writer's evening routine there is another glimpse of Churchill's esteem, plus a shared love of luxury. According to Ted Morgan: 'Dinner at eight was a more formal affair. Maugham wore a velvet jacket, a black tie – and initialled velvet slippers from Peels, a gift from Churchill.'

The Distant Booms

David Lloyd George, 1914

He was the great reformer; a man who reordered the system of government, turning it from a public-school club into a professionally run organization. He believed in the power of the state to alleviate the suffering of poverty. And for a time, David Lloyd George could count himself as a political mentor to Churchill, some ten years younger. Certainly, across forty years, there was mutual friendliness. Yet there were also points at which these two towering figures recoiled from one another. Lloyd George was Chancellor from 1908 to 1915. By 1911, Churchill had succeeded to the Admiralty. And as the horizons darkened with approaching conflict, the two friends diverged sharply in approach . . .

Margot Asquith was not alone in finding Churchill a chilling figure at the outbreak of war. David Lloyd George – who would become prime minister in 1916 – declared of his erstwhile colleague that he had no imagination of the heart.

I shall never forget that night – that 4th August 1914, when war was declared. I dined alone. I was sent for to see the PM around 10.30. I found [Home Secretary Reginald] McKenna and [Foreign Secretary Sir Edward] Grey in the cabinet room with the PM. We were all very serious, very anxious. The PM said 'Midnight abroad is 11 here.' We all looked at the clock and Grey said, 'It's not all over yet.' He then told us that a wire from [German diplomat and Foreign Secretary] Jagow had been intercepted by our Post office saying [British ambassador Sir Edward] Goschen in

Berlin had sent for his passports. I said 'It's all over, then' . . . Big Ben struck 11; very slowly came the Boom, Boom, Boom. We sat in complete silence I should say for 10 minutes after the last Boom. Winston dashed into the room radiant – his face bright, his manner keen; and he told us, one word pouring out on the other, how he was going to send telegrams to the Mediterranean! the North Sea and God knows where. You could see he was a really happy man. I wondered if this was the state of mind to be in at the opening of such a fearful war.

Vanity! All Vanity!

H. H. Asquith, 1914

Even in the calmer tributaries of political history, Prime Minister H. H. Asquith was in some ways every bit as extremist as Churchill. Where the latter had the abiding sins of pride, bellicosity and an enviable verbal flamboyance, the former transgressed in his own ways: firstly through an enthusiastic and unstoppable consumption of any form of alcohol, and secondly through his sexual meandering. Asquith's aching-hearted affair with Venetia Stanley, who was simultaneously thought by some to be the lesbian lover of his daughter, made Downing Street an unlikely hothouse of erotic longing. In the earliest days of the war, Asquith – whose son was to join Churchill's naval brigade, of which we will hear more presently – discussed with his wife, Margot, the temperamental failings of this Lord of the Admiralty.

*

Margot Asquith's diaries – in their roughness – might not be taken as the most concise or precise of historical records. Nonetheless, at certain points when the cold darkness of the Great War hung over the nation, she captured Churchill's disconcerting episodes of zeal. In the aftermath of the declaration of war, Margot and her husband discussed Churchill's recent behaviour. In her diary, she reproduced that conversation in the form of dialogue.

Henry said to me in the motor going out to dine with the Walter Burnses:

[H]: Winston just now is absolutely maddening. How I wish Oc [Asquith's son] had not joined his beastly naval Brigade! He is having a great Review of them today. He inspects the Brigade in a uniform of his own, which will cause universal derision among our soldiers! (Clemmy said some time ago that inventing uniforms was one of Winston's chief pleasures and temptations.) He has just emerged from a fearful row with K[itchener] by the skin of his teeth, and has now got himself into another.

M: Do tell me.

H: K. has just been to see me about it. Sir John [French, Commander in Chief of the British Expeditionary Force] writes from St Omer and tells K. that Winston has offered him 9,000 of his Naval Brigade, ready to go into action at once in the trenches, and a squadron of armoured motor cars; and [Sir John] French asks if he may be allowed to remove the guns and use the motors, which shows what he thinks of the use of these expensive follies!! K. is of course furious, and says to me he wonders what Winston would say if he, K., was always writing to [Admiral of the Fleet, John] Jellicoe, offering to do this and that. Of course, Winston is intolerable. It is all Vanity. He is devoured by vanity.

M: It was curious to me to see how depressed he was when I congratulated him on his remarkably good (naval) speech in the House Monday night (8th Feb. 1915).

H: It was merely because he thought the newspapers would have praised it more – he is quite childish.

The Roar of the Ironclads

H. G. Wells, 1915

Amid the swiftly unfolding horror of the vast, deathly battlefields – and all these hideous innovations in terms of dealing death – there were other inventions which changed the nature of war, and which are still very visible in conflicts today. It is not overstating the case to say that Churchill can claim some of the credit for the invention of the tank; it was in part his experience in Belgium – driving with an officer called Charles Samson in cars with extemporized armour-plating, and shooting from behind this plating – that led to his own thinking on how such a vehicle might evolve.

There was another young officer, Thomas Hetherington, who had been thinking along these lines and who, over dinner with Churchill, described a vehicle of monstrous dimensions that could negotiate a landscape of trenches. Various prototypes came and – more pertinently – went. But then came 'Little Willie' in 1915: the first fully functioning tank, and the original from which all others would develop. But elsewhere, Churchill's friend and Other Club diner H. G. Wells was having none of it; the idea had been his all along. Even if he was happy to credit Churchill with setting these monsters into action in the first place . . .

I was only too eager to give my time and risk my life and fortune in any task that used me effectively. But I meant to be used effectively. I refused absolutely to volunteer and drill and acquire the saluting habit for the protection of railway bridges and culverts against imaginary nocturnal Germans in the by-ways of Essex, or for sentinel-go in prisoners' camps or anything of that sort. But an old notion of mine, the *Land Ironclads* (published in the *Strand Magazine* in 1903) was being worked out at that time in the form of the Tanks, and it is absurd that my imagination was not mobilised in scheming the structure and the use of these contrivances. These obvious weapons were forced on the army by Winston Churchill against all the conservative instincts of the army; Kitchener had turned them down as 'mechanical toys' and when at length they were put into action, it was done so timidly and experimentally and with so inadequate an estimate of their possibilities that their immense value as a major surprise that might have ended the war was wasted . . .

That was H. G. Wells, writing of the war in his memoirs. Churchill had long been an ardent fan of Wells's work; he wrote to the author telling him 'I read everything you write.' This enthusiasm dated back to the science fiction romance *The Time Machine* (1895), which Churchill had admired not only for its imagination but its 'philosophy'. Wells had written to Churchill, just after the turn of the century, that he did not think that men such as him who dwelled in great houses could quite appreciate the pace of the scientific revolution that was coming. 'It will interest me tremendously to make your acquaintance. To me you are a particularly interesting & rather terrible figure. Believing as I do that big slides & new fissures are bound to come in the next few years, I fancy at times that you are a little too inclined towards the Old Game.'

Wells was both right and wrong. In some respects, Churchill's game was very new, even if his resistance to certain innovations – such as Bolshevism – was granite-firm. As the years progressed, both men would enjoy a sometimes-spiky literary friendship.

After Wells's trip to revolutionary Russia in 1920, for instance, when having met Lenin, the author returned with nosegays of praise for him, Churchill used the *Daily Express* to launch a witheringly sarcastic attack. 'When one [Wells] has written a history of the world from nebula to the Third International and of the human race from protoplasm to Lord Birkenhead in about a twelve month, there ought to be no difficulty in becoming an expert on the internal conditions of Russia after a visit of fourteen days.'

Wells was swift to respond with a sharper bite. To Churchill, he said, it must have seemed 'an act of insolence that a common man like myself should form judgments upon matters of statecraft . . . But Mr Churchill not only poses as a statesman; he is accepted as such. He is the running sore of waste in our Government . . . He has smeared his vision with human blood, and we are implicated in the things he abets.'

Yet not too long after this rather shocking exchange, they were back on speaking terms, meeting amiably on holidays in the south of France and in the dappled splendour of the gardens at Chartwell.

The Golden Pagan

Rupert Brooke, 1915

When it came to the defence of the Belgian port of Antwerp against invading German forces at the start of the war in 1914, Churchill – at the Admiralty – had seen the chance to deploy thousands of naval reservists not on the waves of the North Sea but on land. This force would become the Royal Naval Division, and one of its aims was to stop the Germans getting near Calais and threatening an invasive assault on Britain (the plotline of so many Edwardian thrillers). Churchill sailed over himself to inspect the Naval Division, in the honorary costume of an Elder Brother of Trinity House – a naval cap and pea jacket. Then he was back in his astrakhan-collared coat, with a large cigar, paying no heed to flying bullets, driving around in an open-topped car. Days later, over 2,000 men lay dead – many of them from Churchill's extemporized division. Those who distrusted Churchill saw this as evidence of his calamitous misjudgement. Undaunted, he pushed on with more ambitious military plans – for which one already-famous war poet was preparing.

He was drowning in 'mud, rain and a hurricane' – not in the fields of France but rather some exposed heathland in Dorset, in the early weeks of 1915. Drawn into Churchill's circle, the beautiful poet whose gilded image had enraptured women and men alike had returned to Britain, and was throwing himself into preparation for graver landscapes. Rupert Brooke had been serving with the navy off the coast of Belgium, and in Antwerp, and had in that time composed the work that would prefigure his own epitaphs.

Brooke's war sonnets had conferred on him a grave form of fame; a new sense of moral stature for this twenty-seven-year-old whose poetry (including 'The Old Vicarage, Grantchester') had already started to suggest a vanishing world. Unlike the last in his sequence of five war sonnets – 'The Soldier', with its exquisite corner of a foreign field – the first in this sequence, 'Peace', echoed the curious and beatific excitement that Churchill exhibited at the start of the war.

> Now, God be thanked Who has matched us with His hour,
> And caught our youth, and wakened us from sleeping,
> With hand made sure, clear eye, and sharpened power
> To turn, as swimmers into cleanness leaping
> Glad from a world grown old and cold and weary . . .

Here was honour; here was a sense of war as purification; here was an evocation of death as merely the 'worst friend and enemy'. How could Winston Churchill ever have resisted consorting with a warrior who so lovingly looked mortality in the eye?

Brooke was the representative of a curious ideal amid the flesh-pulping violence, and he was feted by London society – and by Churchill. At the beginning of 1915, before the start of the fateful Dardanelles campaign to which he was due to sail, Brooke was in London, suffering from influenza and in the care of Churchill's secretary, Eddie Marsh. Marsh and Churchill hosted a grand dinner for Brooke at Admiralty House, but the occasion did not do his health any good. And so it was, as his biographer Nigel Jones notes, that the Asquiths 'offered to look after him at Number 10 Downing Street'.

His convalescence was aided by a sojourn on the Kent

coast; and upon his return to the capital on 14 February 1915 there was another invitation from Eddie Marsh to dinner at Admiralty House. Marsh had to leave a little early that evening, but Churchill and Brooke continued their conversation deep into the night. According to Jones, 'Brooke told Churchill that he did not expect to survive the coming expedition'. But Churchill would have none of this, and told Brooke that he must put his faith in the navy, which was poised to begin the assault on the Turkish forts in the Dardanelles. Brooke later told a mutual friend: 'He was rather sad about Russia who he thinks is going to get her "paws burnt" . . . but he was very confident about the Navy and our side of Europe.'

Brooke then returned to the Royal Naval Division in Dorset, and Churchill came down for an inspection on a day when the heathland was open to a rain-lashed *King Lear* storm. 'We were hurried to an extemporised performance,' Brooke wrote to Violet Asquith, 'plunging through rivers and morasses. It was like a dream. At one point I emerged from the mud, with my platoon, under the wheels of a car, in the midst of a waste. And in the car were what I thought were two children, jumping about clapping their hands shrilling and pointing. It was Eddie [Marsh] and Clemmie [Clementine Churchill]. It is rumoured that Winston was "pleased", & impressed by our superiority to the other Brigades: & that we shall go out *as* a Brigade. Which gives us more chance of survival.'

Brooke was with the British Mediterranean Expeditionary Force a matter of weeks later, and it was in Egypt that he was struck down not by bullets but lethal sepsis, in April 1915. Churchill wrote an obituary for *The Times* which itself was infused with an autumnal and golden morbidity:

During the last few months of his life, months of preparation in gallant comradeship and open air, the poet-soldier told with all the simple force of genius the sorrow of youth about to die, and the sure triumphant consolations of a sincere and valiant spirit. He expected to die: he was willing to die for the dear England whose beauty and majesty he knew: and he advanced towards the brink in perfect serenity, with absolute conviction of the rightness of his country's cause and a heart devoid of hate for fellow-men . . .

Joyous, fearless, versatile, deeply instructed, with classic symmetry of mind and body, ruled by high undoubting purpose, he was all that one would wish England's noblest sons to be in the days when no sacrifice but the most precious is acceptable, and the most precious is that which is most freely proffered.

The excess of emotion here – the sense almost of a curious envy of this warrior and his death, raised to a mythic level – seems perhaps alien; yet Churchill was throughout his life authentically given to tears. Amid the obscenity of the mass slaughter of the Great War, Brooke and his departure from this earth might somehow have seemed cleaner; the apotheosis of Troilus, or of Siegfried, as opposed to yet one more casualty among millions.

It would not be long before Churchill himself – deposed from the inner war cabinet, following the calamitous Dardanelles naval campaign and the equally harrowing bloodshed of the Gallipoli landings – would be seeking his own redemption in those freezing, squalid mazes of death. The patience of those around him in the wake of the nightmarish 1915 campaign to fight through to Constantinople would be exhausted, and Churchill would appear to offer himself up as a sacrificial atonement.

Regimental Glory

Lady Gwendoline Churchill and Company, 16 November 1915

For all her acid bitterness towards Churchill, the person who observed him with the most careful objective eye in 1915 was the prime minister H. H. Asquith's wife. First there had been Antwerp; now, the flesh-grinding attrition of the Dardanelles campaign was being laid largely at Churchill's feet (and he accepted the weight of the opprobrium, despite being part of a cabinet collective that – together with the military – had agreed to the entire enterprise). She was to observe as he faced a yet sterner test.

'Winston was delightful,' wrote the usually sceptical Margot Asquith. Perhaps as only a man in middle age about to face the guns of the enemy on mass killing fields could be. Churchill was almost forty-one years old – rather older than the average recruit about to throw himself into the mud and the slaughter of France.

On the eve of his departure for those cold trenches, Lady Gwendoline Churchill – his sister-in-law, known as

'Goony' – gave a lunch at her house in South Kensington. Also present was his wife Clementine, his good friend Violet Asquith, and his less good friend, Violet's stepmother Margot, who recorded the occasion in her diaries. She recalled how they 'said goodbye to Winston. He goes to join his regiment tomorrow in France. I felt <u>so</u> sad for Clemmy – poor, lonely, with her husband fallen from his high estate and facing danger. My heart went out to her . . . Winston was delightful – gay, talkative and interesting – and Clemmy brave, but no one except Winston contributed anything.'

Now deposed from the high office which to him had seemed the most natural state, Churchill appeared fixated on a form of martyrdom; the only compulsion for him to don uniform came from within. He wanted to command, and also to lead. He wanted to be among his men.

The rank of lieutenant colonel was deemed to suffice in order that he might get back into the old rigours of soldiering. His imagination must have been filled with romantic nineteenth-century notions of individual heroism and feats of courage. Yet he also knew that death now came on a production line, spitting indiscriminately from mechanized guns, or released from canisters in the form of flesh-searing gas.

His time in the trenches in Ploegsteert was served with customary – yet perhaps this time misplaced – insouciance. Issues such as the availability of alcohol (and how to ensure it), plus supplies of Stilton, sardines and succulent beef sent over by Clementine (because the standard army meat ration, dry and flavour-free, was not the fare to which he was accustomed), seemed to concern him more than creeping barrages and the prospect of bullets burning through bone. Yet none of this is to dismiss Churchill's courage; he genuinely sought to inspire his men, and it is generally agreed that he did so. 'War is a game that is played with a smile,' he told his officers. 'If you can't smile, grin. If you can't grin, keep out of the way until you can.'

He had his share of near-misses – leaving his dugout in order to smoke a cigar, only to witness, moments later, that same dugout obliterated by a shell; disorientating moments lost in no man's land, with bullets flying in all directions; getting close enough to German lines to hear their voices – but he was also using the time on the ground to analyse why it was all going so wrong, and how it had already become such a swamp of filthy slaughter. Churchill was appraising the lines of command – the balance between high military authority and the demands and the desires of politicians. And when several battalions were merged, some six months after his active war began, it was time for this serving MP (at that time for Dundee, which he had represented since 1908) to return to London, and to the apparent ruins of his political life.

Churchill was still out of the war cabinet; but incoming prime minister David Lloyd George was gradually to restore his roles and standing. The repercussive peace to come – for many across the world, from Russia to the Middle East, no peace at all, but further violence and painful death – would test Churchill's newfound experience and judgement.

In the meantime, in the midst of the foulest of all wars, there were – back in Britain – some unintentionally lighter moments. Churchill's social circle was to expand in an unexpected direction.

The Naughty Set

Ivor Novello, 1917

A few years before Noël Coward captured society both high and low with his witty whimsy and sharp playwriting, there was an even more luminous figure who loomed large in London musical theatre and later on the cinema screens. Ivor Novello (born David Ivor Davies) was a Cardiff lad with a precocious ear for complex harmony; by the age of twenty-one he had written the hugely popular wartime hit 'Keep the Home Fires Burning'. In 1916, Novello joined Britain's prototype air force . . . and despite his almost total uselessness as a pilot, won a coveted social invitation . . .

It was thanks to Ivor Novello's great friend Eddie Marsh that Churchill was introduced to him. According to Novello's biographer James Harding:

> Lady Randolph Churchill invited Marsh . . . to dinner for [the song] 'The Home Fires' . . . had become a national asset and her son was interested to meet its young composer. He [Winston] was apparently well versed in the music-hall songs of his Sandhurst days, and though they were of a vintage before Novello's time, the composer was able to keep his end up by singing over the port the ditties whose titles came to Mr Churchill's mind. At one point there came a mutual pause for wonderment. 'Do you know,' said Mr Churchill, 'you'd be far better off in a home?' Marsh and his protégé exchanged glances. Had the young airman been

showing signs of insanity? 'You'd Be Far Better Off in a Home', it transpired, was the only title so far that Novello had not come across before.

But there is also an unlikely-sounding story ascribed to Somerset Maugham about Churchill, Novello and sexual experimentation. According to Harding:

> Maugham got to be on close enough terms with Churchill to once ask: 'Winston, your mother indicated that you had affairs in your youth with men.'
>
> 'Not true!' Churchill replied. 'But I once went to bed with a man to see what it was like.'
>
> 'Who was it?'
>
> 'Ivor Novello.'
>
> 'And what was it like?'
>
> 'Musical.'

Reds Under Every Bed

Clare Sheridan, 1920

Churchill found a form of redemption in war, and in its bitter aftermath. After Lloyd George brought him back into government, he once more began to rise in power and influence. In the post-war era, he was Secretary of State for Air (controlling the nascent RAF) as well as remaining Secretary of State for War.

In the wake of the Russian Revolution, Churchill was determined to strangle communism 'in its cradle'. Bolshevism was an ideology that in his view threatened to overturn the foundation stones of civilization. Domestically, however, Churchill was at peace. By 1920 he and Clementine had three children: Diana, born in 1909; Randolph, born in 1911 and overindulged almightily by his father from the moment of his birth; Sarah in 1914; and Marigold in 1918. The pre-war world of weekends and art and stupendous quantities of drink was shakily re-established; but Churchill never ceased to be haunted by the soldier friends he had lost.

'[He] would remain still for three minutes, after which he'd begin to fidget,' wrote his sculptor cousin Clare Sheridan, who had struggled to get Churchill to pose. In art, they were bonded souls; in politics, they were a universe apart. Clare had been watching with fascination the epoch-defining displacements and violence tearing through St Petersburg and Moscow.

Was the revolutionary fire consuming Russia and its ruling elite a blaze that might spread throughout Europe? In the aftermath of the Great War, there was violent tumult in the city streets of Germany, as its own revolution pitted communists against psychopathic Freikorps soldiers. And from 1918 to 1921, Russia ran with the blood of a vicious civil war. Lenin and Trotsky sought to cement communist rule; so-called White Russians sought to dislodge this fledgling autocracy. Winston Churchill was among those British who very much favoured aiding the White Russians. His cousin Clare – her mother was the sister of Churchill's mother – was very much of the opposite view.

If Clare was ever labelled as 'troubled', it would always be worth pointing out that she had suffered. Her daughter Elizabeth had died as a toddler, in 1914. And Clare was a young widow; her husband Wilfred had been killed in the

Great War. Like so many throughout Britain and Europe in the wake of that conflict, she found that all the certainties of life had been violently upended. Was it perhaps this that led her to develop a sympathetic view of the new world that Lenin was apparently aiming to construct?

Her relationship with her famous cousin was – until later in 1920, when she embarked upon an expedition to the Soviet Union – warm and indulgent. In her memoirs she recalled a short interlude with Churchill and another cousin near Richmond upon Thames; a form of artistic retreat:

In 1920 my career as a sculptor was to find fulfilment: Winston's cousin, Freddy Guest, Minister for Air, commissioned me to do the heads of certain famous people who were his friends. I spent many weeks at Freddy's house, Templeton, near Roehampton. Winston and his wife, and F. E. [Lord Birkenhead, Churchill's great friend] were there, and a big north room had been converted into a studio. There Winston painted and I sculpted. Sometimes Ambrose McEvoy joined us and would try to paint Winston, while Winston painted me, and I modelled him. Not one would keep still for the other, and it was small wonder that none of us got very far.

Of all people, Winston was the hardest to do; it seemed a physical impossibility for him to keep still. He pleaded that Sunday was his only day of the week to paint. Freddy would beseech him: 'Give her a chance, Winston; it's for me'; and Winston would be contrite, he'd promise, say he was sorry, admit he knew it was hard for me . . . Not only would he not keep still for me, but he expected me to keep still for him. Once a secretary arrived from the War Office with a locked dispatch box; Winston took no notice, but went on painting. The secretary, grinning broadly, watched us both, but dared not interrupt.

Now and then, Winston, remembering I was trying to portray him, would stop dead and glower at me with beetling brows; those were the momentary chances he called 'sittings'. As the day faded he abandoned whatever he happened to be working at and turned excitedly to the big window to paint the sunset. His canvas had been prepared, the cedar tree in the foreground already sketched in; he concentrated on the sky. On one such occasion, without looking round, he said wistfully: 'I could *almost* give everything up for it.'

One night, having dined out in London, I arrived back towards midnight, and, hearing voices through a door ajar, I pushed it open. There was Freddy Guest wrapped in a bath towel, F. E. in vivid squashed-strawberry pyjamas and Winston in a Jaeger dressing-gown that Freddy had looted from a German prisoner. I was plied with champagne and Winston, having fixed his contemplative eye on me, observed: 'In my next incarnation I mean to be a woman, I mean to be an artist, I shall be free, and I shall have children.' If this meant he regarded my life as ideal, he knew nothing of its complexities.

Those complexities were melancholic, but shortly afterwards there was to be a form of disbelieving anger from Churchill. In that year, a visiting 'Russian trade delegation' (almost always a cover for espionage and subversion) invited Sheridan to take her sculpting skills to Moscow. And so it was, as the nightmare of the civil war raged, that she became ensconced deep within the Kremlin itself, making busts of Lenin and Trotsky.

It has been alleged that she had an affair with Trotsky. Certainly Sheridan was wholeheartedly in favour of Bolshevism's new society; and upon her return to England she found that she had become a gossip-column character in the newspapers – an object of both derision and chilly contempt. The recently formed domestic intelligence service MI5 considered her to warrant a special file and a measure of surveillance.

And nor was her relationship with her cousin easily repaired; but she persisted, and he was not inclined to bear a long-term grudge. Some six months later (feeling herself shunned by society and after moving to the US), she wrote a hurt letter to Churchill, who replied: 'My dear Clare, I do not feel that you have just cause to reproach me. You did not seek my advice about your going and I was not aware that you needed any on your return. Anyhow it was almost impossible for me to bring myself to meet you fresh from the society of those whom I regard as fiendish criminals. Having nothing to say to you that was pleasant, I thought it better to remain silent until a better time came.'

In one sense, the better time came: in the years that followed, they resumed their old friendship (helped a little by Sheridan renouncing her Bolshevik fervour), and by the outbreak of World War Two they were once more sufficiently close for her to sculpt him once more.

Duckadilly

Marigold Churchill, 1921

'I took the children on Sunday to Marigold's grave,' wrote Marigold's mother, Clementine, 'and as we knelt round it – would you believe that a little white butterfly . . . fluttered down & settled on the flowers which are now growing on it.'

The grief of a parent can never be quantified. To preside over the funeral of a child is a pain that is impossible to simply imagine. Clementine had her first child, Diana, in 1909; Randolph followed in 1911; Sarah arrived in 1914; and in 1918 came Marigold, who Churchill and Clementine referred to by the loving nickname 'Duckadilly'.

At the age of two, Marigold developed a cough that never quite seemed to clear up. In August 1921, the toddler and her siblings and their French nanny Mademoiselle Rose were packed off for a holiday and some fresh air at the Kentish resort of Broadstairs. In the meantime, Clementine travelled to Cheshire to Eaton Hall, home of the Duke of Westminster, for a tennis-playing break. Churchill stayed in London.

In Broadstairs, Marigold's infection very suddenly worsened, and she contracted septicaemia, though the nanny did not have the experience to see the danger. Marigold's throat turned septic, and at last the nanny sent word to the parents. Clementine and Churchill raced to Broadstairs, having engaged the services of a specialist. But this was an age before antibiotics.

They were at the bedside of their two-year-old daughter

when she succumbed. Three days later they were burying her in the north-west London cemetery of Kensal Green. For the headstone, they commissioned Eric Gill to chisel the lettering.

The aftershock of loss can produce a sort of fugue state. Churchill travelled to Scotland on political business after the funeral. He was not there on that first Sunday when Clementine took Diana, Randolph and Sarah to their sister's grave. A man who was usually so open about his emotional states, Churchill now seemed only able to face the power of his own grief at an angle, busying himself so that it would not overwhelm. From Scotland, he wrote to Clementine, but could only manage this fleeting reference: 'Alas I keep on feeling the hurt of the Duckadilly.'

A year later, Clementine gave birth to Mary. In later years, Mary would observe: 'Perhaps I was, for my parents, the child of consolation.'

An Artistic Interlude

Edwin Lutyens, 1921

In 1921 the famous architect Sir Edwin Lutyens – an habitué of Churchill's Other Club and the creator of, among other structures, the Cenotaph in Whitehall and the St Jude and Free churches for Hampstead Garden Suburb – had been 'drawing a lot of pictures for Winston Churchill to show him how to sketch and get shapes', according to Lutyens's biographer Christopher Hussey. Among his absolute surefire techniques: Lutyens 'showed [Churchill] how, from two elongated loops, he could produce either a boat or the brim of a hat; or from three eggs the body of a horse'.

These baby steps sound comical, but in the wake of the war Churchill was both serious and passionate about his art; his developing painting technique had a sensitivity to colour that – to expand on one of Mel Brooks's brilliant jokes in *The Producers* – made him by far the aesthetic superior to Hitler the watercolourist. *Winter Sunshine, Chartwell* – a symphony of rich ochres, oranges and pearl – might be described as both impressionist and expressionist.

After World War Two, Churchill would submit works to the Royal Academy's Summer Exhibition, not under his own name but that of 'David Winter' to avoid any charge of favouritism. They were selected to be shown. And as in other areas of life, Churchill was willing to adapt and learn.

Landscapes of Molten Lava

T. E. Lawrence, 1922

The lines that were drawn by the victorious powers across maps of desert sands continue to send shocks through the Middle East to this day. In the wake of the war, the mighty Ottoman Empire collapsed and dissolved into dust; Churchill – now in position at the Colonial

Office – was among those scrabbling to ensure Britain's influence and power in countries from Iraq to Palestine to Egypt was not diminished.

He had already met the hypnotic, charismatic T. E. Lawrence – known as 'Lawrence of Arabia' – who had fought the Ottomans in the Arab Revolt alongside Emir Faisal. Lawrence had adopted the full flowing robes of Arab dress; as with Churchill, outward costume was intensely important. By 1921, Churchill had persuaded Lawrence to help the Colonial Office and himself in trying to piece together the fragments of these ancient lands, the work of which involved forming the Kingdom of Jordan and consolidating the British mandate in Palestine.

'Do you remember your camel-trotting at Giza,' T. E. Lawrence wrote to Churchill in an exchange of quite extraordinary mutual admiration, 'when you wore out all your escort, except myself, and I'm not a fair competitor at that!' The image – that of Churchill's natural proficiency in the desert being almost, though not quite, the equal of this blazing-eyed young idealist in Arab robes – has a certain colonial potency. How could Churchill have resisted a man whose greed for acclaim was even greater than his own? More: a man who offered Churchill his own admiration?

Incidentally, some lines in *Seven Pillars of Wisdom*, Lawrence's account of his experiences in the Arab Revolt, have not aged especially well. 'Mr Winston Churchill was entrusted by our harassed Cabinet with the settlement of the Middle East; and in a few weeks, at his conference in Cairo, he made straight all of the tangle, finding solutions fulfilling (I think) our promises in letter and spirit (where humanly possible) without sacrificing any interest of our Empire or any interest of the peoples concerned.'

By 1922, Churchill was ordering the aerial bombing of Arabs and Kurdish people to quell bitter uprisings. And a hundred years later, that 'straightness' still seems an irresolute tangle.

Nonetheless, even when wriggling free of his Middle East obligations – he had developed a fixation upon flying, and becoming an airman – Lawrence did so with a reluctance to hurt Churchill or make the older man think less of him. He wrote to a friend: 'If we get out of the Middle East Mandates with credit, it will be by Winston's bridge. The man's as brave as six, as good-humoured, shrewd, self-confident & considerate as a statesman can be: & several times I've seen him chuck the statesmanlike course & do the honest thing instead.'

Lawrence's resignation letter from his quasi-official government role in November 1922 – at a turbulent point when the government had fallen and Churchill had lost his Dundee seat – saw him genuflecting in a variety of different ways:

Dear Mr Churchill,

This is a difficult letter to write – because it follows on many unwritten ones. First I wanted to say how sorry I was when you fell ill, and again when you had an operation. Then I should have written to say I was sorry when the Government resigned. I meant to write & congratulate you on getting better: but before I could do that you were in Dundee and making speeches.

Lastly I should write to say that I'm sorry the poll went against you – but I want to wash out all these lost opportunities, & to give you instead my hope that you will rest a little: six months perhaps. There is that book of memoirs to be made not merely worth £30,000 but of permanent value.

Your life of Lord Randolph shows what you could do with memoirs. Then there is the painting to work at, but I feel you are sure to do that anyhow: but the first essential seems to me a holiday for you. It sounds like preaching from a younger to an elder (and is worse still when the younger is an airman-recruit!) but you have the advantage of twenty years over nearly all your political rivals: and physically you are as strong as any three of them . . . in guts and power and speech you can roll over anyone bar Lloyd George: so that you can (or should) really not be in any hurry.

Of course I know your fighting sense is urging you to get back into the scrimmage at the first moment: but it would be better for your forces to rest & rearrange them: & no bad tactics to disengage a little. The public won't forget you soon, & you will be in a position to choose your new position and line of action more freely, for an interval. I needn't say that I'm at your disposal when you need me – or rather if ever you do. I've had lots of chiefs in my time, but never one before who really was my chief. The others have needed help at all times: you only when you want it: – and let me say that if your tools in the rest of your career to date had been of my temper you would have been now too big, probably, for the country to employ! That's a modest estimate of myself, but you know it doubles the good of a subordinate to feel that his chief is better than himself.

The chief and the subordinate remained friends. Churchill bought his beloved Kent house Chartwell in 1922; Lawrence was a frequent guest. It was recalled that practically only he could out-talk Churchill and dominate a room. But Lawrence had honed his techniques – he would arrive on his roaring motorcycle, go upstairs to change, and appear at dinner in those flowing robes. His death in 1935, a road accident, shocked Churchill deeply. In an obsequy in which his own extraordinary rhetorical palate in all its blazing wonder was deployed, Churchill declared:

Lawrence was one of those beings whose pace of life was faster and more intense than the ordinary. Just as an aeroplane only flies by its speed and pressure against the air, so he flew best and easiest in the hurricane. He was not in complete harmony with the normal. The fury of the Great War raised the pitch of life to the Lawrence standard. The multitudes were swept forward till their pace was the same as his. In this heroic period he found himself in perfect relation both to men and events.

I have often wondered what would have happened to Lawrence if the Great War had continued for several more years. His fame was spreading fast and with the momentum of the fabulous throughout Asia. The earth trembled with the wrath of the warring nations. All the metals were molten. Everything was in motion. No one could say what was impossible. Lawrence might have realized Napoleon's young dream of conquering the East; he might have arrived at Constantinople in 1919 or 1920 with many of the tribes and races of Asia Minor and Arabia at his back. But the storm wind ceased as suddenly as it had arisen. The skies became clear; the bells of Armistice rang out. Mankind returned with indescribable relief to its long-interrupted, fondly-cherished ordinary life, and Lawrence was left once more moving alone on a different plane and at a different speed.

The Ancient Forest

The People of Epping, 1924

Ejected by the voters from the jute city of Dundee, and gazing with ill will at the prospect of the spread of socialism throughout Britain, Churchill once more needed to find a parliamentary seat. In the face of the rise of the Labour Party, it was time for a cautious turn back to the Tories whom he had so dramatically spurned two decades beforehand.

There was an idea he might stand as a 'Constitutionalist' candidate – notionally quasi-independent but very firmly aligned with the Tory Party. The constituency of Epping – the forest lands to the east of London and inside the borders of Essex – seemed in some sense ideal. Though there were some Conservatives locally who objected instantly to the idea of Churchill; not because of his ideological stances, but because in this new post-Great War era, it was surely more fitting to have a prospective Tory MP from a slightly humbler social class – a candidate who had been a working man, with a trade, who understood working-class aspiration. Surely that, rather than a rich aristocrat. would better befit the new world? But older heads in the Conservative Associations deemed otherwise.

From the *Essex Newsman* newspaper: a chatty column entitled 'Reflexions of Reflex', published on Saturday, 27 September 1924 lightly discussed various burning local topics as a means of circling around to the idea of Churchill as an Essex MP:

Then there's the council of West Ham popping on the rates to the tune of 1s, 1d, for the year and Mr Will Thorne

MP declaring that there can be no material reduction until the cost of education is borne by the nation and local authorities have full control of their own traffic. Something will have to be done to give us relief. So says Winston Churchill, whom the Epping Tories have been cute enough to catch as a candidate. My word, I do congratulate them. It's fairly upset the dovecotes of the others.

Probably the Tories in their time have called Winston more names than anybody else, but they're wise to eat those words of old and support probably the greatest figure on the political stage today.

The prospective candidate became – by a narrow majority in the election of October 1924 – the new MP. And from that date until forty years later (he only retired a year before he died), Churchill remained the 'cute' MP, with ever ballooning majorities, for a constituency that widened to Woodford and Wanstead and Aldersbrook and other affluent new London suburbs. There he was to become a fixture in a variety of local schools, community halls, and snug hostelries.

I've Been to a Marvellous Party

Barbara Cartland, 1924

Although her name is now most associated with sugary, sexless romance novels, Dame Barbara Cartland, a daughter of Birmingham, was once a tornado-force power on the social scene. Writing — and reporting — came naturally to her; and her sphere was the glittering kaleidoscope of high society. Before the novels (over the course of her life, she wrote 723 of them, apparently selling some 750 million copies in total — a golden literary age!) she worked for smart magazines, and as a correspondent for the then vastly popular Daily Express. *Her real genius was that she always knew her readership and their desires. The fact that she had not been born into the grandest of families — her background was instead upper-middle-class — gave her the necessary distance to perceive the occasional absurdities of this social world. Churchill, quite properly, was a source of fascination to her in the mid-1920s.*

'As always when Winston was up against it he was very voluble in defence of himself,' wrote Barbara Cartland of his ejection from Dundee (and then his adoption by Epping). 'He was not defeated, he was undefeatable; and yet there must have been some hurt in knowing that his brilliance was unappreciated, that his political acumen hadn't more support in the country . . . he had been chosen as prospective candidate for a rural constituency of West Essex, or the Epping division. He told us about it, extolling its virtues as a place wholly desirable, the sort of people he would want to represent, and which must, without reserve, want him as their representative.'

His confidence in his constituents, though not misplaced, was at that time a little optimistic; there were rebels on his own side in Chigwell who began unsure, and who would grow ever more unsure as the years of wilderness in the 1930s crept along. But Cartland was alive to his energy.

'One thing I learned about Winston Churchill was that he had an amazing capacity for concentrating on what he was doing to the exclusion of all else,' she wrote in her autobiography. 'He would set up his easel in the garden at Cherkley and paint the bushes and the shrubs on the terrace, depicting them in what seemed to me strange colours.'

The interesting detail here is not Churchill's artistic Vorticism, but the unsaid fact that both he and Barbara Cartland were weekending at the Surrey estate of the newspaper proprietor Lord Beaverbrook at the same time. Churchill and Beaverbrook had first struck up a friendship during the Great War, and in the early 1920s they set out across the Channel on gambling missions to Deauville. Beaverbrook, at the helm of the *Daily Express*, was an extraordinary power in the land; and his relationship with Churchill would deepen in this interregnum between terrible conflicts, as the skies slowly darkened once more.

Cartland the society reporter watched Churchill paint. 'When he did this, he didn't seem to be thinking of anything else, he didn't even seem to hear what was going on around him.'

Dame Barbara would also recall a grand fancy-dress ball thrown by Lord and Lady Ribblesdale, which saw, as Noël Coward might have put it, 'the highest society scampering past'. On this occasion, one aristocratic woman was dressed as Little Lord Fauntleroy, and two well-born girls had donned rags and soot to portray 'street arabs' (or urchins). 'There was Rosemary Ednam as the Artful Dodger'; Gerald Berners had expressed an outrageous desire to go as nurse Edith Cavell; and then there was Winston Churchill. How else should he have dressed up other than in the voluminous toga of the emperor Nero?

There was a more piercing family connection a few years later: Cartland's younger brother Ronald – a young Tory MP for King's Norton from 1935, and very much on Churchill's side in the opposition to appeasement – was killed in the war, very early on, during the Battle of Dunkirk, in May 1940. Churchill, who was said to have 'adored him', delivered a moving tribute.

In the mid-1920s, Churchill also entered a forbidding realm combining abstract mathematics and graphs with an infinite series of real-life consequences. By accepting the role of Chancellor of the Exchequer in 1924, he was on the threshold of what was a fast-developing science. But this was also a period of tumultuous global economic uncertainty.

The Naked Economist

John Maynard Keynes, 1925

Among his many glaring faults – the imperialism that teetered on white supremacism, the impetuous bellicosity – Churchill had the consistent virtue of paying careful heed to his more thoughtful critics. More: it was rare that he appeared to take any such opposition to his ideas personally. In 1925, he was Chancellor – and with the economies of Europe and the US still fragile in the aftershocks of war, anyone in his position would have been desperate for the finest advice. Under particular pressure from the US and its incessant demands for the repayment of war debts, Churchill worked with his instincts. The economist who was fiercest in his opposition to those instincts was to become a valued colleague in later years.

*

'The politicians, who have ears, but no eyes, will not attend to the persuasion until it reverberates back to them as an echo from the great public,' wrote the pioneering economist John Maynard Keynes, and he might well have been referring to Winston Churchill – later a good friend and boon dining companion – directly.

In 1925 Stanley Baldwin was prime minister, and Winston Churchill his choice as Chancellor. Keynes's view of Churchill's grasp of economics was that he had 'no intuitive judgement'. It is more than possible that Churchill himself ruefully agreed with this assessment. Yet this particular battleground was far from academic; the world was still suffering the profound aftershocks of war. Poverty was grim and endemic, and Britain had very little in the way of social security: if a man in a northern manufacturing city were to lose his job, he and his family would be facing hunger, cold and destitution. If cotton mills and factories were to close, then that destitution would be spread across entire towns and communities.

The decisions made in cigar-scented meetings in Whitehall, and at the Bank of England, had the most direct bearing on the destinies of working people who had little agency of their own. Miscalculations or misunderstandings of the forces of economics could condemn countless people to lives of freezing misery.

So it is now slightly extraordinary to imagine Churchill – who had spoken of his schoolboy efforts with mathematics as 'an "Alice in Wonderland" world, at the portals of which stood "A Quadratic Equation"' – being appointed Chancellor of the Exchequer, and also absorbing the finely wrought complexities of Keynes's own economic theorems.

The paths of Churchill and Keynes – himself a

philosophy don – had crossed many times before the 1920s. It is thought that one social nexus was Lady Ottoline Morrell, whose salons Keynes regularly frequented. The economist was also, like Churchill, enmeshed with the Asquiths.

In the wake of the Great War, Keynes had delivered a booming denunciation of the terms of the Treaty of Versailles, reproduced as a pamphlet – he ensured that a copy was sent on to Churchill, for on this matter they were both in accord.

In the early 1920s, Keynes had been brooding darkly on the subject of a return to the gold standard – that is, the system whereby a nation's currency is fixed to the literal quantity of gold held by the nation. As with all matters financial, the aim was to ensure stability – in currency exchange rates and in inflation. Britain had left the gold standard at the outbreak of the Great War; in the midst of such swirling calamity it could never be held. But in peace, would a return to the system help to calm the roiling economic waters? Keynes vehemently thought not. He considered the gold standard 'a barbarous relic'.

Yet the fear of inflation – and its nightmare side effects – was not abstract. Weimar Germany in the early 1920s had suffered hyperinflation, bringing a fresh blow of misery to a people already driven into the dust by defeat. At this stage, the landscape of Britain lay under a thick cloud of industrial smog. It was a manufacturing nation, powered by the coal hewn from the earth by vast workforces. It needed cast-iron stability.

Keynes was right: Churchill was not a natural economist. But because Churchill knew that, he was open to advice. He wrote a memo to Treasury officials, name-checking Keynes and outlining his doubts. 'The Treasury have never, it seems to me, faced the profound significance of what Mr Keynes calls "the paradox of unemployment amidst dearth". The Governor [of the Bank of England] shows himself perfectly happy in the spectacle of Britain possessing the finest credit in the world simultaneously with a million and a quarter unemployed.'

And Churchill was acutely aware of the evils of unemployment, having seen outbreaks of it in his former northern constituency; he knew it was a disaster for many working families that was every bit as profound and immiserating as war.

So: which path to choose? In 1925, Churchill hosted a dinner for Keynes, top Treasury official Sir John Bradbury and former Chancellor Reginald McKenna. The arguments ran into the small hours: if Britain went back to the gold standard at its pre-war rates of $4.86 to £1, the pound would be overvalued and the result would be swooping deflation, inevitable unemployment, and also the possibility of vast social unrest.

In the views of Keynes's opponents, and much against his own advice, such a move would be 'hell' but – at the same time, like a terrible operation – necessary for the greater health of the nation. So, mindful of the economic lurch to come, and in spite of Keynes's own inclinations, Churchill took Britain back on to the gold standard; the pound was indeed greatly overvalued, and the near-instant result was appalling unemployment and then, in 1926, the fierce turmoil of the General Strike.

Keynes had pre-empted all this with his fiery pamphlet which – in the way of fiery pamphlets back then – proved to be a bestseller at the railway-station bookstalls. It was called *The Economic Consequences of Mr Churchill*. 'Seven thousand copies were printed priced at 1s a copy. They sold out immediately: several more editions were printed over the summer,' wrote Keynes's biographer Robert Skidelsky.

'*The Economic Consequences of Mr Churchill* was more than the echo of a name . . . Keynes's pamphlet combined a scorching analysis of policy with a passionate denunciation of injustice. He can be criticised, as at Versailles, for seeing the matter more clearly in retrospect than before the fateful decisions were taken. It needed the decision itself to crystallise the indictment . . .'

Keynes continued to be a sharp-toothed critic of Churchill; and Churchill continued to take the criticism mildly. In 1928, Keynes wrote to Churchill on the subject of his new currency bill. 'Dear Chancellor of the Exchequer, What an imbecile Currency Bill you have introduced!'

Churchill's silky riposte read: 'My dear Keynes, I will read your article enclosed and reflect carefully, as I always do, on all you say.'

According to Skidelsky, Keynes never blamed Winston Churchill personally for the return to gold. He wrote that Churchill had taken the decision 'partly because he has no intuitive judgement, partly because of the clamorous voices of conventional finance, and, most of all, because he was gravely misled by the experts.'

Nor did Churchill take Keynes's attack personally: in 1927, Keynes was elected to The Other Club. Meanwhile, the shadows were gathering around the world once more, and the Wall Street Crash of 1929 sent a shock wave that had a ghastly momentum of its own, creating fresh repercussions for months and years afterwards. In 1931, Britain – as shaken as many other nations by the teetering global financial edifice – was once more forced off the gold standard. It was observed that Keynes reacted to the news by 'chuckling like a boy'.

Churchill was not only no longer Chancellor by this stage, he was also out of office – and ever more isolated from old colleagues because of his antediluvian imperial views about the future of India. Nonetheless, he and Keynes met up for lunch.

After they said their goodbyes, Keynes made his way to the country home of Churchill's old adversaries Beatrice and Sidney Webb for another social engagement. And that evening, he relayed to them the gossip that Churchill had told him – that he personally had never wanted to go back to the gold standard in the first place, and that it had all been due to the machinations of the Governor of the Bank of England, Montagu Norman.

The two men – Churchill unintuitive but fast to grasp all arguments; Keynes with his philosopher's capacity for extraordinary feats of abstract thought – were to remain close as darkness stole over the world once more. When Churchill was run over in New York in 1931 (of which we will read more), Keynes was among those who contributed to his convalescence gift: a brand-new Daimler. Their dinners at the Savoy under the umbrella of The Other Club also provided them with a number of fruitful chances for the exchange of views. When it came to the appeasement of Hitler – and the terrible folly thereof – Keynes was very much in support of Churchill's opposition.

Some years later, the outbreak of World War Two – and the creation of the world that would come in its aftermath – would give Keynes his own remarkable centre of gravity. In the 1940s, he would become a form of unofficial economic ambassador for Britain, sailing back and forth to America, taking a hand in the creation of the International Monetary Fund and in crucial summits such as the Bretton Woods Conference. And all of this would be not just with the blessing of Churchill, but also with his admiration and friendship.

The General Strike

May 1926

A bitter conflict that would change little at the time, yet paradoxically echo down through the decades: the General Strike of 1926 was an eruption primarily of anger, but also of anguish and desperation and disbelief. Precipitated by the privately owned coal mines demanding of their workers not only substantial wage reductions but also extra hours labouring underground, the call to strike action across other industries – rail, transport, docks, steel, iron, printers and builders – was understood by huge numbers of workers as a fight for justice. The miners (under their union leader A. J. Cook) had the slogan 'Not a penny off the pay, not a minute on the day.' The mine owners (among them aristocrats) sought to justify themselves by citing the state of the economy, which was struggling in part because of Churchill's stance on the gold standard, making exports more expensive. They felt it was natural that the burden should fall not on them but upon their workers. For nine months, the government was subsidizing mining wages. On 30 April 1926, that subsidy expired. Then the mine owners locked the miners out of the pits.

From 4 May to 12 May, millions of manual workers across the nation downed tools. Factories and foundries fell silent. There were no whistles from steam engines, nor the clanging bells of midnight trams. But there were also scenes of conflict across the country: police leading baton charges on demonstrators near the docks in the East End of London, and in Hackney; crowds in Glasgow and Portsmouth demanding that strike-breaking buses and trains stop, and smashing their windows to ensure they went no further. But while there were disagreements on the left to do with strategy (the Trades Union Congress boycotted the BBC, for instance, on the grounds that it was part of the mass media armoury of capitalism), Stanley Baldwin's government was grimly determined to portray the strike as a larger effort to usurp Parliament – and by extension democracy and the state itself.

Because the printers were on strike, there were no newspapers. Churchill was seconded into producing a strike-breaking state-run free-sheet from the offices of the Morning Post, *called the* British Gazette. *He commandeered stocks of paper from* The Times *and threw himself into writing much of the* Gazette, *with a gusto that repelled his opponents. Even before he had started, his enthusiasm for treating the coming General Strike as a form of military campaign disgusted many – as it would for generations after.*

'I have just spoken in the House of Commons,' announced Labour leader and former prime minister Ramsay Mac-Donald at a meeting in the Kingsway Hall, London, on the evening of 3 May 1926, the eve of the strike. 'After me came Mr Winston Churchill – one of the most sinister figures in our public life today. He is a man of brilliant intelligence, but of a wayward and unsettling imagination. It makes him a sort of Ishmael, who has no permanent habitation on this earth, who by adventure and misadventure is consistently seeking new fields upon which he may exercise his restless and destructive spirit. A literary man – all wild people are good literary men – but as a politician or statesman a man who has never touched anything without turning it to disastrous account.'

Earlier that very same day, Churchill had had a close encounter with hostile public opinion (in the days when politicians were not surrounded by security details). 'Mr Winston Churchill left 11 Downing Street around noon and walked down the street into Whitehall,' it was reported in the *Daily Herald*. 'As he reached the end of Downing Street, a great rush was made by the crowd which had been kept back on the opposite side of Whitehall. Mr Churchill found himself hemmed in completely and a number of police had to be brought from Downing Street to clear a way for him. Eventually the Chancellor of the Exchequer had to take refuge in the Home Office.'

As the strike got underway, the military was called in; there were soldiers taking the place of dock workers unloading cargoes. Middle-class white-collar recruits were drafted in for other duties, including driving and deliveries, in order for food to make it to shops. Others kept the power stations and gasworks going. There was even the ominous spectacle of a military camp and barbed wire in Hyde Park.

It was suggested that Churchill had been given the task of editing a newspaper to keep him away from the temptations of physical trouble. Even though none of the *British Gazette* carried his by-line, its intensely purple rhetoric was distinctly his.

On 7 May 1926, a full-time journalist from the West Country, who wrote a regular 'London Letter' column for the *Plymouth Gazette*, observed Churchill in action. According to the unnamed (and clearly rather admiring) columnist:

Ministers are all leading strenuous lives nowadays, and each has more or less special emergency duty. To Mr Churchill is allotted the onerous task of combining the work of Chancellor of the Exchequer in Whitehall with that of editor of the *British Gazette* in the Strand. Between the two offices there is not a large interim for rest, but Mr Churchill is an old campaigner and has the knack of taking a nap – 'getting down to it' as Tommy says – at odd moments. When I went into the *Gazette* office last night at a late hour, I found his Majesty's Chancellor of the Exchequer curled up on some rolls of paper. Winston was taking 'forty winks' between proof-reading and seeing the paper to bed. Throughout the present crisis Mr Churchill has been one of the active and dominant cabinet personalities and, though he looks weary and worn, his energy never abates.

Senior members of the Trades Union Congress, or TUC, met with the government; by 12 May, the strike was over. There was hope that guarantees could be extended to the miners, but the government would not guarantee that every striker would have a job to return to. (The most outlandish dream of many on the left of the TUC – that the coal mines of Britain could be wrested from private hands and nationalized – would finally be realized in 1946).

In a large cartoon in the left-leaning *Daily Herald*, days after the strike ended, Churchill was portrayed as a fat sobbing boy in shorts, wearing a helmet, standing near a toy tank and holding an axe. Standing over him was a stern, giant figure – holding in one hand a 'bill for damages', listing 'British Gazette', 'Tanks', 'Guns' and 'Specials', and in the other, a birch. 'Father! I can't tell a lie!' exclaims this 'boy' Churchill. ' 'Twas I that did it!'

Churchill was linked inextricably with the paramilitary flavour of the government's response to the strike. This was the image that would stick.

Kingsley Martin, a prominent academic intellectual on the left, was a few years later to invite Churchill to a seminar at the London School of Economics. In his book *Father Figures*, Martin later recalled:

The General Strike of 1926 was an unmitigated disaster. Not merely for Labour but for England. Churchill and other militants in the cabinet were eager for a strike, knowing that they had built a national organization in the [nine] months' grace won by the subsidy to the mining industry. Churchill himself told me this on the first occasion I met him in person.

I asked Winston what he thought of the Samuel Coal Commission [which had been looking into miners' remuneration]. When Winston said that the subsidy had been granted to enable the Government to smash the unions, unless the miners had given way in the meantime, my picture of Winston was confirmed.

That said, Martin conceded, Churchill had been 'a delicious and witty guest' at the LSE, 'quite willing to talk freely to young academics'.

I then regarded him as the most dangerous of all politicians. He combined brilliance with the most foolish and antiquated views, which would have condemned us without hope of reprieve to war between classes and nations; he had tried to make war with Russia in 1919, and he waged successful war against the workers in 1926. The economic disasters of the thirties were inaugurated by his return to the Gold Standard in 1925; he was to be a supporter of Mussolini and Franco and would have carried out a disgracing war in India.

Churchill would have spluttered at this last part at least. In his book *The Gathering Storm*, he stated that while the advent of Mussolini had brought a 'new theme of government', he had 'raised himself to dictatorial power', and from fascism came Nazism. In the case of Franco, much less creditably, Churchill wrote of the Spanish Civil War that 'in this quarrel, I was neutral'.

'All the more remarkable,' Martin added, 'that I was to become [Churchill's] admirer in the later thirties and to write a eulogy of him as our indispensable leader in 1940.'

The Man from Auntie, Part One

John Reith, 1926

And with the debacle of the gold standard, and the overvaluation of the pound, a sharp and painful recession started biting into the British economy. The rippling effects upon the manufacturing and fuel industries – contraction, redundancies, and the crushing misery of unemployment – resulted in a surge of trade union support. Churchill, who two decades beforehand had been proclaiming his sympathies for the privations of working men forced into crisis through no fault of their own, had become flintier. In part, there was paranoia (from him, and others in government and the security services) about Bolshevik infiltration.

At this time, the BBC – which had begun as a radio broadcasting service in 1922 – was still navigating the borders of how much politicians could use the airwaves for party means. The general manager (as the job was then termed) of this nascent organization was a fierce six-foot-six Presbyterian Scotsman – a former soldier called John Reith. In spring 1926, as the General Strike was underway, the government made an effort to take full control of the BBC's broadcasts. Chief among those believing it should cede its power was Churchill. Lord Grey of Fallodon was deeply opposed, however, believing this to be an abuse of governmental reach. He had already won the argument when Reith and Churchill at last met for the first time. But from that point, Reith loathed Churchill – a flame of hatred that would burn ever brighter as the years progressed, as the first of his selected diary entries, below, illustrates.

May 9, 1926: Grey of Fallodon spoke tonight and I had a message asking if I would collect him from Churchill's house, no 11. I had not met Winston before. Hearing that someone had come to collect Lord Grey, he came out and asked me in to have coffee. He asked me if I were connected with the BBC. I said I was the Managing Director. He swung round with – 'are you Mr Reith?' – almost shouted out. I said I was. He said he had been hunting for me all the week. I said I was on the job all the time and he could have asked me to come along, and that he ought to do so when he was feeling indignant with us. He was really very stupid; his wife backed him up but Lord Grey approved the idea of keeping the BBC to some extent impartial. He was quite polite throughout, but I certainly kept our end up. I told him that if we put out nothing but government propaganda we should not be doing half the good that we were. He came to the car with us. He said he had heard that I had been badly wounded in the war. I said that I was but that had no bearing on my actions at present, which embarrassed him.

A Masterclass in Art

Walter Sickert, 1927

Of all the artists for Churchill to turn to for advice, Walter Sickert might at first glance have been unexpected. Here was a pioneer in the realm of urban realism – dowdy Camden Town parlours, rackety music halls, nudes draped over beds in frowsy lodging houses – which created shock in more traditionalist circles. Yet his paintings – suffused and heavy with atmosphere and sensuality – also conveyed a rich humanity. What it is not too much to say is that Churchill was very eager and willing to listen to Sickert's artistic advice, even if he did not take it.

'The most illustrious pupil of all was Winston Churchill,' wrote Sickert's biographer Marjorie Lilly. 'When he was Chancellor of the Exchequer, Sickert used to give him lessons at Hyde Park Gate. The studio was upstairs and although Sickert assured me that his teaching was as drastic as usual, the peals of laughter that the family heard from below seemed to indicate that they were managing to amuse themselves as well as serving their stern taskmistress, art.'

It was stern only as far as the application of technical method, to which Churchill – all instinct and swirling colour – seemed violently allergic.

'Sickert found it difficult to induce Churchill to draw,' the biographer continued. 'As the teacher brooked no compromise and made no difference between advising professional painters and trying to steer a mettlesome amateur who was tremendously committed elsewhere, they argued freely. Churchill always chafed at the discipline of the pencil and found it terribly irksome to build up the foundations of his picture with sufficient care, and when Sickert returned for the next lesson, he invariably complained that the drawing had been scamped' [that is, rendered as a quick, frazzly sketch] 'and that Churchill had indulged in his usual orgy of colour. I fear that this obstacle was never really overcome. Sickert could not teach by halves and Churchill was really happier afterwards with more pliable instructors, but he and Sickert engaged each other's society and spent many hours in art appreciation, especially when the Sickerts stayed at Chartwell.'

The New Generation

Jennie Lee, 1929

A fresh general election loomed. Yet despite this, on top of his duties as Chancellor, Churchill took the keenest interest in all manner of MPs in the House of Commons, whether on his side or in the Labour

Party. The Smoking Room was the centre of his Commons web, where he would initiate encounters with people from whom he wished to hear more. Owing to his actions during the 1926 General Strike — especially the lurid anti-socialist propagandizing of the British Gazette — *and also thanks to the firmly set legend that he had ordered soldiers to open fire upon striking workers at Tonypandy in 1910 — Churchill was reviled by many in the younger generation of rising Labour stars. That did not stop him from trying to make friends.*

'He assured me that we both wanted the same thing, only we had different notions of how to get it,' wrote Jennie Lee of her first encounter with Winston Churchill, in 1929. She was the remarkable, newly elected youngest MP in the House: a twenty-four-year-old Scot hailing from a Fife mining family. Her powers of oratory had been dazzling political meetings for some years. Lee would go on to marry Aneurin Bevan, Labour's totemically prized inaugurator of the NHS, and would bestow her own remarkable contribution to British public life in the 1960s, with the creation of the Open University. In 1929, however, all this lay ahead.

That year's by-election in North Lanark saw her elected as the Independent Labour Party MP, and her maiden speech in the Commons, aimed at Churchill — who was then still in office (the coming election would see him evicted from 11 Downing Street) — was akin to the door of a furnace opening. She accused him of 'cant, corruption and incompetence'.

'I directed my attack mainly against his budget proposals,' Lee wrote in her memoirs. 'Later in the day, in the Smoking Room, he came over to me and congratulated me on my speech. He assured me that we both wanted the same thing, only we had different notions of how to get it. The richer the rich became, the more able they would be to help the poor. That was his theme and he said he would send me a book that would explain everything to me. The book duly arrived. It was *The American Omen* by Garet Garrett, a right-wing economist who was despised by most of us for his extreme views.'

In some ways, her disdain was perfectly understandable: Garrett, a now largely forgotten journalist/author/economist manqué, was then at the height of his powers in the US; he wrote popular novels in which plucky individual capitalists were pitched against the repressive machinations of Big Government, which sought to stifle their honest quests for profit and bring everything under state control. To Lee, this expression of the rawest and most pitiless side of American rapacity would have been appalling.

And given that Churchill sometimes proclaimed genuine social concern, and admitted that some forms of hardship could only be alleviated with state intervention, was it at all possible that he presented Lee with this book as an elaborate tease, knowing that it would make her pirouette with indignation? We will catch up with them again in several decades' time, for an occasion when Lee – by this time married to Bevan – found herself perhaps a little taken aback by the unsuspected sensitivity of Churchill.

What Ho, Churchill!

P. G. Wodehouse, 1929

These were the days before the economic tsunami hit; nonetheless, the general election of 1929 tipped the sitting Tory government out of power. Churchill himself increased his constituency majority in Epping, but he was evicted from 11 Downing Street. This was the start of what were termed the 'Wilderness Years'; Churchill would continue as a local MP but would be out of office until 1939 and the start of World War Two.

Yet the wilderness was frenetic; a time when Churchill was raising his voice about India, about appeasement. He was writing like fury, and the forms that this writing would take even – as we shall see – branched into the realm of screenwriting. He was also perfectly determined that his voice should be heard further in the United States. Certainly there were many who were eager to hear it. Churchill attracted the attention of louche as well as powerful figures. Yet there were also American encounters with famous British expats which were not so smooth.

'I have reluctantly come to the conclusion,' said the prolific and wildly popular comic novelist P. G. Wodehouse, 'that I must have one of those meaningless faces which make no impression whatsoever on the beholder.' Surely, though, this could not have been the case with his fellow Beefsteak Club member Winston Churchill?

In the happy early summer of his life, Wodehouse was a bigger hit in the United States than even Winston Churchill. Poor eyesight had recused him from military efforts in World War One; it was in those years that he made a name for himself for writing the plots and lyrics of light comic Broadway musicals, and also for his new literary creations – the witty, eccentric capers set in and around Blandings Castle, and the escapades of Bertie Wooster and his valet Reginald Jeeves. His evocation of a fantasy England – heedless aristocrats, timeless country seats, faithful servants, and an endless series of sunny farces – was adored. Brilliantly articulate though Bertie Wooster was in recounting his scrapes, those scrapes were frequently as slapstick as anything conjured on the screen in Mack Sennett comedies.

In fact, by the early 1930s Wodehouse would even be under contract to the Hollywood studio MGM to write screenplays. The arrangement did not last – and an interview he gave to an American newspaper about the wasteful racketiness of the movie business caused an industry furore. Nonetheless, Wodehouse was still very much on the smart guest list in film circles, as indeed was Churchill.

Wodehouse was in California in 1929 when Marion Davies – a very popular actress and producer – invited him to a lunch being held at the Montmartre Restaurant in Santa Monica. Also present was media tycoon (and Davies's lover) William Randolph Hearst. Churchill – and his swaggering son Randolph – were the guests of honour.

Churchill was asked to give an after-lunch speech. He did so, and as soon as he was finished, the film producer Louis B. Mayer (of Metro-Goldwyn-Mayer) stood up, announcing: 'That was a very good speech. I think we would all like to hear it again.' And to Churchill's great surprise, his own voice started booming from the bushes; this was the latest in Hollywood-talkie recording equipment.

As Wodehouse's biographer Robert McCrum relayed, what followed was a moment of perfect English embarrassment: 'In due course, the two famous Englishmen were introduced. Amid the crush of Hollywood stars and the astonishing glamour of the moment, Churchill did not recognise Wodehouse, who commented wryly . . . "This was – I think – the seventh time I have been introduced to Churchill, and I could see that I came upon him as a complete surprise once more."'

A little over a decade later – in the desperate clamour of war – Churchill would know only too well who P. G. Wodehouse was: an Englishman giving idiotic radio broadcasts from the heart of Nazi Germany.

Upon the German invasion of France in 1940, Wodehouse and his wife, living in Le Touquet, were interned by the Nazi forces and held for a year. Upon his release, the novelist agreed to give a series of light-hearted and – as he saw it – non-political radio broadcasts from Berlin concerning his time in captivity. He imagined his wry tone would override any disgust. His misjudgement was beyond astounding. The repulsion in Britain was intense, and from the government's point of view, his actions were unforgivable.

Several years later, in late 1944, with France liberated by the Allies, Wodehouse and his wife were back in that country, but the smell of suspicion and the accusations of treachery hung heavily over them both. The French authorities arrested them, and this created a spasm of diplomatic irritation for Churchill – who was asked what sort of action might be taken.

He declared: 'We would prefer not ever to hear about [Wodehouse] again . . . His name stinks here, but he would not be sent to prison. However, if there is no other resort, he should be sent over here and if there is no charge against him, he can live secluded in some place or go to hell as soon as there is a vacant passage.'

Wodehouse was released; he neither lived secluded nor – as far as we know – went to hell. Instead, he and his wife emigrated to the United States, where they were still welcome. And his many adoring readers, in time, forgave.

In the intervening years, Wodehouse's view of Churchill had gnarled into deeper dislike. 'One of the few really unpleasant personalities I've come across,' he wrote. Meanwhile, Churchill's antipathy to the writer was shared by a number of government officials, who blocked efforts to have Wodehouse honoured.

The curious thing to consider is that both Churchill (in some senses) and Wodehouse were masters of comic prose; and that Churchill might surely have been expected to have more sympathy for a man who shared his prodigious gift. But the broadcasts were, in Churchill's view, not just a slip; they were an indication of moral weakness, which could never be tolerated.

The Most Famous Man in the World

Charlie Chaplin, 1929

Charlie Chaplin was the world's most recognizable silhouette: the bowler, the baggy trousers, the cane. In the era of silent films – with all barriers of language torn down and pure kinetic emotion flowing from the screen – a star could be taken into the hearts of every nation. In the 1920s, even Soviet Russia had clasped Chaplin's tramp character close.

Churchill – a cineaste – was a huge fan, having attended with his wife Clementine the gala London premiere of The Gold Rush *in 1925. And four years later, even as the era of the talkies approached, he was fascinated by how Chaplin deployed his 'glittering weapons' of 'wit and pathos'. Chaplin – out of costume – was polished, hand-some, devoutly socialist and effortlessly dominant. He and Churchill would repeatedly cross paths across the years – though without ever quite finding one another's wavelength.*

'I first met Winston Churchill at Marion Davies's beach-house,' wrote Chaplin in his memoirs, in 1964. 'About fifty guests were milling about between the ballroom and the reception room when he appeared in the doorway with [William Randolph] Hearst and stood Napoleon-like with his hand in his waistcoat, watching the dancing. He seemed lost and out of place.'

Churchill was there with his overbearingly confident son Randolph. Hearst saw Chaplin and beckoned him over, so they could be introduced:

Churchill's manner, though intimate, was abrupt. Hearst left us and for a while we stood exchanging the usual comments while people milled about us. Not until I talked about the English Labour government did he brighten up. 'What I don't understand,' I said, 'is that in England the election of a socialist government does not alter the status of a king or a queen.'

His glance was quick and humorously challenging. 'Of course not,' he said.

'I thought socialists were opposed to a monarchy.'

He laughed. 'If you were in England we'd cut your head off for that remark.'

It was a curiously witless exchange between two of the finest wits; almost as though neither of them could quite fathom the level at which to address each other. Though perhaps it is also possible to detect an element of star-struckness in Churchill's initial silence.

The Hollywood encounters were to continue.

'An evening or so later, he invited me to dinner in his suite at the hotel,' recalled Chaplin. 'Two other guests were there, also his son Randolph, a handsome stripling of sixteen, who was esurient for intellectual argument and had the criticism of intolerant youth. I could see that Winston was very proud of him. It was a delightful evening in which father and son bantered about inconsequential things.' The term 'esurient', or hungry, was a kind way of describing Randolph's unlovely teenage habit of boomingly dominating dinner-table conversations with eminent people.

'And now we were in London,' Chaplin continued, 'Mr Churchill invited Ralph [Barton, *New Yorker* cartoonist] and me to Chartwell for the weekend . . .'

It was at Chartwell that Chaplin was introduced to the full, faintly eccentric, range of Churchill's hinterland hobbies: his passion for bricklaying and horse racing and art. There was a painting over the fireplace that caught Chaplin's eye. His keen attention in turn caught the eye of Churchill, who told the star proudly that he had done that. Chaplin said it was remarkable; Churchill responded with an outrageous fib: 'Nothing to it – saw a man painting a landscape in the south of France and said, "I can do that."'

Both Walter Sickert and Edwin Lutyens might have had words to say about that.

There was a dinner that night, at which the fellow guests were Churchill's patience-trying parliamentary cronies Robert Boothby and Brendan Bracken (the latter we shall presently be hearing more from). Chaplin told them all lightly that he was due to meet Gandhi. Bracken exploded that they should put Gandhi 'in jail and keep him there'. Chaplin was unruffled, responding, 'If you imprison one Gandhi, another will arise. He is a symbol of what the Indian people want.'

At this, Churchill smiled at him and said: 'You would make a good Labour member.'

'The charm of Churchill is in his tolerance and respect for other people's opinions,' wrote Chaplin, who would have been too much of a communist for the Labour Party. 'He seems not to bear malice with those who disagree with him.' But again, there were signs that Churchill and Chaplin could not really spark off one another in the way that might have been expected.

'I hear you are interested in filming Napoleon,' Churchill said to Chaplin. 'You should do it – great comedy possibilities: Napoleon taking a bath, his brother Jerome bursting in upon him, arrayed in gold-braided uniform, using the moment to embarrass Napoleon and make him acquiesce to his demands. But Napoleon deliberately slips in the tub and splashes the water all over his brother's uniform, telling him to get out. He exits ignominiously – a wonderful comedy scene.'

Chaplin chose to leave it where it was. Churchill's nascent talent for screenwriting would find other outlets.

The Romantic Cynic

Brendan Bracken, 1929

In 1929 Winston Churchill was already deep into middle age, and told his wife that he did not expect to live very much longer. He had been cast into the political twilight. Yet as the years of the new decade progressed, and as his fears over rearmament sharpened, he would be sustained and supported by some extraordinary friendships. Among them was the enigmatic figure of Brendan Bracken . . .

'Harrow School was no better than a bloody borstal,' Churchill was told, with some swaggering confidence, by Brendan Bracken, who also had the maddening habit of lighting his cigarettes off Churchill's cigar. 'If anyone else had done that,' Churchill said of this tic, 'I would have killed them.'

The outward appearance of Bracken was – on first sight – rather startling. He resembled an outsized, gangling ventriloquist's doll. His hair was a ginger fright, corrugated and, as some remarked, wig-like. His face bore a half-smile; his eyes were small and watchful behind round glasses.

It was this vision – lying fully clothed, stretched out on the drawing-room sofa of her London flat one morning – that Clementine Churchill initially found highly disagreeable. Churchill's friend had stayed the night and slept with his shoes on. Bracken later remarked of his warm relationship with Churchill: 'We were a party of two.'

But if a man may be judged by his friends as well as his enemies, what light does the enigmatic Bracken throw on

Churchill's hinterland? Bracken's background – at a time when background mattered – was mysterious. What were his roots? Bracken waved away curiosity. It was of no matter to Churchill; he found Bracken's company exhilarating and constantly amusing. And Bracken, in turn, regarded Churchill as being wholly correct about all the important political principles, including rearmament, at a time when others were dismissing the former Chancellor as an irksome and noisy eccentric.

By 1929, Bracken was a shrewd media tycoon as well as an MP, with stakes in the *Economist* and the *Financial Times* (the newspaper is headquartered at Bracken House, opposite St Paul's). He was very rich. What made this impressive was that he had summoned it all – emerging from modest beginnings – by sheer force of will.

He was actually Irish-born; the son of a reasonably well-off builder from Tipperary. His father died when he was three. Bracken and his siblings were brought up by his mother but he was ungovernable, even when – or perhaps especially when – he was sent away to a ferocious Jesuit school. He was then put on a boat to Australia to live with a Jesuit relative. There, he absorbed every book he could find; and formed an intensely romantic view of England's eighteenth century. Aged nineteen, he sailed to Britain, arrived at Liverpool and presented himself at Sedbergh School, claiming to be an orphaned fifteen-year-old and imploring the headmaster to take him in to complete his exams. (It was an age when such a gambit might be viewed more innocently than it would now.)

This was the man on Clementine Churchill's sofa. This would also be the man who, throughout the 1930s, was constantly at Chartwell. Sunday at that house became known as

'Brendan's Day'. Stanley Baldwin referred to Bracken as 'Winston's faithful chela' (*chela* is a Hindu term meaning 'disciple'). But he was much more than that; he and Churchill argued freely, and frequently, but always without rancour. According to Harold Macmillan, they 'quarrelled' incessantly 'like an old married couple'. There were rumours that Bracken was Churchill's illegitimate son (the mad red hair appeared to be one giveaway clue). Mrs Churchill became rather vexed on this point, leading Churchill to joke: 'I looked it up, but the dates don't coincide.'

The point was that Bracken had a tremendous and rather touching faith in Churchill at the moment when others were shunning him; and possibly because Churchill was in one sense a reincarnation of Bracken's idealized eighteenth-century man of politics. There was another factor that bonded them: intense autodidacticism. Both read and absorbed and revelled in all the great works and ideas that they could find. 'Brendan was almost more Churchillian than Churchill,' said the newspaper editor Colin Coote. 'And it is a singular tribute to his character that the alliance was forged at the outset of ten of the blackest years in Churchill's career. He was no fair-weather friend.'

Clementine eventually shook off her distaste for this eccentric sprawling figure and instead came to welcome the clouds of cigarette smoke that he trailed into Chartwell. He had a warmth and an engaging manner that even sceptics could not help but like. He was to be the model for Evelyn Waugh's Rex Mottram in *Brideshead Revisited*. But when at last his hour of destiny arrived with the war, Bracken would prove every bit as ingenious with the use of propaganda as Goebbels ever was. We shall meet Bracken again in 1944, in the wake of D-Day.

In the meantime, his constantly amusing friendship gave Churchill succour. 'He was a romantic posing as a cynic,' said one contemporary.

The Amused Amanuensis

Maurice Ashley, 1929

Churchill could always hear the ravening wolf prowling ever closer to his door. His money worries were never the type that would assail working families struggling to pay the rent. Yet he faced some extraordinary financial cliffhangers (one of which led to him considering selling his beloved Chartwell). The Wall Street Crash and the resulting Great Depression laid waste to many of his investments, and he was in constant need of richer friends finding ways to bail him out. His own solution was to write more: articles, essays and especially books, for which he received stratospheric advances. One such great work – begun as he was tipped from office in 1929 – was Marlborough: His Life and Times. *For this Churchill needed a literary assistant who would plough through the archives for him, investigating all first-hand eighteenth-century sources.*

'He did not like the smoking of Virginian cigarettes or pipes about his house,' recalled Maurice Ashley, 'although when a very distinguished guest insisted on smoking a pipe he had to put up with it. Boxes of Turkish or Egyptian cigarettes lay about the place and of course there were boxes of cigars, usually Coronas. He told me: "Help yourself to a cigar whenever you feel like it." I did not often do so, but once when I did, it went out and I started to relight it in his presence. He said firmly, "Never relight a cigar, take another one."'

In 1929, Ashley, then twenty-two and a forthright socialist, was in Oxford subsisting on two research grants, studying for a doctorate. Money was a preoccupation. A friend at Christ Church told him he had learned that Churchill was embarking upon the life of the first Duke of Marlborough and needed a researcher. Ashley had been the chairman of the Oxford University Labour Club, and the very name 'Churchill' made the sky echo with metaphorical thunder claps: the prime villain of the General Strike of 1926!

Yet Ashley was more of an historian than a politician; he dealt in nuance rather than caricature. And after a meeting brokered by Professor Frederick Lindemann, of whom we shall be hearing more shortly, Ashley took the part-time job, which paid the handsome (for that time) sum of £300 a year.

Soon came the invitation to Chartwell. Ashley's background was very solidly middle class; and as such, on his first visit, he was hyper-aware of the more upper-class atmosphere of Churchill's home. He had a middle-class resistance – though he could offer no actual resistance – to ideas such as a valet unpacking his case and laying his evening clothes out, and everyone wearing formal dress to dinner. Ashley also had middle-class drinking tastes: his constitution was not prepared for the succession of sherry, Champagne, wine, brandy and port that accompanied dinner. That night, in his room, Ashley was horribly and embarrassingly ill.

The following evening, Ashley identified the most lethal of the alcoholic refreshments – and politely refused the port. Churchill instead offered him some Madeira. And from that point onwards, on every return visit to Chartwell, Churchill would make an elaborately jokey point of fetching out the Madeira for his young guest.

A little like Jonathan Harker at Dracula's castle in Transylvania, Ashley quickly discovered that the Churchillian day was based upon very irregular hours. He observed Churchill's morning routine: breakfast taken in bed, where he would remain to read the newspapers and deal with correspondence with one of the two secretaries who worked on a shift system. In the late morning, he would head out into the Chartwell grounds, either to build walls or to lure his fish to the surface of their lake by means of a special call (a technique which, as we will see later with his son-in-law, could be rather disconcerting). At noon, the work on Marlborough would begin. Ashley would present Churchill with sheaths of documents that he had sourced, and notes that he had taken from a variety of different books.

By the afternoon, Churchill would be back out in the garden, returning to his manual labours. Then it was indoors, where he would retire upstairs to bathe and then dress for dinner.

Ashley observed that despite the array and range of alcoholic refreshment on offer, Churchill himself was not as prodigious a drinker as legend seemed to suggest – in the sense that he drank constantly, but it was not generally the stronger liquors he favoured. Lunch would be accompanied by beer; there would be un-potent whisky and soda in the evening; and the ever-present motif of Champagne, which had its own sparkling innocence.

Mr and Mrs Churchill had a late-evening, post-dinner

routine: a couple of games of backgammon. But then, come 10 p.m., Churchill's working day suddenly began in earnest.

It took place in his bedroom (Mrs Churchill's quarters were elsewhere), and as well as Maurice Ashley, there was his main secretary, Violet Pearman. What unfolded was a spectacle that sounds hypnotic: Churchill pacing the floor of the room and dictating his book – part of a chapter a night – off the top of his head. This was clearly a process of trial and error. The young historian would refer to his notes throughout and point out factual infelicities. Churchill would give the impression of ignoring this; nothing would interrupt the prose that flowed from him like a stream. But the interruptions had been noted nonetheless; and over the course of subsequent evenings, Churchill would make the subtle adjustments required.

And rather like Jonathan Harker having to sit up with the Count until the small hours, listening to wolves, so Ashley had to adjust to this new world of working into the depths of night. Pearman had grown perfectly accustomed to it, and Churchill always ensured that there was a hired car waiting to take her home at 2 a.m. when at last his perorations evaporated. But after she left the boudoir, Ashley was required to stay on a little longer, to check back through notes and discuss all that had been thus far committed to paper. He was able at last to go to his own room by about 3 a.m.

If Churchill ever harboured any suspicions that he had a committed socialist not only under his roof but in his very bedroom, he was mannerly enough to keep any doubts to himself. In fact, Ashley always found Churchill to be the most considerate of employers. Part of it might have been a respect for Ashley's academic achievements at university:

this young man represented the scholarly life that Churchill had never had, and Ashley was aware that Churchill held him in esteem. He and Churchill discussed how Churchill had missed out on university; he told Ashley that it had occurred to him after Africa to embark on study, but the element that put him off university entrance was the requirement for Latin – that old horror for verb conjugations had never left him.

Ashley also noted how considerate Churchill was towards his secretaries, and how, in the dark silence of the small hours, as he strode back and forth, Violet Pearman was able to forgive his erratic, annoying moments as he growled to himself or appeared to lose his temper over a train of thought. The young man also came to understand that Churchill was not quite the pure villain of the General Strike. Dr Ashley conceded, in a warm speech about his former employer years later, that 'as a matter of fact, as we now know, Churchill was sympathetic to the claims of the miners, who were then paid a pitiful wage, and he did not care for the coal-owners'.

One point in Churchill's disfavour, as Ashley saw it, was his friends. Brendan Bracken, whom we have already met, was 'conceited and ill-mannered'. Frederick Lindemann, whom we are just about to meet, 'fed himself on whites of egg and stewed apple' – in other words, a vegetarian nuisance – and flaunted his inherited wealth by being the only don in Oxford with a chauffeur.

In the years to come, Maurice Ashley pursued a hybrid career that was not entirely unlike Churchill's: he went into journalism, but also wrote high-minded history on the side. A few years after the war, he joined the then highly respected *Listener* magazine, becoming its editor (and

hugely enjoying war memoirs that recounted how Churchill drove his generals mad by insisting on pacing and
perorating until 3 a.m.).

But he also did a very good job for Churchill: the result at
the end of those nocturnal labours was a four-volume life
of Marlborough, which sold respectably if not spectacularly. Ashley had helped keep those wolves from that door.

Atoms and Robots

Frederick Lindemann, 1931

*Churchill's restless mind, when not absorbing great literature and history
and art, would frequently alight upon the glow of scientific discovery (in
contrast to what he would term 'the lights of perverted science' pursued
by Hitler). Technological innovation fascinated him, but not just from a
material or indeed military point of view. While he was always keen to
fathom the possible applications in the battlefield for certain ideas, he was
also fascinated by the philosophical dimension.*

'I need my Prof,' said Churchill of Frederick Lindemann
(later Lord Cherwell). 'He is my adder.' But then, seeming
to regret the venomous snake image, he added: 'No. I can
add – he is my taker-away.'

He might just as well have left the remark where it was;
everyone else regarded the chilly Lindemann as serpentine.
They wondered how Churchill had become such great
friends with a physicist who was renowned as a 'great hater'

(i.e. one who did not disguise his loathing of so many others). Yet as the world moved towards an atomic age, Churchill revelled in the experience of a scientist who had the incomparably rare ability to communicate complex technical ideas in succinct memos.

In the years to come, the wartime skies darkening with bombers, such ability would prove invaluable. Even in the 1930s, as Lindemann and Churchill shared their foreboding of a rearming Germany, their dinner-table exchanges at Chartwell were sparky.

Lindemann, of German aristocratic heritage and an habitual bowler-hat wearer, was only thirty-three years old when he was appointed Professor of Experimental Philosophy (i.e. physics) at Oxford. His presence was so unpleasantly imposing that he was known by some as 'Dracula', because the temperature in the room immediately fell upon his entrance.

He was a pioneer in the research of solar winds, and the effects of hyper-low temperatures, and the use of photoelectric cells to capture astronomical images; and even more of a pioneer – to the extent of risking his own life – in the relatively new field of aeronautics during the course of World War One. Lindemann had taught himself to fly a biplane; the aim was to understand with precision – from the cockpit – the lethal physics of downward spins that killed so many other pilots. His courage could never be doubted, but his capacity for compassion could.

To those he disliked – and this included a very broad swathe of humanity, from the working classes onwards – Lindemann was openly rude and contemptuous. But those few who found his favour basked in an eccentric warmth: Clementine and then Winston were among those happy few.

Lindemann – regarded by colleagues as a social mountaineer and also nicknamed 'the Ferry' because he sailed 'from peer to peer', and who was friends with smart figures such as Duff Cooper and Evelyn Waugh – had first met Clementine at a charity tennis match (he was a superb player). This led to Churchill, and an immediate mutual admiration. As well as enjoying this scientist's company, Churchill sought out his knowledge and intelligence at every turn.

His fascination with the science fiction of H. G. Wells had turned to a fixation on scientific reality, and how it was going to shape the world to come. In 1931 – with Churchill now prowling political wastelands – Lindemann collaborated with his friend on a remarkable article that the former Chancellor was to write about the world that was coming. It was entitled 'Fifty Years Hence'. In it, we hear the fusing of two minds, and the conjuring of some shared demons.

'High authorities tell us that new sources of power, vastly more important than any we yet know, will surely be discovered,' Churchill told his readers (without telling them that Lindemann was that high authority). 'Nuclear energy is incomparably greater than the molecular energy which we use today. The coal a man can get in a day can easily do five hundred times as much work as the man himself. Nuclear energy is at least one million times more powerful still . . . There is no question among scientists that this gigantic source of energy exists. What is lacking is the match to set the bonfire alight, or it may be the detonator to cause the dynamite to explode. The scientists are looking for this.'

Churchill was radiantly optimistic about the coming nuclear revolution. 'The discovery and control of such sources of power would cause changes in human affairs incomparably greater than those produced by the steam engine four generations ago. Schemes of cosmic magnitude would become feasible. Geography and climate would obey our orders.'

There were also predictions – inspired by late-night conversations at Chartwell, with Churchill on brandy and the normally teetotal Lindemann persuaded into a wee drop himself – that seem astounding for 1931. 'Wireless telephones and television, following naturally upon their present path of development, would enable their owner to connect up with any room similarly installed, and hear and take part in the conversation as well as if he put his head in through the window,' Churchill told his readers. 'The congregation of men in cities would become superfluous. It would rarely be necessary to call in person on any but the most intimate friends; but if so, excessively rapid means of communication would be at hand.'

There was dystopian warning, though, too. Given Lindemann's chilly dismissal of the intellectually inferior, which for him was in essence the great number of mankind, it is interesting to see how Churchill diffused their discussions on the potential future of eugenics and where it could lead:

> But equally startling developments lie already just beyond our finger-tips in the breeding of human beings and the shaping of human nature. It used to be said, 'Though you have taught the dog more tricks, you cannot alter the breed of the dog.' But that is no longer true.
>
> A few years ago London was surprised by a play called *Rossum's Universal Robots*. The production of such beings

may well be possible within fifty years. They will not be made, but grown under glass. There seems little doubt that it will be possible to carry out in artificial surroundings the entire cycle which now leads to the birth of a child. Interference with the mental development of such beings, expert suggestion and treatment in the earlier years, would produce beings specialized to thought or toil. The production of creatures, for instance, which have admirable physical development with their mental endowment stunted in particular directions, is almost within the range of human power.

A being might be produced capable of tending a machine but without other ambitions. Our minds recoil from such fearful eventualities, and the laws of a Christian civilization will prevent them. But might not lop-sided creatures of this type fit in well with the Communist doctrines of Russia? Might not the Union of Soviet Republics armed with all the power of science find it in harmony with all their aims to produce a race adapted to mechanical tasks and with no other ideas but to obey the Communist State? The present nature of man is tough and resilient. It casts up its sparks of genius in the darkest and most unexpected places. But Robots could be made to fit the grisly theories of Communism. There is nothing in the philosophy of Communists to prevent their creation.

Within the next two years, it was less the spectre of communism than fascism that would come to absorb the two friends. And Churchill would start widening his scientific acquaintanceships swiftly.

A Near-Miss with His Maker

New York City, 13 December 1931

'There was a moment – I cannot measure it in time – of a world aglare, a man aghast,' Churchill wrote. He was referring to an occasion in Manhattan, having been driven in a taxi to the house of his friend Bernard Baruch. Churchill had lost the exact address but remembered how to get there from Central Park and Fifth Avenue. He stepped from the cab into the cold air. But by instinct, he looked left rather than right.

The car that hit him, driven by a Mr Mario Contasino, was travelling at thirty-five miles per hour.

'Then came the blow,' recalled Churchill. 'I felt it on my forehead and across the thighs. But besides the blow, there was an impact, a shock, a concussion indescribably violent. It blotted out everything except thought. I do not understand why I was not broken like an eggshell, or squashed like a gooseberry.'

Mr Contasino, by some accounts a young man, was distraught. He lifted Churchill into his car to take him to the closest hospital, near Lexington Avenue. Churchill, understandably, was woozy. He declared that he was a British statesman, that he did 'not wish to be hurt any more' and that he wanted 'chloroform or something'. He had lacerations to the face and serious bruising to his torso, arms and legs, and was bedbound in hospital for a week.

The horrified Mario Contasino – who was questioned and then immediately released by the police – rather affectingly, in his terrible anxiety, came to visit Churchill's bedside. His presence was appreciated by both Clementine and Churchill. The 'British statesman' showed there were no hard feelings by giving him a signed copy of one of his books.

And his friend Professor Lindemann wrote to Churchill, explaining helpfully, via the medium of physics, that the impact of the crash on his body would be 'equivalent falling thirty feet on to pavement'.

Even in the aftershock of the accident, Churchill's instinct for earning never left him: he immediately secured a lucrative commission from the *Daily Mail* to write of his near-death encounter, and of how he was vividly conscious throughout it all. Even his proximity to heaven's gates had to be carefully curated for posterity.

Upon his return to Britain, Churchill was dazzled with an extraordinary gift: a Daimler 35 limousine. Brendan Bracken had organized what we would now term the crowd-sourcing for it, though for Churchill this involved the highest in the land, from the Prince of Wales to the Duke of Westminster – and even Charlie Chaplin and John Maynard Keynes – among some 150 contributors. Many were members of his still-popular dining society The Other Club. Some of these friends went back years: General Sir Ian Hamilton was among those who chipped in.

The car cost £2,000. Churchill never had difficulty accepting gifts – he was grateful, but he was also immodest enough to think that it was perfectly natural that people should want to be outlandishly generous – and this extraordinary car was no exception.

A Near-Miss with Hitler

Ernst Hanfstaengl, 1932

It was not merely through the crystalline lens of hindsight that Churchill later recalled his deep unease about Germany in the early 1930s. He immediately understood Hitler as being the conduit for a manifestation of a darkness that – as Churchill saw it – had long been there in the soul of Germany. It had roared through the Great War; and that rage was about to menace Europe once more. But in 1932, Churchill – whose furious views on Indian independence had estranged him from party and friends – could not make his voice heard. Later that summer, while writing the biography of the Duke of Marlborough, he took the opportunity to jump on a boat with 'the Prof' (Lindemann) and drive to 'old battlefields' near the Danube and the Rhine as part of his research. This excursion led to the closest he came to meeting Hitler.

'At the Regina Hotel, a gentleman introduced himself to some of my party,' Churchill later recalled. 'He . . . spoke a great deal about "the Fuehrer", with whom he appeared to be intimate . . . He had probably been told to get in touch with me.'

There was no shortage of British fans of Hitler as his ascendency began, and he had American fans too. One especially curious figure – a dual German-American called Ernst Hanfstaengl – tried to broker a 1932 meeting between Churchill and Hitler. It came within a whisker of happening. Such a face-to-face encounter would surely never have changed the course upon which they were set;

quite apart from the ideological distance, and cultural antipathies and suspicions stretching back to the Great War, neither could speak one another's language. Nonetheless, the prospect still intrigues. As Churchill journeyed through Germany that summer, he had 'naturally asked questions about the Hitler Movement, and found it the prime topic in every German mind. I sensed a Hitler atmosphere.'

And in Munich, this elegant stranger Ernst Hanfstaengl – known as 'Putzi' – had spotted Churchill and was eager to convert him. Before his waltz with Nazism, Hanfstaengl had been a very well-connected businessman who composed popular music on the side (including stirring anthems for baseball teams). His godfather was a Saxe-Coburg duke; his father was an art publisher. It was in New York that Hanfstaengl continued the family business after studying at Harvard and entering the social orbit of Franklin Roosevelt. He also married an American woman.

His seduction into Nazism was in part the result of a Harvard pal inveigling him into a spot of light intelligence-gathering: could Hanfstaengl, who had returned to Munich in the early 1920s, pop in to a local beer hall to see what all the fuss involving the National Socialists was about? Hanfstaengl did so, and was enraptured. So much to his liking was it that he sought out Hitler, and they were to become good friends. Hanfstaengl was precisely the sort of smart social veneer that Hitler needed for his party.

Then in 1932, at the glamorous Regina Palast Hotel in Munich, as Hitler was on the march but not yet in power, Hanfstaengl swiftly sidled over to Churchill and Lindemann to introduce himself. Possibly because of his

American background and experience, Churchill was won over by this stranger – describing him as 'lively' and 'talkative' – and asked him to dine. Throughout dinner, Hanfstaengl sang hymns of praises to Hitler. 'He spoke as one under the spell,' observed Churchill drily. Hanfstaengl then literally sang – commandeering the lounge piano and performing a medley of Churchill's favourite popular songs. He also suggested that Churchill should meet Hitler. The Führer came to that very hotel every day, and such an encounter would be easy to arrange.

Churchill claimed in his account of those years that, at that stage, he knew little of Hitler's 'doctrine' and 'nothing' about his character; that he had a 'perfect right' to want to defend his country. But there was one question that Churchill had to put to Hanfstaengl: why was Hitler so 'violent' about the Jews? How could he be against a man 'simply because of his birth'?

The question, Churchill reasoned later, must have been relayed to Hitler, for the previous enthusiasm to meet evaporated. The next day, Hanfstaengl, the go-between, had to tell Churchill lamely that Hitler would not in fact be visiting the hotel as promised. There was a suggestion elsewhere that Hitler had in fact been there, in another lounge, taking coffee; and having heard Churchill's question, announced to Hanfstaengl dismissively that Churchill, out of power, was of no account and not worth seeing.

'Thus Hitler lost his only chance of meeting me,' wrote Churchill wryly. 'Later on, when he was all-powerful, I was to receive several invitations from him. But by that time a lot had happened, and I excused myself.'

A Genius at Chartwell

Albert Einstein, July 1933

As Hitler's Nazis first were handed power in political manoeuvres, and then seized it entirely for themselves in 1933, German citizens who were Jewish immediately had to face the hideous choice: to emigrate, to lands which scarcely seemed any more welcoming or friendly, in search of security which might never be found; or to stay in Hitler's Germany, with the desperate hope that the anti-Jewish rhetoric was merely some form of populist trick. One exceptional Berlin resident made his choice quickly: the physicist Albert Einstein, in America as the Nazis gained ascendancy, understood that he could not return. Back in Britain, Churchill and Frederick Lindemann became involved in a scheme to bring Jewish scientists over to Oxford and Cambridge. Einstein, greatly interested in this initiative, paid a visit to Kent . . .

'Eminently wise,' was the verdict of Albert Einstein on Winston Churchill – rather than the other way around. There is a marvellous photograph – black-and-white but radiating fresh, bright Kentish summer sun – which shows the two men standing side by side in a quintessential English garden (this was Chartwell). On the right is Albert Einstein – a shock of white hair defying his own laws of relativity, wearing a crumpled white suit, shirt and tie, and a relaxed, eyebrow-raised smile. Next to him, Churchill is wearing an early version of his siren suit – a zip-up onesie, with pockets, rough in texture – paired with a white shirt. His face is in shade, chiefly because it is in the dark eclipse of his vast hat brim (another of those curious hats – this one a kind of jumbo fedora – never seen elsewhere). If we look especially closely, we see the hint of a smile through that shadow.

It would have been wonderful if they had also had the chance to discuss the cosmological mysteries: curves in space–time, the qualities of entropy and heat death. But Einstein's visit to Chartwell was very particularly and singularly about the urgent need to help Germany's Jews.

Frustratingly, there was no one present who thought to record the encounter beyond the photograph; in any case, since Churchill's German was non-existent, and Einstein's English an infinitesimal point of singularity – and since their conversation had to be relayed haltingly by one translator – there may not actually have been all that much said. In a sense, it did not really matter; the meeting was about the symbolism of friendship. And it was clearly a success on all levels. Later on, Einstein wrote to his wife about it and described Churchill thus: 'He is an eminently wise man, and it became quite clear to me [through their meeting] that these people have planned well ahead and will act <u>soon</u>.' Positions by that stage had been found for around twenty Jewish scientists in the great universities.

Churchill at the Movies, Part One

Alexander Korda, 1934

It was in Churchill's youth – when he was twenty-one – that popular cinema was born, in France in 1896. According to hoary and unlikely legend, the short film of a train arriving at La Ciotat station caused Parisian audiences to jump out of their seats for fear of the train smashing through the screen. If that was so, they cannot have been familiar with the earlier technology of magic lanterns, which deployed all sorts of trickery to suggest moving images. Churchill, as a magic lantern devotee, took to cinema with even greater passion, his eyes brimming at every sentimental scene.

The winter of Churchill's Wilderness Years was brightened by encounters with a remarkable director/producer/studio owner called Alexander Korda, who in 1933 had scored a tremendous hit with The Private Life of Henry VIII *starring Charles Laughton. The two men embarked upon a collaboration in 1934.*

'Preliminary outline really splendid and I am most happy about it,' trilled the film mogul Alexander Korda to Churchill, who was making his debut in the film industry. After the two men shared epic quantities of wine and brandy over an ideas lunch, Churchill had subsequently written the outline for a script about the reign of George V and had sent it to Korda from a yacht in the Mediterranean where he was holidaying. 'Only criticism', added Korda, 'that in this version politics play too big a part . . . But no doubt this can be easily corrected . . . Interest in picture tremendous.'

Hungarian-born Alexander Korda had been making silent films in his native land when there was still an Austro-Hungarian Empire. The tides of history swept him to Vienna, and thence to Hollywood and – by the 1930s and the inception of the talkies – to London. By this time he was established as a fine director, perceived as having a particular skill for working on glossy romances. And the expertise that he brought to Britain – where he adopted a bowler hat – also included that of running a studio; he established his own at Denham, in Buckinghamshire, and here entire worlds and epochs were conjured. He was at last his own man, and under the banner of 'London Films' would across the next two decades furnish the screen with some extraordinary classics such as *The Thief of Baghdad* (1940) and *The Third Man* (1949), plus the luscious partnership of Powell and Pressburger.

Churchill had very much enjoyed the Henry VIII film; though when he and Korda met, he commented on the famous scene where the King, gnawing at a chicken leg, throws it over his shoulder. 'A little less chicken-bone-chewing and a little more England building' was his idea of how the film might have been tweaked. It was in part Churchill's energetic and imaginative enthusiasm for the form that inspired Korda to commission that previously mentioned epic screenplay from him: a film that would span the life of the then reigning King George V.

It was a curious idea – a grand romance – inspired by the King's forthcoming silver jubilee (he had ascended to the throne in 1910). Churchill envisaged a story told against the vast backdrop of recent history: a screenplay that would march though the 'Irish problem' to the suffragettes, from the trenches of the Great War to a new era of 'social advance' and 'inventions and change'. This wasn't a documentary, however; Churchill's idea was that we would celebrate the reign of George V by following the story of 'the son of a nobleman' who – before going 'off to the wars' – would become engaged to a young lady of 'good family'. The nobleman's father – a duke – would be thrilled that he was 'affianced' to a beauty who was 'virtuous withal'.

It is difficult not to wince at the all-too-obvious and idealized projection of Churchill's own life, recast as a glossy celluloid epic, where the young hero has a living father that he can turn to for approval and praise.

More: the salient recent historical events would be narrated by Churchill himself, and 'essential statistics' of George V's reign would be conveyed by means of animated cartoon sections. In some parts, the vision was spectacular: vast naval battles, startling images of skulls becoming visible beneath the skin. Churchill brought a painter's sense of colour to the project.

And it paid: Korda offered him an advance of £10,000 (a colossal sum then), which subsequently had to be reduced to £5,000 when the accountants of London Films began dancing with agitation.

There was a full-time screenwriter – Eric Siepmann – assigned to the project with Churchill, and Churchill set aside his ongoing work on Marlborough to throw himself into it. There were, however, two fundamental obstacles: in order for an epic to be shot and screened in time for the 1935 Jubilee celebrations, pre-production should have really started a year earlier. Churchill completed his screenplay – with its 'cataract of impressions and emotions' as he put it – in the opening weeks of 1935; a rather tight turnaround. Churchill himself was conscious of this, urging Korda that they would have to get a move on 'with the preparation of the sets'.

But on top of that, as Siepmann later recalled, with the best will in the world a narrative following a young aristocrat – and his rather eighteenth-century-sounding romance and adventures – through the extraordinary social changes of modern industrial Britain was not the recipe for a vast cinematic hit. Nonetheless, a third screenwriter, brought in to give the project further shape, was taken aback by Churchill's ability to summon visions.

Lajos Biro observed Churchill in the full flow of his creativity:

That is a man with a brilliant mind. In my presence he started dictating. For two hours without stopping, he dictated. After one hour one secretary went and another came. Again, for another hour he dictated, walking up and down, up and down. I remember there was a mirror at the end of the room, and every now and then he would stop. And look at the mirror, but blankly, as if he didn't see himself. I believe he saw nothing but the story.

Churchill described scenes that were perfect scenes, pictorially as well as dramatically perfect. He would shape a line, first whispering it as a phrase, trying it out as an orator might, looking at it impersonally in that mirror. Then he would dictate it.

To no avail! It could not work. And quietly, the project was shelved. 'I am rather embarrassed in writing you this letter . . .' Korda sheepishly wrote to Churchill. At first, Churchill was distraught – all his enthusiasm had come to nothing. But it did not damage his friendship with Korda in any way; in the years to come, he would continue to offer advice to the increasingly powerful producer. And Korda continued to seek out his expertise – for a dramatization of the life of Lawrence of Arabia (which also came to naught – though the later 1960s David Lean version would be a cinematic milestone), and for an epic about the story of aeronautics which eventually became 1940's *Conquest of the Air*.

In 1937, Churchill visited Denham Studios to watch Korda's new historical epic *Fire Over England* in production. Here was the life of Elizabeth I; Churchill was there on the day when the Spanish Armada had been ambitiously recreated on one of Denham's lakes. The casting was perfect – Vivien Leigh and Laurence Olivier, both of whom would also become friends of Churchill, as we shall see later.

Slightly to the frustration of the production crew, Churchill lingered a long time on set, questioning the team on technical matters. But this was not stargazing on his part; he understood better than many politicians just how powerful the medium of film was, and the extent to which audiences could be infused with grand passions. Without any of the heavy-handedness of fellow cineaste Joseph Goebbels, who took complete control of the German film industry, Churchill was analysing the extent to which even historical epics might be turned to more determined national purpose. He also ensured that Alexander Korda was knighted in 1942.

The Reign of George V is a fruitful 'what if?' prospect, not merely for what the screenplay would have revealed of Churchill's flair for fiction, but also for what it would have revealed of his soul.

Churchill at the Movies, Part Two

The Grand Opening of the Woodford Majestic, 1934

The following report featured in the film business newspaper Kinematograph Weekly *on 8 November 1934 – a fine example of a meeting between Churchill, some of his eager constituents, and more pertinently the art form to which he was addicted. It is also one of those moments from the Wilderness Years of a certain bathos; he was by turns a mighty statesman warning of the shadows of war creeping once more over the earth, and a slightly vulgar showman, very much at home with the pleasures of his more ordinary constituents. His enemies might have declared this occasion – the gala first night of a new cinema in the suburb of Woodford – akin to the old joke about public figures eager to turn up to the opening of an envelope.*

The Majestic, Woodford, the opening of which on Monday night was attended by a brilliant gathering of political, social and trade personalities, is the fifth and most luxurious theatre of the Majestic chain of kinemas sponsored by W. E. Greenwood.

In addition to Winston Churchill, the Member of Parliament for the division, who performed the opening ceremony, there were present Mrs Winston Churchill, Randolph Churchill, James Hawkey, chairman of the local council . . .

Long before the programme began, every one of the 1,200 seats of the theatre were filled, the majority having been booked several days ahead. There were many hundreds of disappointed would-be patrons turned away before the curtain rose on the opening ceremony . . .

Winston Churchill, in declaring the building opened, spoke very highly of the film trade. 'The kinema,' he said, 'enables many thousands of people who cannot regularly attend the legitimate theatre to obtain education as well as entertainment in very luxurious surroundings.'

Mr Greenwood, replying, regretted that he could not offer Mr Churchill a contract to appear at the kinema regularly as he had performed wonders in 'pulling in the crowds'. However, he was booking films which Mr Churchill is now editing, and which he sincerely hoped would possess the same powers of attraction.

And the films that were projected that night for Churchill, his family, and the enraptured audience? 'British Paramount News', a 'Walt Disney cartoon' – and then, as the main feature, *Cleopatra*. For the VIPs, there then followed supper and music in the cinema's ballroom on the second floor.

Churchill was exactly right not to be snobbish or standoffish about such occasions. This was a fantastic boom era for cinema, with theatres such as the Majestic opening in their thousands up and down the country, all offering invaluable escapism – and warm, plush surroundings – for audiences whose own homes were very far from either warm or plush. This is to say nothing of the comforts that cinema would provide to millions when war came again. Among those with an intense craving for that escapism was Churchill himself.

Is Vic There?

Vic Oliver, 1936

By 1936, Churchill's eldest daughter, Diana, had been married and divorced; her first union was with John Milner Bailey. Divorce was relatively unusual in the 1930s (though Diana's subsequent marriage

*to the politician Duncan Sandys in 1935 would last a great deal longer).
Churchill's son, Randolph, though a keen romancer, did not marry
until 1939, when he was twenty-eight. Churchill's second daughter,
Sarah, however, was to place the clan at the centre of the most extraordinary show-business soap opera; in some ways, she was decades
ahead of her time. Her romance with — and subsequent marriage
to — a popular theatre comedian called Vic Oliver led to some vivid
scenes between Churchill and his unexpected son-in-law.*

As Vic Oliver wrote in his memoirs:

> Mr Churchill was plainly embarrassed, but it was equally
> clear that he felt impelled to say something. He cleared his
> throat. There was a pause. Then he said . . . 'Well, you're a
> married man now. I hope you realise you have responsi-
> bilities.' I made what I hoped were appropriate noises. He
> spoke again. 'What are your plans for the future?'
>
> The words came out a shade gruffly, in those deep
> tones to which all of us were later accustomed in his his-
> toric war-time speeches over the air.
>
> 'Well, I have four weeks booked at the Holborn
> Empire,' I said tentatively.
>
> 'Good – what else?' he asked.
>
> 'Then I have three weeks at the Metropolitan Theatre
> in the Edgware Road,' I replied, feeling vaguely that if
> I spelled out in full the name of the old 'Met' music hall it
> would somehow acquire the status of a major opera
> house.

Of all the mannerisms that Churchill ardently disliked in
his daughter's new husband, he shuddered most violently
when Vic Oliver insisted upon addressing him as 'Popsie'.

How had such a wanton (yet winning) vulgarian managed to infiltrate the Churchill clan?

The story began with twenty-two-year-old Sarah Churchill searching for her calling. She had taken to the stage; and given the immense quantities of limelight that her father appeared to require, could there have been any other direction for her to move in?

The 1930s were a lustrous age for the stage revue – comedy, music and spectacular dance troupes. One such show, entitled *Follow the Sun*, was playing at the Adelphi in the Strand in 1936. Its star was a thirty-eight-year-old Austrian-born musician who had turned to comedy by mistake. His birth name was Victor von Samek, the Jewish son of a Viennese baron.

After World War One, the saturnine young man had roamed Europe performing classical works, as well as jazz. He was a lively pianist, but one night, after accidentally falling off his stool (which got a huge laugh from the audience) and making a clumsy apology (which got an even bigger laugh), he had a lightning moment of inspiration: he would continue making audiences laugh, and he would do so on Broadway, under a new name.

Vic Oliver – who in appearance had the firm-jawed dignity of the straight man, rather than the fast-quipping back-chatterer that he portrayed in his act – was soon a transatlantic stage success.

It was at the Adelphi that Sarah Churchill fell swooningly for him. But he had to return to New York to star in *It's the Tops*. She followed him there, announcing her intention to marry him (he was sixteen years her senior). In turn, Sarah's father – frantic with anxiety and distaste, regarding him as 'an itinerant vagabond' – commissioned his son,

Randolph, to follow *her* to get her to change her mind. The affair became what would today be termed a tabloid sensation: a steamship chase across the Atlantic, the tawdry glitter of stage romance. There were on-board press conferences. Randolph commissioned a New York private eye to dig for dirt. Save the matter of two previous marriages, there did not appear to be much.

Sarah and Vic got their way and they married. Churchill had to reluctantly accept it even though he considered Oliver 'as common as dirt'. This much now seems slightly puzzling; he had never previously been averse to chancers, of whatever social class. Was it a hateful discrimination against Oliver's Jewish heritage? Extremely unlikely, given Churchill's lifelong and proud philosemitism. Was it simply protectiveness towards his daughter? Did he think Vic Oliver had no prospects?

A reluctant invitation to Chartwell was issued. Churchill could not stand Oliver's 'horrible mouth' and his 'foul Austro-Yankee drawl'. Of their first meeting, Churchill confessed 'I did not offer to shake hands'. Yet Oliver himself was marvellously forgiving. 'I was of course very raw at this time and very Americanized too,' he noted self-deprecatingly, diplomatically eliding the fact that Churchill himself was half American. 'I often delivered myself of some clangy turn of phrase which almost made the gentle Churchill shudder.'

Both men made an effort, though. At an early meeting, Churchill granted Oliver the full personal tour of the Chartwell grounds, introducing him to the black swans Pluto and Persephone and the white swans Juno and Jupiter. And away from the water, there was an animal nearby that seemed malevolently eager to make Oliver's acquaintance.

Towards us across the grass trotted a friendly-looking goat. Mr Churchill warned me to be careful of it. Gaining a sudden confidence in myself and all my surroundings I patted the little beast on the nose and said with some bravado: 'Oh, he's all right. In fact he likes me.'

Mr Churchill chuckled: 'Oh yes, he's all right,' and said no more. We turned away and changed the subject. I had walked only a few yards, admiring the Chartwell scenery, when suddenly a mild tornado struck me in the seat of my pants. I leaped a foot into the air and came to earth a little ruefully, to be greeted by Mr Churchill quipping amid the general amusement: 'As you say, he's quite all right.'

Oliver wrote in his memoirs that, as they got to know each other better, he would seek out Churchill's wisdom and Churchill 'was often pleased that it was to him I directed my questions'. Yet Oliver also neglected to mention that he addressed Churchill as 'Popsie'. Might this calculatedly infuriating term have been his own gentle and satiric reprisal against Churchill's very clear outbreaks of hostility?

In this light, it takes some comic courage to continually call the grand old man 'Popsie' in order to see Churchill's features redden with rage. But if there was any bitterness, time healed; the comedian later insisted that Churchill 'grew to be fond of me', that he was always included in 'family functions' and that – though he cannot have believed this to be true for one moment – Churchill never displayed 'a hint of snobbery or discrimination' towards him.

And as it happened, Churchill's fretfulness about the durability of his theatrical career and his ability to make a living was wrong: Oliver *did* have prospects. By 1942, he was sufficiently famous to be the first-ever guest on the

BBC's *Desert Island Discs*. He was one of the main stars of the BBC wartime radio comedy *Hi Gang!*, which drew guest stars as diverse as John Gielgud, Michael Redgrave and Ronald Reagan. He founded a concert orchestra that gave light music performances, and years later was the host of another huge radio hit, *In Town Tonight*.

Nowadays Vic Oliver is almost wholly forgotten, but there was a time when all knew his name. The marriage to Sarah foundered by 1945, however; her own lively involvement in war work (including a spell at the top-secret aerial photography unit at Medmenham) underscored her firework independence, while Oliver wanted her to stay at home. There were other secret sadnesses too; her increasingly fraught relationship with alcohol being one. Yet Oliver himself was not wholly irredeemable in Churchill's eyes. And as the world's skies darkened with coming conflict, the comedian would occasionally glimpse Churchill's vulnerability.

I Danced with a Boy
Who Danced with a Girl

Edward VIII, 1936

The snow lay around the grand Norfolk house, silver-blue in the dark; and there was silence throughout the grounds. A king lay dying, his life about to be taken by his own doctor. George V was at Sandringham, suffering terribly with lung problems. That physician, Lord Dawson of Penn, looming over his bed, took matters into his own hands with an injection. The King was dead – long live the new King, Edward VIII.

As Prince of Wales, Edward – forty-one years old when he inherited the throne – had been hugely popular with the public but a worry to government ministers. A source of incessant fascination to the mainstream press, Edward seemed happy to defy a range of protocols. He made visits to poverty-stricken communities in Wales and the north-east, and made plain his deep sympathies with the unemployed; and for this he earned shouts of praise. At the same time, he was unabashed about his own life of glamour. His keen awareness of clothes, for instance – plus-fours, woollen knitted tops – made him a most unlikely setter of fashion for men.

In his private life, Edward appeared to have an erotic fixation with married women. In the 1920s, he conducted a long affair with Freda Dudley Ward, wife of Liberal politician William. That was an age when such matters – even when widely known in aristocratic circles – would not be relayed in the press. Edward's father had given him his own home, Fort Belvedere, in Windsor Great Park, adding layers of discretion (though that was not his father's intention – and George's frustration with his son and heir would grow as the years went on). There was also an affair with Thelma Furness, American wife of a British peer.

In time, Thelma was to introduce Edward to an American friend of hers: Wallis Simpson. What followed was not a simple question of love versus convention or constitution, but a crisis that threatened the Crown itself. It was a crisis that was to engulf Winston Churchill as well.

'Dear Winston,' wrote the King. 'Thank you for your book. I have put it on the shelf with the others.'

As an unconscious dismissal, it could be seen as quite funny, were it not quite so rude. Yet it is possible that no rudeness was intended; that the Prince of Wales, turned

Edward VIII, turned Duke of Windsor, was simply mulishly dense.

Churchill imagined that he was a friend of the man who had brought the monarchy to its gravest moment of twentieth-century crisis. Yet is it ever really possible for anyone to be a friend to a king? Perhaps Churchill, having first met Edward when the king-to-be was still a schoolboy, came to see himself in the style of John of Gaunt, who in the fourteenth century exercised a fatherly eye over Richard II. Certainly – as in Shakespeare's version of that history – Churchill would have much cause for subsequent bitterness.

Their first real encounter was at Edward's 1911 investiture as Prince of Wales (when Edward was sixteen). Churchill was there as Home Secretary, 'proclaim[ing] his style and titles . . . amid the sunlit battlements of Carnarvon Castle'. Churchill observed to Clementine that 'he was a very nice boy – quite simply and terribly kept in order'. That 'very nice boy' was subsequently present at Balmoral when Churchill was visiting King George, now as First Lord of the Admiralty. The boy prince – himself an enthusiastic naval cadet learning the craft of the sea at the Royal Naval College in Dartmouth – hovered around Churchill as the politician went through the red-box dispatches sent up from Westminster. 'He is a wonderful man,' proclaimed the prince, 'and has a great power of work.'

Yet, as is the way with dense, impulsive and sparsely informed princes, the young man soured melodramatically after the ill-fated 1915 Dardanelles campaign and the disaster at Gallipoli, telling anyone who would listen, with swaggering self-importance (as if he knew anything about it), that Churchill was actually 'an interfering politician . . . an intriguing swine' and 'nothing short of a national danger'.

The prince's tempestuous views were then remarkably calmed and turned again by Churchill's return to government. They met at polo matches; both had an affinity with horses. They exchanged words over cigars. Churchill arranged for Edward to have public-speaking tutorials with the baroquely named Cortland MacMahon. He also observed the prince with the married Freda Dudley Ward and told Clementine 'his love is so obvious and undistinguishable'.

Then came the also-married Wallis Simpson, and the death of the King. Edward was already regarded with nervousness by the government because he was so intensely careless with his own confidential briefing papers, which he left lying around at Fort Belvedere. But the presence of Mrs Simpson (together with some extraordinary rumours concerning her sexual techniques, one of which she allegedly learned in the Far East and was termed the 'Shanghai squeeze' or 'China clinch') went far beyond security. When her divorce came through, it was his intention to marry her. But would she be Queen?

This was not just a national question; this divorcee would be the queen of an empire too, with its dominions and millions of worldwide subjects. If Edward could not have his own way, he would abdicate. The answer from the vast majority of politicians and the public appeared to be: so be it. If you marry her – you walk. Conversely, while Churchill also did not want to see Wallis Simpson as Queen, he had a distinctly medieval idea of monarchy. Edward's infant reign had to be saved, in his view, because a monarch could not be lightly cast aside. When crowned, he would be anointed by God; this was a tapestry that had been woven for a thousand years. Could Wallis Simpson not be given a morganatic position? Like Duchess of Cornwall?

The answer was: no. So the King forswore his crown. His younger brother George would take his throne. In December 1936, in Parliament, as Churchill tried to explain his impossible support for Edward, the House took it as evidence of Churchill's mad and terrible judgement – part and parcel with his mad and terrible views on India, and his deranged views on the danger of a rearmed Germany. In vain, he sought to declare to the House – in a moment of agonizing bathos, sounding more like Falstaff than John of Gaunt – that he had enjoyed King Edward's 'personal kindness' and 'friendship'; that he might have had a 'glorious reign' which would have had a lustre in the 'ancient annals of monarchy'.

It was a matter of weeks before Churchill at last saw what everyone else saw: that Edward was both stubborn and arrogantly insensitive. Now the Duke of Windsor, Edward and his wife embarked upon an insane red-carpet tour of Nazi Germany, complete with tours of 'labour camps' and tea with Hitler at Berchtesgaden. There was no possibility that the Führer was going to allow such an opportunity – the stamp of legitimacy from a British royal – pass without full exploitation. It is said that Churchill attempted to dissuade the duke from visiting. But Edward – a fluent German speaker, and intensely romantic about his own Germanic roots – would not be told.

The reaction in Britain was chilly; the new King thought it 'a bombshell' and 'a bad one' at that. As war loomed closer, nervousness about the duke's apparent susceptibility to the Nazis increased.

When Edward and Churchill met once more before the outbreak of war, Churchill told him flintily: 'When our kings are in conflict with our constitution, we change our kings.'

Royal Postscript: The King and I

George VI, 1937

The spring of 1937 brought the prospect of a different coronation: Edward's younger brother George. As Churchill at that stage was contemplating the wreckage of his political career, and as Edward and Wallis faced a future of echoing emptiness, he received a letter on the morning of the coronation. It was from the new King. That new King then granted him permission to reproduce it so that the world might see.

The Royal Lodge
The Great Park
Windsor, Berks
18.V.37

My dear Mr Churchill,

I am writing to thank you for your very nice letter to me. I know how devoted you have been, and still are, to my dear brother, and I feel touched beyond words by your sympathy and understanding in the very difficult problems that have arisen since he left us in December. I fully realise that great responsibilities and cares that

I have taken on as King, and I feel most encouraged to receive your
good wishes, as one of our great statesmen, and from one who has
served his country so faithfully. I can only hope and trust that the
good feeling and hope that exists in the Country and Empire now
will prove a good example to other Nations in the world.
Believe me,

Yours very sincerely,
George R.I.

When Churchill was returned to power, then made prime minister in May 1940, his relationship with King George VI was a crucial point of stability at a time of the darkest tumult. Even if the King and Queen were occasionally taken aback by Churchill's superiority. According to Jock Colville – who was Churchill's private secretary, on and off, throughout the 1940s and 1950s, and later his faithful chronicler – the royal couple were 'a little ruffled by the offhand way he treats them – says he will come at six, puts it off until 6.30 by telephone, then comes at seven'.

Oh, Those Russians!

Ivan Maisky, 1937

Omsk-raised Ivan Maisky, the Soviet Union's ambassador to the
United Kingdom from 1932 to 1943, was in part an Anglophile.
A diplomat with a warm smile, fuzzy moustache and exquisitely

lacquered comb-over, he adored the works of Shakespeare and Lord Byron, and he had a fascination (occasionally tempered with communist distaste) for the complex threads of English society.

Born in 1884 to bookish parents, Maisky studied in St Petersburg and came to London before World War One, making friends with Sidney and Beatrice Webb and H. G. Wells. Then, initially displaced by war, by the roil of revolution, by severed diplomatic relations between the UK and Russia, he was installed as ambassador in 1932. Intensely sociable, he moved slickly through influential circles – he was friends with John Maynard Keynes, George Bernard Shaw and Lord Astor, among others. He was also intensely alive to Churchill. Maisky's portraits of his meetings with Churchill – below is his first meeting, followed by his first outing to Chartwell – are a delightful evocation of the way the older man could flummox communist true believers . . .

16 November 1937: The Moscow Devil

'There was a sudden commotion in the Bow Room,' wrote Ivan Maisky. 'I looked up and realised what was happening.' The Bow Room was in Buckingham Palace; the grand occasion was that of the state visit to England of King Leopold of Belgium. As well as the new King, George VI, the room was swarming with ambassadors and politicians. There were the young princesses Elizabeth and Margaret, who at that stage were only children. Also present was the German ambassador Joachim von Ribbentrop, who gave 'a Nazi salute'. But that was not the reason for the commotion; it was the entrance of Winston Churchill, with Lord Cromer, bringing a sense of colour and interest and vivacity that the ceremonials had not. It was also immediately clear to this fascinated former Menshevik turned loyal

Stalinist that Churchill would not play by convention. As he later recalled:

> Churchill moved away from the kings and bumped into Ribbentrop. Ribbentrop struck up conversation with the famous 'German-eater' . . . Ribbentrop was, as usual, gloomily pontificating about something and Churchill . . . was joking in reply, eliciting bursts of laughter from the people standing around. Finally Churchill seemed to get bored, turned around and saw me . . . in full view of the gathering, and in the presence of the two kings, Churchill crossed the hall, came up to me and shook me firmly by the hand. Then we entered into animated conversation, in the middle of which King George walked up to us and made a comment to Churchill. The impression was created that George, troubled by Churchill's inexplicable proximity to the 'Bolshevik ambassador' had decided to rescue him from the 'Moscow devil'. I stepped aside and waited to see what would happen next. Churchill finished his conversation with George and returned to me to continue our interrupted conversation. The gilded aristocrats around us were well-nigh shocked.

What followed was an exchange where Churchill – voice lowered – told Maisky of the pressing need for a 'strong Russia' in the face of Germany, the 'chief enemy'. This was the time of Stalin's purges – of terror arriving in the night, generals and civilians alike, in their many tens of thousands, spirited from their homes to face torture, death or exile to slave camps. Churchill demanded of Maisky 'what was happening in the USSR?' Was it not being 'weakened' by this ruthless exercise in mass killing?

Maisky held the Stalinist line: that the removal of 'disloyal' officers and factory managers 'engaged in sabotage' could only strengthen the USSR. Churchill, in response, 'shook his head distrustfully'.

This was almost two years before the shock Molotov–Ribbentrop pact between Hitler's Germany and Stalin's Russia – the non-aggression treaty that meant that Russia would not be siding with Britain in the initial stages of the war. Even through his detestation of communism, and Stalinist rule, Churchill never stopped praying for the stronger Russia.

4 September 1938: Vodka Diplomacy

At last Maisky had received the summons: the invitation to Kent. Churchill was still crying in the wind in the wake of Anschluss and just before Chamberlain's flight to Munich to try to buy guarantees of peace from Hitler. But his hinterland remained both lively and life-affirming. That hinterland – Chartwell – was the physical expression of his inner psyche. Maisky was to receive the grandest of tours.

'I visited Churchill on his country estate,' Maisky wrote. 'A wonderful place! Eighty-four acres of land. A huge green hollow. On one hillock stands the host's two-storey stone house – large and tastefully presented. The terrace affords a breathtaking view of Kent's hilly landscape, all clothed in a truly English dark-blue haze.'

Maisky was also very taken with Churchill's artful landscaping, the fish ponds arranged in tiers on the gentle slope of a hill, flashing with the golden sheen of fish of varying sizes. Churchill, he would later recall, was rather hypnotized by his fish, and could hold forth on them for some time.

More than this: the grounds of Chartwell featured a small swimming pool and a tennis court. There were also orchards and an 'abundance' of plums and peaches. Maisky loved the 'cages with blue birds that can speak in human voices'. And he was naturally given the full tour of the pavilion that Churchill used as a painting studio, filled with his own works. But the point that Churchill especially wanted to show off to the Soviet dignitary was a tiny brick cottage, half-built – which, Churchill explained, he was constructing with his own hands.

'"I'm a brick-layer you know," Churchill said with a grin. "I lay up to 500 bricks a day. Today I worked half the day and look, I've put up a wall." He slapped the damp and unfinished brickwork with affection and pleasure.'

(There is a pleasing symmetry in Churchill's insistence on showing off his labouring-class credentials to two dedicated communists – Maisky, and Charlie Chaplin before him. However, a modern note: there are suggestions at the Chartwell estate today that a great deal of the brickwork concerned is not as stable as it should be – indeed, workmen have had to insert steel rods to prevent collapse.)

'It's not a bad life for the leaders of the British bourgeoisie!' mused Maisky. 'There's plenty for them to protect in their capitalist system!'

However, he noted, 'Churchill must have guessed my thoughts because, taking in his flourishing estate with one sweeping gesture, he said with a laugh: "You can observe all this with an untroubled soul! My estate is not a product of man's exploitation by man: it was bought entirely on my literary royalties."'

On this, Maisky commented wryly, 'Churchill's literary royalties must be pretty decent!'

Then it was time for refreshment. Tea things were laid out, and by their side was 'a whole battery' of 'alcoholic drinks'. 'He drank a whisky-soda and offered me a Russian vodka from before the war,' said Maisky. (There are wide variations between different accounts of Churchill's drinking habits – the quantities he gulped down, and the variety. It is possible that his rate and style of consumption changed across the years).

'He has somehow managed to preserve this rarity,' wrote Maisky of the vodka. 'I expressed my sincere astonishment, but Churchill interrupted me. "That's far from being all! In my cellar I have a bottle of wine from 1793! Not bad, eh? I'm keeping it for a very special, truly exceptional occasion."'

When asked by Maisky which bottle, exactly, he had kept, 'Churchill grinned cunningly, paused, then suddenly declared: "We'll drink this bottle together when Great Britain and Russia beat Hitler's Germany!"'

The visit, naturally, was not merely social. Churchill sensed – correctly – that Ambassador Maisky was using him as a conduit to the ears of Number 10. This was the time of the Czech crisis, Hitler's grab for the Sudetenland. In those days before the Molotov–Ribbentrop pact, Maisky, it seemed, was very tentatively suggesting that Britain and Russia and France might prepare to join forces as a gesture for 'peace', with the possibility of some Russian troops funnelled through Romania.

'I realised he was making a declaration to me, a private person, because the Soviet government preferred this channel to a direct offer to the Foreign Office, which might have encountered a rebuff,' Churchill said of Maisky's visit. 'It was clearly intended that I should report what I was told to His Majesty's Government.'

Churchill conveyed the message; it was considered; and then 'ignored'. He noted the 'disdain' with which the

Soviets were treated, and fervently anti-Bolshevist though he was, he understood this to be a mistake.

The Ghost of His Ancestor

Harold Macmillan, 1938

Even in the thickets of the wilderness, Churchill's growls were attracting attention from a new political generation. Harold Macmillan – whose family business was publishing – had fought with terrific valour in World War One, sustaining injuries that would remain with him for the rest of his days, and yet he had returned to the battlefield with all speed. Now, as MP for Stockton-on-Tees, Macmillan – who would himself rise to a certain elegant greatness – was mesmerized by the older man's acute vision . . .

'The debate . . . was chiefly memorable for Churchill's remarkable speech,' wrote the man who would be one of Churchill's successors as prime minister. Harold Macmillan continued: 'He was listened to with rapt attention, and many Members, at last beginning to face reality, were entranced by his picture of the gradual unfolding of what he called "the programme of aggression nicely calculated and timed".'

This was in the wake of Hitler's Germany clamping its jaws into Austria by means of Anschluss. Macmillan was one of the few younger Tory MPs who were now looking at Churchill and his warnings about Germany in quite a different way (a great many others were not, and possibly for honourable reasons: the slaughter of World War One had been such – so filthy, so desperate, so chillingly nihilistic – that the desire to avoid sending a new generation of young men into conflict was simple compassion). Macmillan – like Churchill – was starting to see how the darkness could not be avoided:

> He asked how long we were to go on waiting upon events. How long was bluff to succeed until, behind the bluff, the forces which Germany was creating had become irresistible? [Churchill] spoke with gravity and authority, but without bitterness or recrimination. He displayed full command of his subject, based upon his profound study of history and the art of war. I had just been reading the first three volumes of his splendid life of Marlborough and was looking forward to the publication of the last. This work, the finest in my judgement of all Churchill's writings, appeared suddenly topical. The spirit of his ancestor seemed to have descended on the biographer. He spoke as a man outside and above party, only for his country. This occasion moved me deeply.

The Grasshoppers of Chigwell

Colin Thornton-Kemsley, January 1939

Of all the taverns in his Epping and Woodford constituency – the 1930s was a golden age of cultivated pub cosiness, and there were

*fireplaces and inglenooks from Theydon Bois to Snaresbrook —
Churchill had a particular soft spot for Ye Old King's Head, a
sixteenth-century establishment, half-timbered, in the hilltop village
of Chigwell. We will meet him there a little later on. But also to be
seen drinking and debating amid those wall-mounted horse brasses
were some in the local Conservative Party associations who were
becoming increasingly uncomfortable with their MP's bellicose stance
on world affairs. In the thunderously oppressive approach of war in
1939 — Austria annexed, Czechoslovakia invaded, and Prime Minister Neville Chamberlain still clutching in his hand the Munich
agreement with Hitler that meant 'peace in our time', Churchill could
not refrain from crying out against appeasement. In turn, many of
his local party members were infuriated by Churchill's refusal to
back the prime minister and the party. It fell to a young businessman
called Colin Thornton-Kemsley to raise the metaphorical dagger . . .*

'Mr Churchill's post-Munich insurrection was shocking,'
declared Colin Thornton-Kemsley — sleek, moustached,
hair thinning, perhaps skirting the edges of caddishness in
appearance — in a speech that was reported in various
Essex and national newspapers. He was addressing a special dinner of the Chigwell Unionist Association.

[Churchill's] deplorable broadcast to the USA was about
as helpful to this country as Mr Lloyd George's writing to
the Hearst Press at the time of the General Strike. His
castigation of the National Government, which we
returned him to support, would in any other party but the
Conservative Party, have earned his immediate expulsion.

Loyal Conservatives in the Epping Division have been
placed in an intolerable position. I feel that unless Mr
Churchill is prepared to work for the National Government

and the Prime Minister, he ought no longer to shelter under the goodwill and name of such a great Party. Most of us in the Epping Division agree that Mr Churchill has over-stepped the line.

Thornton-Kemsley came close to suggesting that if Churchill did not step back from that line, then perhaps someone else might be better serving the constituents of this Essex seat. As such, the businessman was briefly caught in the flare of national limelight; the younger generation inveighing against the grand old man. Thornton-Kemsley was saying on a local level what numbers of Tory MPs in the House seemed to be saying nationally: that Churchill, in his ever-more apocalyptic warnings, was being disloyal, and should be shunned.

Yet this was at a point when newspapers were also carrying articles on how civilians might prepare for war; on everything from gas masks to bomb shelters in back gardens. Loyalty to Prime Minister Chamberlain was one thing, but Churchill was receiving numbers of letters from his Epping constituents agreeing with his own line and telling him to hold firm.

Churchill went to Chigwell himself a few days afterwards and addressed a packed meeting at the manor house. Thornton-Kemsley was absent (he was in the process of being selected for another Tory seat, this one in the north-east of Scotland). In his place, a Mr E. C. Finch introduced Churchill thus: 'We cannot help realising that we are dealing with a man who has wisdom and courage and who cannot deny that he is a man who is first for Britain and the Empire.'

Bucked up, Churchill declared to the audience: 'Five years ago I began to warn this country of the great dangers into which we are being drawn by the rearmament of Germany. I have a book here – a book full of my speeches covering the whole of these five years. All of these speeches are directed to one idea – namely a stronger Britain armed and prepared to unite with other peace-loving countries.'

He went on to deploy a marvellously poetic (and contemptuous) image, contrasting his own position and that of his supporters with the noise made by his opponents. 'Because half-a-dozen grasshoppers under a fern make the field ring with their importunate chink,' Churchill declared, 'whilst thousands of great cattle, reposed beneath the shadow of the English oak, chew the cud and are silent, pray do not imagine that those who make the noise are the only inhabitants of the field; that of course, they are many in number, or that, after all, they are other than the little, shrivelled, meagre, hopping, though loud and troublesome, insects of the hour.'

Thornton-Kemsley, one of those 'insects of the hour', won his seat in Kincardine; it was only a matter of weeks before he was in the army, preparing for the conflict to come, and also preparing to write to Churchill an apology. As soon as war was declared on 3 September 1939, Churchill was recalled to government by Neville Chamberlain, resuming his old role of First Lord of the Admiralty.

And from this perspective, the MP-turned-soldier Thornton-Kemsley's letter to his former bête noire was rather touching. 'I have opposed you as hard as I knew how. I want to say only this. You warned us repeatedly about the German danger and you were right. Please don't think of replying – you are in all conscience busy enough in an office which we are all glad that you hold in this time of Britain's danger.'

But Churchill did write back; he could never resist demonstrating grace towards those who had wronged him. In a way, it was the opposite of humility; more the lofty demonstration of final superiority. Nonetheless, as a letter from the First Lord of the Admiralty to a soldier in training at army camp, it was still rather moving. 'I certainly think,' wrote Churchill, 'that Englishmen ought to stand fair with each other from the outset in so grievous a struggle, and so far as I am concerned, the past is dead.'

Mad About the Boy

Noël Coward, Summer 1939

Noël Coward occupied a unique and highly lucrative position in British popular culture throughout the 1920s and 1930s: his plays, from The Vortex *and* Hay Fever *to* Cavalcade *were vast hits (in the US too). His songs, such as 'Mad Dogs and Englishmen', were also insanely popular. As with so many hugely witty people, he desired most strongly to be taken seriously. With the drums of war now beating, he had already undertaken some freelance intelligence work – this largely meant keeping his ears open in the grander salons. But he wanted to do more. Thanks to an intermediary – a Canadian called Campbell Stuart, managing editor of* The Times *– a meeting with Churchill loomed. They had met before at Chartwell; Churchill had* *taught Coward to paint with oils. This was the point at which Churchill had begun to transform in the popular imagination; even before he arrived in 10 Downing Street, the rebel had become the warrior, and he started to inhabit the daydreams of others.*

'I was aware . . . that he was misunderstanding my motives,' wrote Noël Coward, 'and had got it firmly into his mind that I wanted to be a glamorous secret service agent.' It was an evening amid the cosy lamps and sofas of Chartwell, and it was spinning out of Coward's control. Though in fairness to Churchill, the idea of spying was not beyond the realms of possibility; it would have been quite shrewd casting in its own way.

In fact, Coward had already been a spy, reporting back to Sir Robert Vansittart at the Foreign Office; as Coward moved through Europe, from Warsaw to Stockholm, ostensibly for stage work, he'd taken the political temperature at diplomatic and aristocratic gatherings, and assessed matters such as England's perceived prestige and strength. But the more brutal side of espionage – sabotage, assassinations – might have been a trickier proposition for one of Europe's most famous faces.

This was the prelude to war: a population being mobilized into action; men preparing to join regiments; women readying themselves to take their places in industry. Naturally the smart set and the show-business crowd were eager to throw themselves in too. But what sort of war role might best suit a playwright and singer with a cigarette holder?

Coward's preference was for some form of position with the Royal Navy, possibly a continuation of his previous quasi-diplomatic efforts in international embassies, spreading influence.

I had known Winston Churchill for several years but never very well. We had met from time to time, with Anthony and Beatrice Eden, with Diana and Duff Cooper, at Maxine's villa in the South of France, and I had been once or twice to Chartwell, where he had lectured me firmly but kindly about painting in oils instead of dabbing away at water-colours. He had always been courteous and agreeable to me, although I had a gnawing suspicion that there was something about me that he didn't like. This of course worried me, because the thought of there being anything about me that anybody doesn't like invariably worries me and, naturally, the possible disapproval of Winston Churchill, whom I so admired and respected, ceased to be a mere worry and inflated itself into a major disaster. However, I determined not to allow these hypothetical doubts to impair my natural poise and make me uneasy in his presence. After dinner I played and sang to him some of my lighter songs which he always liked, 'Mad Dogs and Englishmen' being his favourite, with 'Don't Put Your Daughter on the Stage, Mrs Worthington' as a close runner-up.

But Coward was not there for pleasure alone; the evening had a purpose. Eventually he left the piano and asked Churchill if he might have a private talk with him. 'He led me into another room and we sat down with a whisky and soda each, and I proceeded to explain . . . my own feelings as to the best service I could give to the country if it came to the point of war.' Coward spoke of his own 'creative intelligence', and later recalled that the word 'intelligence' set Churchill off.

He leapt to the assumption that Coward wanted to be a

spy. Coward tried to deny this, claiming that the 'very fact of my celebrity value' would make any form of under-cover assignment rather complex. But Churchill was now fixated – and was set upon dissuading Coward from the course of espionage.

> [Churchill] said irascibly: "You'd be no good in the intelligence service." I endeavoured, with growing inward irritation, to explain that I didn't mean 'The Intelligence' in inverted commas, but my own personal intelligence, which was not in inverted commas. He would have none of it . . . Finally, warming to his subject, he waved his hand with a bravura gesture and said dramatically: 'Get into a warship and see some action! Go and sing to them when the guns are firing – that's your job!' With, I think, commendable restraint, I bit back the retort that if the morale of the Royal Navy was at such a low ebb that the troops were unable to go into action without my singing 'Mad Dogs and Englishmen' to them, we were in trouble at the outset . . .

Despite this heroic misunderstanding, Coward did eventually manage to serve his country in a manner close to his original idea: in the early weeks of the war, he was established in Paris to set up a Ministry of Propaganda. Even before the Nazi invasion, this quickly fizzled – but Coward spent more fruitful time in America, seeking out politicians and journalists, expounding on Britain's war effort to drum up more concrete support. And his wider artistic contribution – including the eye-prickling Blitz song 'London Pride' and the heart-thumping 1942 film *In Which We Serve* – was terrific, and in terms of morale quite unquantifiable. The fact that the songs and the films still resonate today gives an idea of how powerful they were back then. Churchill and Coward stayed friends; and we shall meet Coward again upon a more sombre occasion.

The Secret Weight

Vic Oliver's Flat, 3 September 1939

Despite the early apparent ill will between Churchill and his son-in-law, it is worth brooding on one small episode that hints at mutual respect: the day that war was declared with Germany, on 3 September 1939.

The day had begun for Churchill and Clementine in their London flat listening to Neville Chamberlain's grave radio broadcast. He had 'scarcely ceased speaking when a strange, prolonged wailing noise, afterwards to become familiar, broke upon the ear'. Clementine, on hearing the air-raid siren, remarked that the Germans had been very prompt. It was an exercise; the sky above was already plump with silvery barrage balloons.

Taking 'a bottle of brandy and other appropriate medical comforts', Mr and Mrs Churchill went down to their local air-raid shelter: the first and only time they would do so as civilians. 'Everyone was cheerful and jocular,' Churchill recalled, 'as is the English manner when about to encounter the unknown.' Yet he was under no illusions about the darkness that lay ahead. In that shelter, 'my imagination drew pictures of ruin and carnage and vast explosions shaking the ground, of buildings clattering down in dust and rubble'.

Then, the all-clear: out into that September sunshine. Churchill went to the Commons, where Neville Chamberlain had asked to see him. He was being recalled to government and reinstalled as First Lord of the Admiralty. Churchill's first act was to send word to the Admiralty that he would arrive at 6 p.m. The fleet was signalled with the message 'Winston is back.'

Before taking up this role once more, Churchill arranged an impromptu lunch involving Clementine, Diana and her husband Duncan Sandys, and Sarah and Vic Oliver. The location: the Olivers' home in Marsham Street, which was not far from the Commons.

There was Champagne; the toast was to 'victory'. And yet it was to Vic Oliver that Churchill suddenly turned. 'No one would listen to my warnings,' he told the comedian, and Oliver later remarked that he was 'sadder than I have ever known him'. After lunch, Churchill retired for a long afternoon nap in Vic and Sarah's marital bed, prior to shouldering these vast new responsibilities.

Into the Storm

Charles de Gaulle, 9 June 1940

Chamberlain had fallen (and was terminally ill); Churchill entered 10 Downing Street on 10 May 1940. On the same day, Hitler unleashed his lightning strike on France. Charles de Gaulle, a colonel, had been promoted to general and brought into Paul Reynaud's government. He was sent as part of a desperate delegation to Downing Street to ask for more help from the RAF.

'Mr Churchill seemed to me equal to the greatest task,' wrote Charles de Gaulle years later, 'provided it had grandeur . . . the humour, too, with which he seasoned his acts and words and the way in which he made use, now of graciousness, now of anger, contributed to make one feel what mastery he had of the terrible game in which he was engaged.'

On that initial occasion, the two appeared to be in surprising agreement: Churchill told the delegation there was no possibility he could send more British air squadrons for the Battle of France. As the delegation made to leave, it was de Gaulle who turned and told Churchill: 'I think you are quite right.'

That would be pretty much the last time their accord would be so honeyed. De Gaulle, later based in Britain, leader of the Free French, was explosively intransigent. His position – an exile whose forces were dependent upon whatever military equipment Britain could spare – was intolerably humbling for a proud man. His desire – that despite invasion, France might somehow after the war hold on to its imperial territories and be regarded among the victors – was quixotic. Churchill would later be asked what he thought of de Gaulle and whether he could be described as a great man. 'He is selfish, he is arrogant, he believes he is the centre of the world,' answered Churchill. 'You are quite right. He is a great man.'

There was tension over the Middle East lands of Syria and Lebanon in 1941, where French Vichy forces (allied with the Nazis) fought with de Gaulle's Free French troops. When the British stepped in – not recognizing the Free French as a government in exile – de Gaulle was berserk with rage against Churchill; Churchill advised his military commanders to let the French leader 'stew in his own juice'. After a little more rancour, Churchill arranged to meet de Gaulle in Downing Street, alone and in private. When the door remained shut for an hour, officials feared that Churchill had been murdered. They burst in to find Churchill and de Gaulle sitting together, looking startlingly content and smoking Churchill's cigars.

De Gaulle's constant bitter attacks on the shortcomings of British efforts – plus his own desire to wrest Churchill away from American influence and an 'Anglo-Saxon' alliance – led to a colourful harangue from Churchill in 1943 when the general was told: 'Every time we have to choose between Europe and the open sea, it is always the open sea we shall choose.' Yet on D-Day, with de Gaulle broadcasting an address calling on the sons of France to rise up and to thank Britain for her help in France's liberation, Churchill started crying. He was observed by General Hastings Ismay. Churchill shouted through his tears: 'You great tub of lard! Have you no sentiment?'

And de Gaulle was not above sentiment himself. Throughout the tempestuous storms of his relationship with Churchill, he did find the time in 1942 to show a rather sweet kindness to Churchill's daughter-in-law Pamela (then married to Randolph, and later the US ambassador in Paris): a book of historic sketches intended as a gift for Churchill's grandson (also called Winston). 'Dear Madame,' he wrote to her. 'I permit myself to send you an old book of pictures of Marlborough for your son

Winston. It is about the only thing that I brought with me from France. When the young Winston Churchill looks at these Caran d'Ache sketches he will possibly think about a French general who was, in history's greatest war, the sincere admirer of his grandfather and the loyal ally of his country.'

Beyond all the words said in heat, this gesture and message were intended for the ages.

'He Asked Me What I Would Drink'

Bernard Montgomery, Summer 1940

Throughout the winter of 1939–40, the British Expeditionary Force based in France – soldiers standing with their French allies in anticipation of German invasion – had been running through drills. None of them were of any use in May 1940, when the Wehrmacht storm hit. The retreat from Dunkirk – little ships ferrying more than 330,000 British soldiers back from France under heavy bombardment from the air and siege conditions on the beaches – was an extraordinary national moment. The boats, and their courageous crews, seemed to summon some alchemical blend of Sir Francis Drake and the Battle of Trafalgar. Among those returning soldiers was Lieutenant General Bernard Montgomery, and he was full of bile. He understood that the truth of the situation was darker: Hitler was mulling over plans for an invasion of Britain. Would the nation be ready to fight off such an attack?

*

'The real trouble in England in the early days after the fall of France was that the people did not yet understand the full significance of what *had* happened, and what *could* happen in the future,' wrote Field Marshal Montgomery years later. 'The fact that the BEF had escaped through Dunkirk was considered by many to be a great victory for British arms. I remember the disgust of many like myself when we saw British soldiers walking about in London and elsewhere with a coloured embroidered flash on their sleeve with the title "Dunkirk". They thought they were heroes, and the civilian public thought so too. It was not understood that the British Army had suffered a crushing defeat at Dunkirk and that our island home was now in grave danger.'

Lieutenant General Montgomery, as he was in 1940, understood better than most the terrible rhythms and velocity of war; he had been shot through the lung in World War One, feigning death with a corpse on top of him as further bullets thudded into that lifeless body. Recovered, he had returned to the Western Front. That war had taught him about the then snobbish hierarchy of the army – the generals who never addressed their men. This, he was certain, was not how war should be fought. And in the rich, skylarked summer of 1940 on the south coast of England, as Montgomery would recall years later in his memoirs, he was making ready for the ordeal to come.

It was in that summer of 1940 on the south coast, near Brighton, that I first met Winston Churchill and his wife. We were to become great friends as the war went on, and today I regard him as chief among all my friends . . . I would like to describe that first meeting, as my thoughts often return to it and he and I have often recalled it.

My Divisional Headquarters were near Steyning, in a house lying to the north of the downs. I was told the Prime Minister wished to spend the afternoon of the 2nd of July with my division; he would arrive by car and I was to finish the tour in Brighton, so that he could return to London by train in the evening. I was not impressed by politicians in those days; I considered they were largely responsible for our troubles. But I was keen to see this politician who had for many years before the war been telling a series of governments what would happen . . .

He arrived with Mrs Churchill . . . and some others, one of whom was Duncan Sandys. I have never discovered what Churchill thought of me that day; I know I was immensely impressed by him [there are suggestions elsewhere that Churchill initially heartily disliked him – but this was soon to change] . . . I took him to Lancing College, inhabited by the Royal Ulster Rifles, and showed him a counter-attack on the small airfield on the coast below which was assumed to have been captured by the Germans; he was delighted, especially by the action of the Bren-gun carrier platoon of the battalion. We then worked our way along the coast, finishing up in Brighton around 7.30 p.m. He suggested I should have dinner with him and his party at the Royal Albion Hotel, and we talked much during the meal. He asked me what I would drink at dinner and I replied – water. This astonished him. I added that I neither drank nor smoked and was 100 per cent fit; he replied in a flash, that he both drank and smoked and was 200 per cent fit . . . From the window of the dining-room we could see a platoon of guardsmen preparing a machine-gun post in a kiosk on Brighton pier, and he remarked that when at school near there he used to go and see the performing fleas in the kiosk.

In 1942, Lieutenant General Bernard Montgomery was in the sands of North Africa, poised to play an extraordinary part in turning the fortunes of war. This general was attentive to his soldiers; not only talking to them and making time for them but also, on occasion, distributing cigarettes. They were soon to start cutting into Rommel's German forces.

As the conflict roared on, Montgomery would command the British Eighth Army through the Battle of El-Alamein, through Tunisia, through Sicily, and thence the 21st Army Group into north-west Europe, where he would face fires of controversy with the heroic failure of the September 1944 campaign to seize bridges over the Rhine. Churchill remained his friend throughout, although the prime minister's advisers were profoundly sceptical of a man who appeared to chronically lack any kind of tact. General Hastings Ismay once remarked of Montgomery: 'I have come to the conclusion that his love of publicity is like a disease, like alcoholism or taking drugs, and that it sends him equally mad.' Tact, or lack of it, aside, Montgomery was there towards the end of Churchill's days, his friendship faithful and profound.

The Department of Death-Rays

Reginald Victor Jones, 13 June 1940

The twenty-eight-year-old Dr R. V. Jones – whose determined-jawed, crinkle-haired appearance curiously suggested that of a running-track hero in the 1940s boys' comic Wizard *– was a protégé of Frederick*

Lindemann. Assistant Director of Intelligence at the Air Ministry, Jones was developing 'beam bending' – a means of sabotaging the Luftwaffe's navigational signals that would ultimately prove a triumph. He would later take on even greater responsibilities. Jones's first meeting with Churchill in Downing Street gave him a euphoric shot of confidence; a form of rocket fuel to spur ever greater inventiveness and ingenuity.

'From our encounter, I of course felt the elation of a young man at being noticed by the Prime Minister,' Reginald Victor Jones wrote years later, 'but somehow it was much more. It was the same whenever we met in the war – I had the feeling of being recharged by contact with a source of living power. Here was strength, resolution, humour, readiness to listen, to ask the searching question and, when convinced, to act. He was rarely complimentary at the time, handsome though his compliments could be afterwards, for he had been brought up in sterner days. In 1940 it was compliment enough to be called up by him in a crisis; but to stand up to his questioning attack and then to convince him was the greatest exhilaration of all.'

One of those compliments came after the war, when Jones was offered a professorship at the University of Aberdeen. Churchill said of him: 'He did more to save us from disaster than many who are glittering with trinkets.' And Jones – who had an anarchic, prank-loving sense of humour – had been a true believer in Churchill from the start.

When he was pulled from Oxford into secret war work for the Air Ministry in 1936 he cultivated great contacts within Bletchley Park, working from the intelligence they gleaned about German aircraft. One of his revolutionary ideas – termed 'Window', and involving British bombers scattering metal strips throughout the skies to confuse German radar – was eventually adopted with great success.

But through all this, Professor Jones (as he became) recalled with the greatest delight his pride at sitting in the Cabinet Room with Churchill for the first time in June 1940. In a speech, Jones remembered:

> As I presented the evidence in the Cabinet Room – so Churchill told me – it was for him one of the blackest moments of the war. He had reckoned that we should just be able to win the coming Battle of Britain by day, but then he had this young man [here Jones was referring to himself] come and tell him that even if that battle were won, the Luftwaffe would be able to strike our cities accurately by night, when we had virtually no defence. He felt the clouds gathering about him, but then they were quickly lifted when the young man told him that it would be alright, we could do something about it by radio countermeasures.
>
> I could see at the time how deeply he was absorbing my words, and the episode made a lasting impression on him – all the more so, fortunately, when it transpired that the radio countermeasures we then instituted had blunted the Blitz to the extent that only one bomb in five fell on their intended targets. Ever afterwards, he would summon me when Lindemann told him that I had perceived a new threat, most dramatically, of course, in the German development of the V-1 and V-2 weapons in 1943 and 1944.

The two men remained sufficiently close that young Professor Jones was even able to visit Churchill at Chartwell after the war, when he was in bed with a cold, and distract him with debate on the Classics and history.

The Word of God

Cosmo Gordon Lang, 1 August 1940

Churchill was not a churchgoer. In this sense, we might see him in fact as a very traditional Anglican. Churches were there for christenings, weddings and funerals. He also claimed that he had in his twenties rather lost his Christian faith. 'I passed through a violent and aggressive anti-religious phase which, had it lasted, might easily have made me a nuisance.'

But as much as he let his mind explore 'the paths of thought and logic', he was never an atheist and was happy to countenance 'a supreme creator'. Still, even in moments of national extremity – and the Battle of Britain was precisely one of those moments – he did not turn to prayer. There were others to do that for him.

'On August 1st I had a long talk with the Prime Minister. He had just awakened out of his afternoon sleep, which he regards as the best protection of his health.'

Thus recalled Cosmo Gordon Lang, the Scottish-born Archbishop of Canterbury, who was a good ten years older than Churchill but not in so much need of that siesta himself. Lang had been at Lambeth Palace since 1928, and his austerely moral view of Edward VIII's relationship with the divorcee Wallis Simpson was one of the factors that had prevented Edward being crowned. Yet Lang – who had originally trained as a barrister before one day hearing 'a masterful inward voice' that proclaimed, 'You are wanted. You are called. You must obey' – had very swiftly approved of the idea of Edward's champion, Churchill, becoming prime minister in this, the nation's darkest hour.

The retreat from Dunkirk had taken place days beforehand. The RAF was poised to begin the battle for Britain in the skies above. Yet the archbishop – rather winningly – was in Downing Street in order to remind Churchill that, as prime minister, he had other responsibilities.

'It was his first introduction to his ecclesiastical duties in the appointment of a new Bishop of St Edmondsbury and Ipswich,' wrote Lang in his diary, lightly aware that this Anthony Trollope-esque scenario was some distance from the overwhelming weight of war. 'Evidently, he knows almost nothing of the Church and its personalities, but his comments were entertaining. He said very little about the business in hand but discoursed on things in general with immense vitality, as he puffed the inevitable cigar, as inevitable as Stanley Baldwin's pipe. He seems confident that things are going well, though as ignorant as any of us about Hitler's intentions, and pleased with his team. He spoke very generously about Neville Chamberlain [the former prime minister] and has no wish to lose him.'

The archbishop came away with a glowing impression of the nation's new leader. 'He told me he had just finished a book about Henry VIII! *What* a man he is – such amazing vitality and confidence! But before I left I could see there was depth beneath this brilliant surface, when he spoke with real emotion about the honour of being alive at this greatest moment in British history, and when, remembering his immense responsibilities, I said, "God bless and guide you."'

Lang's delight in Churchill's company never faded,

although his mild irritation with Churchill's ignorance of church politics became rather more intense as the months went on. It was charming of him to imagine that the man with the fate of so many in his hands would also have been giving intense thought to the vacant sees at Hereford and Worcester.

'He knows nothing whatever about the Church, its life, its needs or its personnel,' Lang noted a few months later, graciously conceding that there were other matters upon the prime ministerial plate. 'The result is much provoking delay and uncertainty.' The charm lay in the fact Churchill seemed so inspirational at this precise national moment, that many – not just the archbishop – initially imagined him to have a kind of omniscience.

Red Churchill

Ivan Maisky, 22 August 1940

Ambassador Ivan Maisky's fascination with Churchill naturally intensified upon the latter's ascension to Number 10; and as the Battle of Britain was fought ferociously in the summer skies, he began projecting on to the prime minister. Might the state of war trigger a transformation in the British state itself? Might a world of rationing, of state-led industry, of every aspect of life being controlled by the government, lead Churchill to realize that perhaps the Soviet way was best after all . . . ?

*

'Lunch with Sir Walter Monckton [then Director General of the Ministry of Information],' Maiskey noted in his diary. 'The conversation . . . turned to Churchill's role in this war. As leader of the military offensive, Monckton said, Churchill is good. But can he become leader of a political offensive as well? Monckton can't yet say, but he doesn't rule out the possibility that Churchill's romantic affection for Empire plus his love of power might make him such a leader. How far would Churchill go in this direction? This is also unclear to Monckton as yet. Churchill would probably be inclined to curtail sharply the privileges of the capitalist upper crust, but would he do so sufficiently *to win the war*? Of course, everything in England will be done the English way.'

Here a note of wishful wistfulness crept in. 'The introduction of a Soviet system may not be necessary here to achieve "victory". The introduction of a particular, intermediary form of socialism may be enough. Perhaps Churchill will prove capable of "accepting" or "creating" such a form: he is, after all, neither a banker nor a businessman – he is not a man of the City. Churchill is a politician and a writer, who makes his living with his pen. He is not as steeped in the capitalist system as, for example, Chamberlain. He does not depend on shares, interest, landed property, etc . . .'

Churchill at the Movies,
Part Three

Vivien Leigh, Late 1940

In one respect – and one only – Hitler and Churchill might well have enjoyed shared evenings together, and that was their passion for popular film. Churchill was mesmerized by the vaster Hollywood epics. One in particular was especially hypnotic because of its star, the English actress Vivien Leigh, whom Churchill had already seen at work at Alexander Korda's Denham Studios. This 1939 production, from Selznick Studios, brought the stormy passion of Rhett Butler and Scarlett O'Hara to record-breaking numbers of cinema-goers. That film, of course, was Gone with the Wind . . .

'It ran [in London] for four years,' wrote Leigh's biographer Hugo Vickers, 'and Vivien was dubbed "the greatest star England ever gave Hollywood". At the end of the year [1940], Winston Churchill . . . sat up until 2 a.m. watching it on Ronald Tree's private screen at Ditchley [Park, a stately home of which we shall learn more presently – it was a thinking space for the PM in the early months of the war]. His private secretary Jock Colville recorded in his clandestine diary: "The PM said he was pulverised by the strength of their feelings and emotions."'

A year later there was another Vivien Leigh production that haunted Churchill on an even deeper level: Korda's *That Hamilton Woman*, a sumptuous historical drama based on the life of Emma Hamilton, mistress of Lord Nelson, that was part love story, part epic wartime morale-booster depicting naval triumphs against Napoleon.

It was again at Ronald Tree's private cinema at Ditchley to which Churchill repaired. Tree wrote: 'Whether it was the story of Lord Nelson or the beauty of Vivien Leigh, this film appealed enormously to the Prime Minister. He was delighted with it and on future occasions wanted it shown again and again.' According to Leigh's biographer, Churchill also took the film with him when he set sail across the Atlantic in 1941 for a summit with Roosevelt. He had the film screened for all the officers on board, claiming that its chief interest lay in its depiction of Britain's triumph at Trafalgar. 'Though seeing it for the fifth time, the Prime Minister was still moved to tears. He declared: "Gentlemen, I thought this film would interest you, showing great events similar to those in which you have been taking part."'

Churchill and Leigh would retain a warm connection. We shall join Leigh and her husband Laurence Olivier later, as – in the midst of their own often terrible personal crises – their post-war friendship with Churchill deepened.

The Man from Auntie, Part Two

John Reith, 2 October 1940

Reith had stepped down from the helm of the BBC in 1939; and at the start of the war, in the dying days of Neville Chamberlain's government, he won a parliamentary seat in Southampton and was appointed Minister of Information. But with the RAF victorious in holding off German invasion in the Battle of Britain, Churchill had his own ideas about that ministry. Reith was to be reshuffled. As the Blitz began in early September 1940 — London's docks and East End streets transformed into nocturnal infernos — Reith's strained relationship with the prime minister did not improve; and at the meeting to be told of his new job, Reith opened his heart to his old foe.

From the diaries of John Reith, 2 October 1940: 'Message to see PM at 5.00. Told [fellow MPs Brograve and Fred] Beauchamp and Montague what was in the wind. PM meeting put off till 5.15, then 5.30, then come at once at 5.20, and then waiting in the secretary's room until 6.00. I went to the Athenaeum [the smart Pall Mall gentlemen's club] at 6.00; then, come at 7.00, then at 6.35 come at once. Works Ministry job [this was the department overseeing the requisitioning of property during the war] and Lords.'

Given that Churchill was trying to run a war, it is oddly amusing to see Reith in a rage about the perceived slight of hanging around (the Athenaeum being a step up from the pub around the corner from Downing Street, but similar in principle). It is also telling that Reith was in a rage about elevation to the House of Lords, which would have filled lesser souls with giddy vanity.

'I told him I didn't think much of it,' he said about his talk with Churchill, 'and that I thought I might have stayed in the House of Commons after the war. I said I wanted a Service ministry [that is, directly related to the conflict out in the field], and he replied that the war might go on a long time, with Japan and America in.'

And it was then that Reith showed — for him — a

startlingly emotional hand. 'I said I had wanted to be more in touch with him [Churchill] and that he didn't really like me. He said he had a great admiration and respect for my qualities. I said I would do what he wanted me to do and he said he would command me.'

At their first encounter, in 1926, Reith had – in his contempt for Churchill – silenced him. Now, this gangling granite-eyed Scot was prostrating himself. Yet it was still very much the same Churchill that stood before him now.

There would be other love/hate encounters, seethingly unrequited. Reith's diary mentions an instance barely a few days afterwards, on 17 October 1940: 'PM's meeting [of ministers] 5.30 to 6.45. He never shows any friendliness to me and I therefore dislike him intensely, which is a pity – especially as he reminds one so much of myself in his methods.'

A Portrait of the Artist

Cecil Beaton, 10 November 1940

As Churchill understood the power of film, he was also keenly aware of the impact of photography. Cecil Beaton – the son of a timber merchant – had captured the aesthetic of the Bright Young Things of the 1920s, and in the 1930s he was a staff photographer for Vogue *and* Vanity Fair. *He had an apparently easy rapport with various royal families. Yet it was the war that would take his work into new moral dimensions, as he was commissioned by the Ministry of*

*Information to capture images of the Blitz. He also had some deli-
cate assignments with the Churchill clan . . .*

'At the centre of an immensely long table sat the Prime
Minister, immaculately distinguishedly porcine,' wrote
Cecil Beaton in his diaries, 'with pink bladder wax com-
plexion and a vast cigar freshly affixed in his chin. Fat,
white tapering hands deftly turning through the papers in
a vast red leather box at his side.'

The timing of such an appointment was always going to
be tricky. How could you persuade the man devoting all his
focus to Britain's war effort – all this in November 1940, at
the height of the Blitz – to give up some time to strike
poses? And, as ever, Churchill was a most unwilling sitter
from the start.

Yet Beaton had already made inroads into the Churchill
family. He had been commissioned by *Vogue* for some portraits of Clementine Churchill a couple of months
previously, in September – also taken at Downing Street.
Her hair, he later recalled, was 'set like Pallas Athene'. He
had been asked by Pamela Churchill, wife of Winston's
son Randolph, to photograph Winston's five-week-old
grandson too. All this, it was hoped, would smooth the
way into his assignment with Churchill in the Cabinet
Room.

When Beaton arrived, Churchill seemed displeased that
he was being asked to step away from his work. Beaton
deftly produced several different studies of that tiny grandson, which had the effect of softening the prime minister.
Beaton tried to arrange Churchill at the cabinet table, and
Churchill responded to every effort to make him pose 'with
growls'. At last the prime minister composed himself, and

Beaton noted that he looked like 'some sort of an animal gazing from across the back of its sty'.

Yet shortly afterwards, Churchill became animated with a larkier spirit; in the minutes before a cabinet meeting, with various ministers gathering, Churchill interacted more with Beaton's camera, happily walking up and down the corridor repeatedly until the photographer had the image he wanted.

The most famous shot is now to be seen in the National Portrait Gallery: Churchill at the table of the Cabinet Room, turning to his left to face the lens with a jutting jaw and steely eyes, a cigar in his right hand, the glint of a clanky watch chain against his waistcoated midriff; a projection of pugnacious determination. It brought Beaton less trouble than some of his shots of Clementine Churchill, which one of her friends had unhelpfully told her made her look like 'a hard-bitten virago who takes drugs'.

The Wild Weekend Whirl

Lady Diana Cooper, February 1941

She was a crop-haired magazine-cover beauty, wide eyes grave yet with a hint of amused irony; an aristocratic actress, nominally the youngest daughter of the Duke of Rutland, though actually fathered by a writer called Harry Cust. Before the Great War, Lady Diana Manners's crowd had been the very smartest of London sets; in that war, many of that set were slaughtered. By the 1920s, she was being cited as a paragon of poshness in music-hall lyrics. She married Duff

Cooper; by World War Two, he was Churchill's representative at the Ministry of Information. Her path would cross Churchill's on various colourful occasions.

'Golly!' wrote Lady Diana Cooper for the benefit of her teenage son John Julius Norwich, 'what a to-do!'

On 19 February 1941, as the onslaught of the Blitz continued over Britain's cities and ports, Churchill was summoning his thoughts at a grand Georgian house in Oxfordshire called Ditchley. As he worked, he gathered colleagues around himself for the weekend. Lady Diana described the intense and charged atmosphere to her son thus:

> Great excitement last week-end! We went to Ditchley where Winston was staying . . . To start with, the Prime Minister has a guard of fully equipped soldiers. Two sentries at every door of the house to challenge you. I look very funny in the country these days in brightly coloured trousers, trapper's fur jacket, Mexican boots and refugee headcloth, so that on leaving the house I grinned at the sentries and said: 'You will know me all right when I come back.' However, when I did return, the guard, I suppose, had been changed. I grinned at what I took to be the same two soldiers and prepared brazenly to pass, when I was confronted with two bayonets within an inch of my stomach. They no doubt thought that I was a mad German assassin out of a circus.

The point about Ditchley Park (quite apart from its proximity to Churchill's birthplace of Blenheim Palace, just four miles away) was that, for a time, the usual prime ministerial weekend retreat of Chequers was out of bounds. It was simply too obvious a target for the Luftwaffe – positioned in the Chilterns just a little to the north-west of London – and on moonlit nights its wide gravel driveways would have been as conspicuous as lit runways.

This meant that the prime minister, plus ministers, advisers and security, needed another country headquarters: Ditchley, belonging to the Conservative MP Ronald Tree, was essentially requisitioned, like practically every other country house in the war.

It was nestled discreetly amid a rich array of trees; deer roamed in the parkland; and as well as the unending business of war work, there were opportunities for strolls and also for companionable dinners.

In her correspondence to her son, Lady Diana Cooper also offered this glimpse of the dramatically changed Churchill – a man who just several years beforehand had been a political outcast, and was now one of the most influential figures in the world. How did he wear this new mantle of power?

'Winston does nearly all his work from his bed. It keeps him rested and young, but one does not see so much of him as in the old Bognor days [she and Cooper had a house there]. There is also a new reverence for so great a leader, and that creates an atmosphere of slight embarrassment until late in the evening. Also,' she added, 'instead of old friends the guests included people called DMO and DMI (Director of Military Operations and Director of Military Intelligence) and an enchanting Commander-in-Chief of the Air Force, Sir Charles Portal, with a wizened little wife with whom I used to play with as a child because she lived at Denton near Belvoir.' (The then forty-three-year old Mrs Portal – who lived until 1996 – would not have been thrilled by that description).

'Brendan [Bracken] of course was there,' added Lady Diana, 'and Venetia [Stanley], also Winston's wife and beautiful, animated daughter Mary. Then on Sunday a flood of Poles rushed in – President Sikorski, the Polish ambassador, and some other splendid Polaks. After lunch the little procession, headed by Winston, followed by the upstanding Poles and brought to a finish by your exceedingly reluctant and rather sleepy Papa [Duff Cooper] walked off to a private room for a conference on Polish publicity.'

There was a carnival of misunderstanding when Churchill decreed that the Polish president should have a guard of honour. No one had thought of providing any ceremony, and no one at that moment could find anyone who would be capable of assembling one. But Churchill was not to be denied this wish. As a result, several young inexperienced soldiers were rustled up; and as they rehearsed, the Polish contingent sat on the doorstep with good-humoured indulgence and declared: 'Mr Churchill is so great a man that we must let him do what amuses him.'

'I tried to remember things that the Prime Minister said that would interest you,' Lady Diana added as a postscript to her son, 'but my brain is like a sieve and I can only think of one thing which I thought very touching and disclaiming of his power. When I said that the best thing he had done was to give the people courage, he said: "I never gave them courage, I was able to focus theirs."'

There was also the obligatory film show (Ditchley's owners, the Trees, had had a private cinema installed, and arranged for prints of the latest popular films to be sent up to Oxfordshire).

'We had two lovely films after dinner – one was called *Escape* and the other was a very light comedy called *Quiet*

Wedding,' wrote Lady Diana. 'There were also several short reels from Papa's Ministry. Winston managed to cry through all of them, including the comedy.'

Three years later, Lady Diana Cooper and Churchill were to share some rather more exotic escapades, in North Africa.

No Love Lost

Nancy Astor, 2 May 1941

American-born Nancy Astor – wife of Waldorf Astor – presided over the grand Thames-side house of Cliveden, and its smart social set, and became a pioneering female MP in 1919. Though Churchill normally formed strong friendships with strong women, he and Nancy Astor always seemed more like rivals. Her intense antisemitism, among other grim prejudices, might not have helped. By spring 1941, her constituency city of Plymouth had been smashed and burned, its people the victims of a ferocious Blitz. The prime minister and his wife scheduled a visit. But there was quite extraordinary conflict behind the scenes.

It was once claimed that Nancy Astor had told Churchill: 'Winston, if I were married to you, I'd put poison in your coffee.' To which he tartly replied: 'Nancy, if I was married to you, I'd gladly drink it.' That was in the 1920s. By 1941 the relationship had not improved.

There were nights when the bombing was so intense the fires so searing, that hundreds of citizens of Plymoutl left their shelters. Carrying blankets, they made their way out of the targeted city and on to the moorland hills around. As in London, Coventry, Birmingham and Shef-field, the suffering had been intense. Their MP, Nancy Astor, knew about the importance of morale. One night, when visiting a shelter, she startled the assembled citizens by performing cartwheels to lighten the atmosphere.

Now the prime minister was to visit, with his wife and US representative Averell Harriman. Nancy Astor, in a spirit of intense territorialism, had devised a programme whereby she and Mrs Churchill would exclusively pay visits to Plymouth's women, leaving Churchill to his own public meetings alone.

Churchill, dressed in the pea-jacket costume of an Elder Brother of Trinity House, an outfit he was last seen sporting at the opening of the Great War in Belgium, was brooding at the Plymouth naval base, and at last decided to overrule Astor's proposed programme for morale-building, arguing that in war, the supreme decisions were his to take. Mrs Churchill, he announced, would be accom-panying him around the city. All this was explained with gravity – but as he turned to Harriman, he suddenly gave a mischievous wink. Nancy Astor sourly observed: 'Isn't he an old repertory actor?'

'They drove around the city which Churchill knew well,' wrote Astor's biographer Christopher Sykes, 'and at the sight of the cheering crowds along the streets of ruined houses, he could not restrain his tears.' In the cold wind, Churchill stood at the back of the open-topped car, his eyes were visibly brimming. He raised his yachting cap to them. At one point he told the crowds: 'Your homes are low but your hearts are high.'

'Nancy was in a hard indignant mood,' wrote her

biographer. 'At one point she said in the hearing of others: "It's all very well to cry, Winston, but you've got to do something."'

The Start of a Special Relationship

Franklin D. Roosevelt, 9 August 1941

The prospect of his first official meeting with the President of the United States was making Churchill almost levitate with excitement: he, Professor Lindemann, and others in his entourage set sail from Scapa Flow for a rendezvous in Newfoundland. America was still not yet in the war; Britain desperately needed her aid. The prime minister sported, for part of the voyage, a sky-blue siren suit and a yachting cap. The officials and crew were made to sit through more screenings of That Hamilton Woman. *Then, sailing towards the pearl-and-green vistas of Newfoundland, cobwebbed with mist, Churchill approached a meeting that had been more than twenty years in the making – for he and Roosevelt had been warily acknowledging each other since 1918.*

'He is a tremendously vital person,' wrote Franklin Roosevelt in a letter to a cousin, going on to compare Churchill favourably with La Guardia, a former notably diminutive mayor of New York. This opinion was an improvement on a dinner in London in 1918 at the end of the Great War, when the younger Roosevelt had found the younger Churchill insufferably high-handed. Yet both verdicts were true; and they reflected knots of ambiguity in the relationship between America and Britain that remain to this day. There is friendship, but it is spiced with rivalry, superiority, snobbishness and suspicion.

President Roosevelt – who for some years had suffered a debilitating paralysis of the legs caused by polio, but who contrived ways via knee braces to make himself partially mobile – hosted Churchill and his party aboard the USS *Augusta*. The president, in his welcoming speech, recalled when he had first met Winston Churchill, at that 1918 dinner in Gray's Inn. For him, it was a 'treasured recollection'. This, diplomatically, was a step up from his view back then, which was that Churchill was 'a stinker'.

Answering this speech, Churchill chose not to recall that 1918 episode at all, proclaiming that 'frankly . . . it had slipped my memory'. Nonetheless, this, their first lunch together, was felt to be a tremendous success, and Roosevelt confessed in a letter to his cousin: 'I like him – & lunching alone broke the ice both ways.'

That ice had been melting across the years. In 1929, when Churchill was on a literary tour of the States and Roosevelt was mayor of New York, a meeting between the two had been mooted; one reason it never came off was because of the apocalyptic crisis of the Wall Street Crash. In 1933, by which time Roosevelt was president, one of his sons, James, was in England and Churchill shrewdly invited him to stay at Chartwell. He instigated a dinner-party game that night: it involved each guest declaring to the others their fondest wish. When it came to Churchill, he declared: 'I wish to be prime minister and in close and daily communication with the President of the United States. There is nothing we could not do if we were together.' Ever the artist, he then took hold of a piece of paper, and drew upon it a dollar and a pound sign cunningly intertwined, handed it to James, and asked him to tell his father that this should be the currency of the future. In addition to this, James received a going-away present: a copy of Churchill's biography of Marlborough, which he was asked to pass on to his father. Churchill understood about soft power.

In December 1941, the Japanese attack on the US base at Pearl Harbor in Hawaii brought America into the war, and Churchill and Roosevelt found themselves side by side. Churchill was to romanticize the relationship; the Americans, by contrast, were flinty about Britain and the future of its empire.

This hauteur would be felt most concretely in the development of atomic weapons. In their early meetings in the 1940s, Churchill expressed his anxiety to Roosevelt that the Germans might be thinking along the same lines. Then, when it became clear that it was possible to create chain reactions, Churchill told Roosevelt he was concerned that, while the US was being kept abreast of British atomic research (under the code name 'tube alloys'), the American scientists were largely silent in return. Churchill was an occasional visitor to Roosevelt's home, Hyde Park; cousin Daisy Suckley observed the 'special little ice pail for his Scotch' and that the PM 'wore a huge 10-gallon hat' and gamely jumped into the pool in a pair of shorts, looking like a 'kewpie' – that is, a rather sinister, naked and bulbous baby doll; a toy that was extremely popular then.

It might be swiftly noted that the British were also adept at keeping partners in the dark: before 1941, they had covered up Bletchley's incredible triumph of cracking the German Enigma codes. But Churchill's pride in the establishment that pulled off this feat was immense, as we shall see.

Tales from De-Crypt

The Bletchley Park Codebreakers, September 1941

It was a slightly eccentric and dowdy country house – a long way from the grandeur that Churchill was accustomed to. And within its grounds was the gravest secret of the war. Bletchley Park, in the north of Buckinghamshire, was where codebreakers were cracking the Nazi Enigma codes. In these grounds worked thousands of young people: mathematicians, chess players, crossword enthusiasts, super-posh debutantes, eager Women's Royal Naval Service recruits (Wrens). But the work was intense and unforgiving, and morale in 1941 was flagging. The establishment needed a visit from the keenest of cipher-cracking enthusiasts.

'Winston Churchill himself came to visit us,' wrote senior cryptographer Gordon Welchman decades later (when the subject was still strictly in the shadows of the Official Secrets Act). '[Edward] Travis [Bletchley's deputy director] took him on a tour of the many Bletchley Park activities.' This included popping his head round the doors of Hut 8 – where Alan Turing and his team were fathoming naval

Enigmas – and Hut 6, where army and air encryptions were being unravelled.

'The tour was to include a visit to my office,' continued Welchman, 'and I had been told to prepare a speech of a certain length, say ten minutes. When the party turned up, a bit behind schedule, Travis whispered, somewhat loudly, "Five minutes, Welchman." I started with my prepared opening gambit, which was "I would like to make three points" and proceeded to make the first two points more hurriedly than I planned. Travis then said "That's enough, Welchman,' whereupon Winston, who was enjoying himself, gave me a grand schoolboy wink and said "I think there was a third point, Welchman."' That giddy pleasure never quite left Welchman, who recalled that Churchill's 'oratory had a powerful effect'.

The prime minister also looked in on Hut 7, dominated by cupboard-sized Hollerith tabulating punched-card machines, which were an aid for checking through code combinations and operated by dedicated young Wrens. 'The visitor was presented with a scene of intense activity,' one eyewitness remembered. 'There were 45 machine operators in action at as many machines. Then all the machines were halted at the same instant, and in the complete silence that followed, Mr Freeborn [in charge of that section] gave an introductory explanation . . . At the conclusion of the demonstrations, all machines were brought back into action as the visitor was conducted to the exit, but all brought to rest as Churchill paused on the threshold to make his farewells.'

There was no possibility that Churchill – with his phobia of calculus – could ever have begun to understand how Welchman, Turing and the other geniuses had applied intensely abstruse mathematics to the apparently insoluble problem of a code-generating machine that could produce some 178 million million different combinations of encrypted letters. But he could see very well how draining the effort was, and how important it was that all these recruits – from the professors theorizing about new cryptanalytic attack methods to the young women working the Hollerith code-checking machines in Hut 7 – were looked after.

Churchill saw to it that a request for the refurbishment of Bletchley's old tennis courts was granted. He was also introduced to an intense twenty-three-year-old mathematics graduate who was not expecting an encounter with the prime minister. John Herivel had – the year previously – cracked the Luftwaffe Enigma codes, giving the RAF an invaluable boost in the Battle of Britain. He recalled Churchill coming to Hut 6: 'The sound of many voices was heard in the distance, gradually becoming louder and louder and reaching a crescendo immediately behind me before subsiding when Welchman's voice was heard saying, "Sir, I would like to present John Herivel, who was responsible for breaking the German Enigma last year." On hearing my name spoken by Welchman in this totally unexpected manner, I turned automatically to the right to find myself gazing straight into the eyes of the Prime Minister! We looked silently at each other for a moment or two before he moved on . . .'

Churchill was also introduced to Turing, who was reportedly 'very nervous'. The prime minister then went outside into the chilly air, climbed a small hillock in the gardens and 'spoke very briefly, but with deep emotion'. Herivel remembered the image he presented: 'a rather frail, oldish looking man, a trifle bowed, with wispy hair, in a black pin-striped suit with a faint red line, no bravado, no large black hat, no cigar'.

For all Churchill's adoration of the entire subject of cryptography, he could not resist teasing Bletchley's director Alastair Denniston about the eccentricity of his youthful cohort. 'About that recruitment,' Churchill told him through a lowered car window just before he left, 'I know I told you not to leave a stone unturned, but I did not mean you to take me seriously.'

The perceived bond between Churchill and his code-crackers was so strong that, a month later, the senior cryptographers, including Turing, felt emboldened enough to write directly to the prime minister in their request for more staff and more funding for specialized proto-computing machinery. Bletchley – in common with all other areas of war work – was up against stringent red tape. The letter was delivered to the door of Number 10 personally by chess champion Stuart Milner-Barry. There was an initial flurry of exasperated confusion; he had neglected to bring any form of identification with him.

Yet this amusing manifestation of slightly otherworldly eccentricity seemed to connect with Churchill directly (even if he was not available to see Milner-Barry that day). As he read the letter, he declared: 'Make sure they have all they want on extreme priority and report to me that this has been done.' On the letter went a sticker: 'Action This Day'.

Close – Yet Many Cigars

Evelyn Duncan, October 1941

An early autumnal visit to Blitzed Birmingham was, as might have been expected, a success, with crowds turning out to cheer Churchill as he was driven around in an open-topped car. He added a touch of theatricality by sitting on top of the rear car seat and placing his bowler hat on his cane, raising it into the air and waggling it. After this came a short walkabout where he was on the receiving end of some fannish attention.

As reported, and syndicated, across various Midlands local newspapers, 4 October 1941:

> Miss Evelyn Duncan, holder of the world's ammunition production record – she made 6,150 anti-aircraft shell parts in a week – who last Friday broke through a police cordon when Mr Churchill visited Birmingham and gave him a box of twenty-five cigars – yesterday received a present from him in turn.
>
> It was a signed portrait of the premier and an autographed copy of his book *Into Battle*.
>
> With it was a letter which said 'Dear Miss Duncan, Thank you for your kind thought, which I greatly appreciate. Please accept in return this small token from me. Yours sincerely, Winston S. Churchill.'

It is impossible not to wonder what Churchill did with that gift of cigars: would they have been the very particular – and luxurious – type that he favoured? It seems unlikely. And a few days later, cigars were one of the leitmotifs of another press portrait that somehow contrived to make his eccentricities seem perfectly normal.

At this time of bombing raids, there was public appetite for domestic details of Churchill's life. Moreover, this appetite seemed to be present in America too. In October 1941, a US correspondent called Paul Manning furnished his readers with an illuminating behind-the-scenes look at a typical day in the life of the wartime leader, which was duly shared with the British readers of the left-leaning *Daily News*.

At dawn, Manning reported, Churchill would return to Downing Street from an unspecified shelter. 'While he does sleep occasionally at another address, which is secret, he hurries back as early as possible to his Downing Street bedroom in which he feels he can really relax,' Manning divulged. 'The bedroom is roomy, and from the large mahogany bed facing the window Churchill commands a view of the small grass plot at the rear of Number 10.'

The day started with paperwork to be read. 'At 8.30 he rings for his breakfast. Like all his meals, there's nothing fancy about it. Bacon and egg, sometimes with a little kidney. And always coffee. He doesn't drink tea – at any meal.' Then one of his rota of 'six secretaries' entered to begin dictation with a 'noiseless' machine. At 10 a.m., she was dismissed. 'Springing out of bed, he shaves, using a safety razor. He is too old-fashioned for an electric razor, he says. He takes baths because showers have not yet been introduced to Downing Street.'

The cabinet meetings would begin; following domestic and foreign policy discussion, a war cabinet met in session.

Then: 'Lunch at one o'clock is a simple meal. First an aperitif with ice, then cold roast beef as the main dish finished off with black coffee, brandy and a cigar. Cigars are his one real luxury. They're all very expensive and outsize. When asked by an inquisitive visitor how many he smoked a day, he replied "Fourteen, and I like every one of them."'

Manning commented: 'He is a Tory, an imperialist, a member of the Old School Tie group, a descendant of the first Duke of Marlborough . . . yet he is an earthy man of the people such as perhaps no other Prime Minister has been. He is "Mr England".'

But Manning also cosily reported that Clementine Churchill was in domestic despair over fraying carpets. There 'runs the clear, beaten track of Winston's feet. "But it's no use getting new rugs," says Mrs Churchill. "If we do, he'll quickly wear them out too."'

Projection

Eric Ambler, November 1941

It is one of the quirks of the war that Churchill was once guarded by the nation's finest spy-thriller writer. Eric Ambler, bestselling author of The Mask of Dimitrios *and* Journey into Fear, *had enlisted as a motorcycle instructor and then for a time became a gunnery officer at Chequers, the prime ministerial retreat in Buckinghamshire. Given that the countryside was not at that point – or at any point – teeming with Nazi commandos, the position had its quieter moments, and Churchill always liked to show his appreciation for his military security team. The main treat was film nights. Ambler – as the quote from his autobiography below shows – was there for the screening of a film starring the then intensely popular screen siren Deanna Durbin. But inevitably and equally fascinating to him was the behaviour of Churchill in the front row.*

The Prime Minister enjoyed Hollywood films . . . there was a roomy projection theatre upstairs at Chequers and off-duty officers from the guard company and our battery would sometimes be invited up for the weekly film shows. On Mr Churchill's birthday in November 1941, I was one of those who went . . . We found the theatre full except for the front row. That was where the Prime Minister was sitting; we could see that from the landing outside. Over his siren suit he was wearing a vast padded and quilted dressing gown made of a beige material. Under the projection beam and in the flickering reflections from the screen he looked like a rumpled bed.

Mr Churchill had a cigar in one hand and a brandy glass in the other. For a time, as the second projector took over from the first, I thought the film had his undivided attention. Then I became aware of an intermittent sound coming from the dressing gown. It wasn't snoring, he wasn't sleeping. By listening more carefully and leaning towards him slightly, I understood what I was hearing; he was rehearsing a speech.

I could not distinguish the words; what he was rehearsing was the way he would deliver the words; what I could hear from the rhythms and cadences of delivery being hummed in a nasal tonic sol-fa of his own.

A Class Apart

James Chuter-Ede, February 1942

If the Soviet ambassador Ivan Maisky was daydreaming that Churchill was secretly thinking socialist thoughts, what of his Labour colleagues in that wartime coalition government? Despite the global situation – in February 1942, British forces in Singapore were routed by the Japanese army; and in North Africa the bitter struggle between the Germans and the British was intensifying – there were those at home who were already starting to imagine the land after war, and the society that they wished to build.

Labour MP James Chuter-Ede – later to be Home Secretary – was at that time Parliamentary Secretary to the Board of Education. Churchill wanted to promote him to War Transport; Chuter-Ede wanted to stay where he was. As Churchill waited to consult with his deputy Clement Attlee over this act of unexpected and insubordinate daring, he gave Chuter-Ede a short and heartfelt speech about his own surprisingly progressive views on education.

'The PM was glad to know that the public schools were receiving our attention,' Chuter-Ede noted in his diary. 'He wanted 60–70 per cent of the places to be filled by bursaries – not by examination alone but on the recommendations of the counties and the great cities.' He also recorded Churchill's pronouncement that '"we must reinforce the ruling class" – though he [Churchill] disliked the word "class".'

Churchill (in Chuter-Ede's paraphrasing) continued: 'We must not choose by the mere accident of birth and wealth but by the accident – for it was equally accident – of ability. The great cities would be proud to search for able youths to send to Haileybury, to Harrow and to Eton.'

The terms were such that any socialist would initially flinch: a ruling elite being bolstered. Yet, at the same time, Chuter-Ede could recognize that the underlying sentiment – that public schools should be open to talented children of any background, and not simply left as the preserve of inherited privilege – was quite arresting coming from a Conservative prime minister who was himself the apogee of inherited privilege. But this was also the prime minister who firmly believed in relieving strict rote learning and instead showing children films and magic lantern shows, the better to fire up their imaginations.

The Four-Poster Nightmare

Dwight D. Eisenhower, Summer 1942

As a younger soldier, Dwight David 'Ike' Eisenhower had been eager to serve in France as soon as America entered the Great War in 1917; yet interminable hold-ups meant that he only received his orders to go a week before the Armistice was signed. He stayed with the army in the interwar years, gaining experience by working with the Philippine government in the 1930s, aiding them in building their military. A certain sense of genial, witty optimism would eventually carry him to the presidency of the United States in the 1950s: to some, a golden age.

When the US entered World War Two in 1941, Eisenhower was

soon sent over to Britain, initially as Commanding General, European Theater of Operations. He was swiftly mesmerized by Churchill's leadership style.

'Ike himself was fascinated by Churchill's dinnertime performances,' wrote Eisenhower's biographer Piers Brendon. 'especially the battle he had with his soup, on which he vented the fury he felt for his own generals. The prime minister crouched over his plate, wielding his spoon rapidly, and the soup disappeared with "raucous gurglings" which, when Ike tried to imitate them for [a friend's] benefit, "almost made him choke".'

The late nights, however, exhausted Eisenhower. 'So did the relentless pertinacity with which Churchill pressed home his arguments – in order to convince Ike, he drew on everything from the Greek classics to Donald Duck. As the prime minister cordially ushered [him] out after his marathons into the small hours, Ike . . . would almost run for the door, fearful of a valedictory harangue, which could last thirty minutes or more.'

Then there was the matter of the English countryside. Eisenhower received an invitation to spend the weekend with Churchill in Buckinghamshire. 'Staying at the prime minister's country house, Chequers, was even more of an ordeal because Ike was a captive audience in what he called a "damned ice-box". On one occasion when he did finally get off to sleep, in the huge oaken four-poster bed in a room said to have been occupied by Cromwell, Ike was awakened by a terrible dream in which he was being strangled. [His subordinate] had forgotten to pack his pyjamas and Ike was wearing one of the prime minister's capacious night-shirts which had worked itself into a noose around his neck.'

The Bull-Dog and the Bear

Joseph Stalin, August 1942

On the morning of 22 June 1941, the citizens of Leningrad were among those Russian citizens who heard with disbelief the news of German invasion; and they would soon hear the distant terrible thunderous booms. The Molotov–Ribbentrop pact had been ripped up; Hitler's attack on the Soviet Union – Operation Barbarossa – had begun. Back in England, Churchill – who for the last few years had tempered his loathing for Bolshevism with a greater pragmatism – took to the radio. 'The cause of any Russian fighting for his hearth and home is the cause of free men and free peoples in every quarter of the globe,' he declared. Britain and Russia were allies. But in the face of that murderous Nazi onslaught (the siege of Leningrad resulted in the deaths of over a million people), Joseph Stalin wanted Britain – and later the US – to open a second front against Hitler's forces. When he and Churchill met for the first time in Moscow, in August 1942, the power struggle was intense and personal.

'At times both were very blunt,' wrote diplomat Sir Archibald Clark Kerr of the extraordinary first meetings between Churchill and Stalin, 'as if each one sought by his bluntness to make a dint upon the other. I think that each succeeded and that the dints were deep.'

On Wednesday, 12 August 1942, Churchill flew from Tehran to Moscow, the plane soaring above vast landscapes of collectivized agriculture. It was still, in Churchill's eyes a 'sullen, sinister' communist state; but this was diplomacy and he had the difficult job of telling Stalin that the Allie were not ready to make any kind of landings in France. He was going to try instead to sell the Soviet leader the virtues of Operation Torch, the North African Allied landings: strength in the Mediterranean would loosen Hitler's axis with Italy. At their first dinner, Churchill produced some paper and drew Stalin a picture of a crocodile; this was a way of explaining, without interpreters, the strategy of aiming for the beast's soft underbelly before attacking its hard snout.

Churchill and his entourage were based at State Dacha No. 7, which was assumed to be bugged. Conversations were held outside, or near a bath being run. The first encounter appeared to have gone well. But the next day, Stalin was suffused with fury – accusing Churchill and the British of cowardice in refusing to open up a second European front. According to Colonel Ian Jacob, who observed the meeting, many bitter words were exchanged and Churchill found himself in the vortex of a diplomatic nightmare. The tension felt by the interpreters can quite easily be imagined.

Stalin declared that 'higher sacrifices were called for. Ten thousand men a day were being sacrificed on the Russian front . . . The Russians did not complain of the sacrifices they were making, but the extent of them should be recognised.'

Churchill said that he 'envied the Russians their glory' and 'hoped that we very soon would show by our deeds that the democracies were neither sluggish nor cowardly and were just as ready as the Russians to shed blood'. He maintained that 'the existence of the oceans and the need to move over them in ships were facts for which it hardly seemed right that we [Britain] should be reproached'.

More: Churchill 'earnestly desired to hear the ring of comradeship in the discussions' and 'well knew what the Russians were going through: we ourselves had fought alone for a year . . . He had come a long way in the hope that he would receive the hand of comradeship and that he would be believed in a spirit of loyalty and friendship . . . It grieved his heart that the Russians did not think we were doing our utmost in the common cause.'

Stalin replied that 'it was not a case of mistrust, but only of a divergence of view'. In his opinion, 'if the British Army had been fighting the Germans as much as the Russian Army, it would not be so frightened of them. The Russians, and indeed the RAF, had shown that it was possible to beat the Germans. The British infantry could do the same provided they acted at the same time as the Russians.'

This accusation of cowardice was beyond infuriating, though Churchill said that he 'pardoned the remarks which Stalin had made on account of the bravery of the Russian Army'. He later described the meeting as a most unpleasant discussion, writing that Stalin 'had said a great many insulting things: I repulsed these squarely, but without taunts. I suppose he is not used to being contradicted repeatedly, but he did not become at all angry or even animated . . . He kept his eyes half closed, always avoiding mine, uttering at intervals a string of insults . . . He will have to go a long way to do any good with me.'

In the midst of all this, there were Red Army troops to review and banquets to be sat through. Churchill, who normally enjoyed his food, appeared less than keen on the quantities of vodka and suckling pig involved. On his host's part, there was some consternation that the prime minister was attending a Kremlin state banquet in a siren suit when everyone else present (other than Stalin) was in formal dress.

Churchill's offence was – perhaps – as calculated as Stalin's anger. Stalin asked if he might stay in Moscow a little longer; Churchill told him that diplomacy had carried him as far as he could go. There was a remarkable moment, as Churchill left, when Stalin was observed to 'jog' to the door to apprehend him. Churchill was persuaded. One more day and night.

The conclusion of this secret conference came in Stalin's private apartments in the Kremlin, where his daughter had prepared more pork and vodka. Like Churchill, Stalin kept vampiric hours. This more private occasion, witnessed by the diplomat Sir Archibald Clark Kerr, was startling in its apparent affability:

> It was interesting to watch the impact of the two men. Clash and recoil and clash again, and then a slow but unmistakeable coming together as each got the measure of the other, and in the end, much apparent understanding and goodwill. To me who am in a way responsible for the meeting it meant some very anxious moments. But at the end of today's meeting I felt satisfied that it had been abundantly wise. Now the two men know each other and each one will be able to put the right value on the messages – and they are very frequent – that pass between them . . .
>
> Each one was very restless. Stalin kept getting up and walking across the big room to a writing table into which he delved for cigarettes. These he tore to bits and stuffed into his absurd curly pipe. In his turn the PM, when he had shot a bolt, got up and had a walk, pulling from his heated buttocks the seat of his trousers which had clearly

stuck to them . . . There was something about this dumpy figure plucking at his backside which suggested immense strength but little distinction . . . The PM was in very good humour, he felt that he had got away with it.

Stalin's colossal consumption of alcohol had to be matched, but was even Churchill up to the endless glasses of vodka? It seems he found an ingenious compromise. When the diplomat Lord Cadogan looked in on them in the early hours, they were still at the table. Stalin pressed Cadogan to have a glass of what he was having. Cadogan described it as 'savage'. But he noted that Churchill, 'who by that time was complaining of a slight headache, seemed wisely to be confining himself to a comparatively innocuous effervescent Caucasian red wine'.

'Everything', added Cadogan, 'seemed to be as merry as a marriage-bell'.

A Prime Ministerial
Heart-to-Heart

Stanley Baldwin, 15 February 1943

Stanley Baldwin had retired from the role of prime minister aged sixty-nine, in 1937. By the outbreak of war, he was being vilified by the newspapers for having been chief among the appeasers who gave so much ground to Hitler, and started receiving hate mail from members of the public. In those days, former prime ministers were not afforded special allowances for office staff. Baldwin had no secretary, and so he faced the daily arrival of increasingly vituperative and sometimes poisonous letters himself. War brings out the most atavistic emotions, and Baldwin was receiving the scorching fury.

There was extra fury when – in response to an appeal for all iron and steel railings and fences to be requisitioned for the war effort, he tried to save the ornamental gateway to his Worcestershire home. So when the invitation to Downing Street arrived in early 1943, the grim clouds parted a little for this genial seventy-five-year-old.

'On 15 February 1943, Baldwin lunched with Churchill and James Stuart, the Government Chief Whip, in the "dug-out" which served as a dining room at 10 Downing Street,' wrote Baldwin's biographer H. Montgomery-Hyde.

The meeting, which had been tactfully arranged by Stuart, happily put an end to the strained relations which had existed between Churchill and Baldwin for some years. Their talk, which was continued in the Cabinet room, lasted for almost three hours. Baldwin called Churchill 'PM', a form of address to which Churchill demurred. But Baldwin insisted it was due to the greatness of his office, he said.

With considerable tact, the Prime Minister asked the older man his advice. Should he speak out against Southern Ireland's neutrality in the war and the de Valera government's refusal to let Britain use the old treaty ports as anti-submarine bases? He handed the notes of his intended speech to Baldwin, and while Baldwin read them Churchill sipped his brandy and smoked a large cigar.

'I wouldn't make that speech,' said Baldwin, and in the event Churchill did not.

Baldwin refused the offer of one of Churchill's famous cigars and lit up his pipe, explaining that he had given up cigars long ago as he could not afford them. 'Oh,' said Churchill, puffing away, 'I flatter myself that I have democratised cigars!'

Then there was an episode that poignantly emphasized the age of both men. A Guards officer was admitted into the Cabinet Room to tell Churchill that there was to be an exercise – a new beret had been designed for the troops and some of the men were in the garden to demonstrate how it would be worn in the field. Churchill was ever alive to the curious importance of sartorial appearance in military life: the way that it demonstrated dignity and confidence. As a result, he leapt up in order to go out to the Rose Garden.

According to his biographer, Baldwin was ready with an old man's warning. '"Don't go without your coat, PM . . . It is very cold and this room is very hot." However, Churchill chose to disregard this advice with near fatal results for himself and the country. The first of the berets to be demonstrated blew off and during the time it took to retrieve it and try it on again, Churchill stayed in the garden and in the event caught pneumonia.'

In general, though, the meeting meant a very great deal to the elderly former prime minister. Baldwin later told Harold Nicolson: 'I went into Downing Street . . . a happy man. Of course it was partly because an old buffer like me enjoys feeling that he is still not quite out of things. But it was also pure patriotic joy that my country at such a time should have found such a leader. The furnace of the war has smeltered out all base metals from him.'

The World Is Not Enough

Henry Wallace, May 1943

Was there ever a moment during the war when Churchill realized with a pang that his beloved British Empire would not survive the conflict? Did he ever expect, as he talked with President Roosevelt, that the deeper American political establishment was watching him with cold eyes and planning for the time when the US would end that empire, and take much of its influence and strategic richness for its own purposes? Could Churchill have guessed that the post-war years would be characterized by Great Britain doing the bidding of the United States? His visit to the White House in 1943 included an encounter with Roosevelt's vice-president, Henry Wallace, who later committed the details of Churchill's pungent imperial views to his diary.

Henry Wallace wrote of the lunch at the White House:

> [Churchill] made it more clear than he had at the luncheon on Saturday that he expected England and the United States to run the world and he expected the staff organizations which had been set up for winning the war to continue when the peace came, that these staff organizations would by mutual understanding really run the world even though there was a supreme council and three regional councils.
>
> I said bluntly that I thought the notion of Anglo-Saxon superiority, inherent in Churchill's approach, would be offensive to many of the nations of the world as well as to

a number of people in the United States. Churchill had had quite a bit of whiskey, which, however, did not affect the clarity of his thinking process but did perhaps increase his frankness. He said why be apologetic about Anglo-Saxon superiority, that we were superior, that we had the common heritage which had been worked out over the centuries in England and had been perfected by our constitution. He himself was half American, he felt that he was called on as a result to serve the function of uniting the two great Anglo-Saxon civilizations in order to confer the benefit of freedom on the rest of the world.

Recently, there has been controversy over St Paul's Cathedral using some online material to describe Winston Churchill as a 'white supremacist'; that the accusation traduces him. It is just possible in this encounter with Henry Wallace that Churchill was arguing about political – rather than racial – superiority; that he was focused on traditions and institutions rather than racial characteristics. Yet his language concerning India made even old friends wince; there was a part of Churchill that had never left those Victorian sunsets. More than this: those wartime White House politicians had apparently constructed their own narrative – that the US was a future-facing bright land of equality (their own racism somehow unacknowledged) that stood far above the British Empire in terms of morality, and it would be forging ahead with Britain not so much as a partner but as a supplicant.

The Lions and the Virgins

Anthony Eden, July 1943

'Sir, it is my duty to report that the Tunisian campaign is over,' wrote General Alexander to Churchill. 'All enemy resistance has ceased. We are the masters of the North African shores.'

The victory of the 8th Army over the German forces in the desert was the decisive turning point. Now the Allies could contemplate Sicily and Mussolini's fascist Italy. Churchill had been in America addressing Congress, and his eyes were firmly fixed upon the victorious future: the plans for the invasion of Europe in 1944, and the perils that awaited in the war with Japan in the East. But it was also time to address the British and American troops in Tunisia.

'They were relaxed and happy in their victory,' recalled Anthony Eden, then Foreign Secretary, 'as they had every right to be.' And so, as Eden noted, was Churchill. These days 'were the happiest of the war for him', and it was the task of the younger (and rather more glamorous) Eden to ride around with him in Tunisia, and to walk behind him at inspections of the troops.

In the military arenas of the desert, both men looked comically and Britishly incongruous: Eden in a sharply cut double-breasted suit, hair flopping in the warm wind; Churchill in a bright white suit, topped with a topee (a form of pith helmet).

Even though the visit to the troops was secret, Pathé News was there to record the general jubilation of the soldiers. Churchill was filmed addressing lines of men, and

Eden came on afterwards 'to give them more good stuff' as the news narrator put it, with Churchill 'nodding in agreement'.

This was a moment of sweet accord between Churchill and the man who had long been promised his job. Eden had been told by Churchill many times that the prime minister would not 'do a Lloyd George'; that when the conflict was over, Churchill would step away, leaving Eden to become leader of the Tory Party and – voters willing – prime minister. And Eden would be told this many more times to come (indeed, until 1955). Their relationship was such that they could both argue with terrific heat for some hours without lasting ill will. At the end of one argument in Downing Street, Churchill apologized; and Eden apologized in turn. 'Oh you,' said Churchill, 'you were bloody.'

But here, in this sunny moment, they were in ancient Carthage for one of the most startlingly theatrical moments of Churchill's war. Standing in a ruined Roman amphitheatre, its rows now filled with some 3,000 British and American troops, Churchill required no microphone – the acoustics were such that his voice carried perfectly under the blazing Tunisian sun.

This was, he said, 'a long step forward towards peace, home and honour'. After he had spoken, the troops raised a vast chorus of three cheers, waving their caps. In answer, Churchill placed his topee upon his cane, raised it into the air, and wiggled it about.

Later, Churchill – briefly reunited with his soldier son Randolph, who would shortly afterwards be parachuted into Yugoslavia – and together with Eden and Generals Alan Brooke and Hastings Ismay, declared of that amphitheatre: 'I was speaking where the cries of Christian virgins rent the air whilst roaring lions devoured them. And yet I am no lion and certainly not a virgin!'

Shandygaff for our Old Baby

Lady Diana Cooper, Algiers, 1944

After Duff Cooper was made the British Representative to the French Committee of National Liberation in Algiers, he and his wife Diana made their home out there for some months in 1944. When they arrived in January, they were greeted by Churchill, who had returned to North Africa and whom Diana referred to as 'The Colonel', plus his daughter Sarah (not far off from her divorce from Vic Oliver). Churchill had just been with General de Gaulle at a summit in Marrakesh; now he was going to enjoy several days of arid winter sun. Diana Cooper was to capture the occasion vividly in her letters.

10 January 1944

'Here I am on top of the deep romantic chasm, where Alph the sacred river runs,' wrote Diana Cooper, quoting Coleridge. 'It's wonderfully hot: the sky is without blemish of cloud. We've just had a terrific lunch *al fresco* – stuffing ham and chickabiddy [chicken] smothered in mayonnaise, fruit and *gateaux*, washed down with shandygaff [lager and ginger ale]. It's been a most wonderful *entr'acte* in the grim, cold misery of Algiers.'

That account alone – had it been seen at the time by those bearing ration coupons back in grey, banana-less Britain – would have set off a national tsunami of saliva. But this was Churchill's world, where excess was unself-conscious. And there was more colourful detail:

We flew here in the Colonel's fine plane. Four hours it took, and I weathered them. An ample champagne colla-tion was served, and three charming young gentlemen were thrown in for good measure.

The party is a circus. It's lodged in a millionairess's pleasure dome, all marble and orange-trees, fountains and tiles . . . At the villa there is a big set-up of decoders, WAAFs, map-room, secretaries at two a penny, your old doctor of the Yeomanry, Lord Moran.

The Colonel's wife and WAAF daughter Sarah were on the airfield to meet us and buzzed us by US car, com-plete with immense white star on its camouflaged side, to the pleasure dome.

Here she added an immortal description of Churchill: 'There was our old baby in his rompers, ten-gallon cowboy hat and very ragged oriental dressing-gown, health, vigour and excellent spirits. Never have I seen him spin more fan-tastic stuff, the woof of English and the warp of Slang . . .'

Churchill, though he gave no outward indication, had suffered an epi-sode of pneumonia in Tunis one month previously, when he was making a tour of the Mediterranean theatre visiting troops and bases. Now, he was accompanied to Algiers by his doctor Lord Moran; and Diana Cooper was keeping her own anxious eye on him – convinced, like others were, that the prime minister had suffered a heart attack.

13 January 1944

Later, after the [military] review, which seemed gruelling enough on Winston in one day, we had our eighth and last picnic. The picnic consists of eight cars with white stars and US drivers (the whole town is run by the US exclusively) with two or three guests in each, some [security men] distributed around, and a van laden with viands, drinks, cushions, tables, chairs and pouffes. The advance party leads off an hour before the main body, reconnoitres and selects a valley miles away, windless, comparatively fertile and green, with water if possible.

We drove some eighty miles through the country . . . very beautiful, olive-green and fertile, with towns walled and fortressed by their *kasbahs*. We came climbing to a famous gorge . . . and there we decided to pitch our pleasure . . . the cocktail was shaken up, rugs and cushions distributed, tables and buffets appeared as by a genie's order, and as we finished our preparations the main party arrived.

The Colonel is immediately sat on a comfortable chair, rugs are swathed around his legs and a pillow put on his lap to act as table, book-rest etc. A rather alarming succession of whiskies and brandies go down, with every time a facetious preliminary joke with Edward, an American ex-barman, or with Lord Moran in the shape of professional adviser. I have not heard the lord Doctor answer: perhaps he knows it would make no difference.

A lot of whisky and brandy, good meat and salad, and 'little white-faced tarts' (to use Winston's expression) are consumed.

But in the heat of the sun, Churchill got an idea into his head: he was insistent that he would clamber down the gorge and stand on one of its vast boulders to take in the view of the plains around. Dr Moran was immediately uneasy and told him that it was not a good idea. Churchill was in no mood to listen. He began the descent into the gorge, closely followed by his faithful bodyguard Inspector Thompson. The prime minister attained his goal of that boulder, but those in the party above were now thinking: getting down was the easy part. How would an almost seventy-year-old man who had recently suffered a heart scare – and was now boiling himself under an angry sky – possibly get back up again?

'It seemed to me that if a rope or strap could be found to pass behind his back, while two men walked in front pulling the ends, it would be better than dragging him by his arms,' wrote Cooper. 'I could find nothing but a long tablecloth, but I wound that into a coil and stumbled down with it. Big success! He had no thought of being ridiculous (one of his qualities) so he leaned back upon the linen rope and the boys hauled our saviour up, while old man Moran tried his pulse at intervals. This was only permitted so as to prove that his heart was unaffected by the climb.'

'The Flaming Interior
of the Stars'

Niels Bohr, 1944

With D-Day in June 1944 and the Allied invasion of German-occupied Europe, the war against Hitler moved decisively into its final stages, even though the Wehrmacht was continuing to fight with real venom. London was being hit with Hitler's new wonder-weapons: the V-1 missiles and then the V-2 rockets. But the real future of warfare was now in the hands of the physicists. Even as top-secret work on the atomic bomb continued in the bleak deserts of Los Alamos, New Mexico, it was possible that neither Churchill nor Roosevelt completely understood at that point that nuclear warfare was not just a rather bigger explosion but in a different philosophical and moral realm altogether. The physicist Niels Bohr – whose Nobel Prize-winning thinking on quantum theory and atomic structures and whose contribution to the 'Manhattan Project' (as the Los Alamos experiments were known) was so crucial in bringing this new nuclear age into being – made a plea to Churchill.

'I will not tire you with any technical details,' wrote Niels Bohr to Churchill in May 1944, following his visit to see the prime minister in person, 'but one cannot help comparing the situation with that of the alchemists of former days, groping in the dark in their vain efforts to make gold.'

The two men had met weeks previously at 10 Downing Street: the grand old man of the Victorian steam age, and the scientist summoning Wellsian visions. The meeting, brokered by Frederick Lindemann (now Lord Cherwell) had not gone well. Bohr was not especially good at explaining himself to unscientific laymen; and Churchill – despite his general enthusiasm for science-fiction-like futurism – did not have the capacity for absorbing intense technicality. Thus it was, as Bohr spoke in a 'low' voice, that the prime minister became impatient and wondered why he was not being more succinct.

But Bohr was there on a vital mission: to teach the prime minister about the full, terrifying potential that the new age of nuclear weaponry could eventually release. He also had a political mission: to plead with the prime minister to share these atomic secrets widely (yes, even with the Soviet Union). For the possibility of one side or bloc holding a monopoly on such weaponry could unleash apocalyptic evil, and even bring civilization itself to an end. But how could he convey this within a half-hour meeting that was already being eaten up by Churchill snapping at Cherwell?

He couldn't. In desperation, as he was ushered out, Bohr asked the prime minister if he could send him a written memorandum instead. 'It will be an honour for me to receive a letter from you,' said Churchill. 'But not about politics.' Had he been under the impression that Bohr was solely there for ideological reasons? Bohr later proclaimed: 'We did not even speak the same language.'

But he sat down to write; and he used the kind of language that Churchill understood very well indeed.

To-day physicists and engineers are, on the basis of firmly established knowledge, controlling and directing violent reactions by which new materials far more precious than gold are built up, atom by atom. These processes are in fact similar to those which took place in the early stages of development of the universe and still go on in the turbulent and flaming interior of the stars . . .

I hope you will permit me to say that I am afraid that, at the personal interview with which you honoured me, I may not have given you the right impression of the confidential conversation in Washington on which I reported. It was, indeed, far from my mind to venture any comment about the way in which the great joint enterprise has been so happily arranged by the statesmen; I wished rather to give expression to the profound conviction I have met everywhere on my journey that the hope for the future lies above all in the most brotherly friendship between the British Commonwealth and the United States . . .

The President is deeply occupied in his own mind with the stupendous consequences of the project, in which he sees grave dangers, but also unique opportunities, and . . . he hopes together with you to find ways of handling the situation to the greatest benefit of all mankind.

But, for Bohr, handling the situation meant sharing the secret of atomic weaponry with Stalin, and that – even for his then limited grasp of what an atom bomb could do – was something that Churchill would never have acceded to.

Ironically, the matter was already in hand: physicist Klaus Fuchs, based in Britain but seconded to Los Alamos, was secretly and treacherously passing nuclear intelligence on to the Soviet Union via the spy Ursula Beurton.

To Normandy!

Alan Brooke, 12 June 1944

Six days after D-Day – the extraordinary landing operation of some 133,000 troops on the beaches of Normandy under the onslaught of enemy fire – Churchill was beside himself with desperation to see what was happening over in France with his own eyes. There were some around him who thought this unwise – what a target he would have made – but his will prevailed. Setting sail on HMS Kelvin, *the prime minister was accompanied by Field Marshal Alan Brooke.*

Churchill's costume that day, carefully chosen as ever, was the pea jacket and yachting cap previously seen in Plymouth. His companion, Field Marshal Alan Brooke, had been torn throughout the war when it came to his feelings towards Churchill. 'Never have I admired and disliked a man simultaneously to the same extent,' he declared. 'Without him England was lost for a certainty, with him England has been on the verge of disaster time and again.'

And on that sunny 12 June – as their vessel ploughed across the Channel and the skies overhead vibrated with Allied bombers – both men might fleetingly have thought of the tremendous row involving the term 'hate' that they'd had just weeks before in 10 Downing Street.

As General Hastings Ismay's personal assistant Joan Bright recalled:

Brooke in the company of other ministers was far ruder to the PM than he had any right to be – and Churchill was shocked. He broke up the meeting and said to Ismay: 'I have decided to get rid of Brooke. He hates me. You can see the hate in his eyes.' . . . Ismay left then to see Brooke and said: 'The PM is frightfully upset and says you hate him.' Whereupon Brooke said: 'I don't hate him. I adore him tremendously. I do love him, but the day that I say that I agree with him when I don't, is the day he must get rid of me because I am no use to him any more.' . . . Ismay went back and told Churchill what had been said and his eyes filled with tears. 'Dear Brookie.'

Throughout the war, Brooke had also seen moments of strange Churchillian vulnerability for himself: there had been an episode in the Downing Street bedroom where the two men were deep in discussion as Churchill emerged from his bath and got dressed in a 'white silk' vest and 'white silk' underwear which had the curious effect of making him look like Humpty Dumpty. There had also been an earlier evening at Chequers where Churchill – well refreshed – decided to show off some bayonet moves to the general in the main hall. 'It was one of the first occasions on which I had seen Winston in one of his really light-hearted moods,' Brooke later wrote. 'I was convulsed watching him give this exhibition of bayonet exercises, dressed up in his romper suit and standing in the ancestral hall of Chequers. I remember wondering what Hitler would have made of this demonstration of skill at arms.'

Yet despite the comedy, Churchill never lacked for physical courage – as he was proving on board the HMS *Kelvin*, ordering the crew to aim their guns at German gun emplacements he spied on the French coast. He and Brooke were conveyed to land on an amphibious vehicle, and were there met by Field Marshal Bernard Montgomery. Despite the tremulous security fears about the prime minister entering a combat zone, this visit to Normandy was a moment of fantastic historic symbolism.

As they were driven to the coastal town of Creully, where Montgomery had established his headquarters, Churchill gazed upon the fields and remarked with astonishment to Brooke that 'we are surrounded by fat cattle lying on luscious pastures'. He had been expecting a deathlier prospect, more akin to that of the Great War.

Yet he was still close to the front line: the distant air blue and hazy with smoke from the battle raging in Caen. The prime minister watched vast quantities of supplies and fresh troops being brought in along the waters of the River Orne, and he was greeted with such levels of adulation that as another onlooker, Admiral Cunningham, noted, Churchill was 'looking a bit exuberant' and 'was a bit childish at times'. It might be said that youthful exultation in an almost seventy-year-old man was – at this moment in history – delightful rather than unseemly.

Nonetheless, there was criticism back home in Parliament of the prime minister having run the risk at all of venturing so close to the front line. It was Churchill's singular MP friend Brendan Bracken who made this trumpeting defence of the journey:

I doubt whether anyone in this House has any knowledge of the appalling burden of work borne by the Prime Minister. He labours over sixteen hours a day, and I should say that his daily routine is more dreary and arduous than has ever fallen to the lot of any man. There are, I suppose, degrees in risk-taking, but I hold that working long hours in a frowsy office is much more dangerous to a man's health, than going to sea under the protection of the Royal Navy, or being wafted to far countries by the Royal Air Force. There are other risks in leading a sedentary life. A sizeable number of bombs have been dropped very near the Prime Minister's office home in Whitehall . . .

The conclusion of the whole matter is that, in war, no one can avoid risk. For this reason, the Prime Minister's colleagues are always pleased when he gets out in the fresh air, and gladdens his heart by contact with the fighting men. The Prime Minister has run risk in this war, and he may have to run many more. There is no sacrifice of health or of comfort that he will not make in the service of Britain. He has been the leader of a brave nation, in the darkest hours of its history, and no one can deter the Prime Minister from taking risk if he feels that, by doing so, he can do something to save the precious blood of our fighting men, who are our saviours and, I hope, will be our redeemers.

There was more blood to be spilled, as the push towards the Rhine and Germany met with desperate Wehrmacht counter-attacks. Yet the tide, now turned, was becoming a torrent. And after a winter of fighting through freezing forests, and with the Red Army on its terrifying march from the east, Churchill could look forward to tasting victory with his people.

'We're Going to Get Lit Up'

The London Crowds, 8 May 1945

The church bells had rung out; Hitler was dead, a squalid suicide in a dripping bunker. The Nazi regime was vanquished and Germany had capitulated. The war in the East against the Japanese continued – but in London, victory in Europe led to an extraordinary day. After making the broadcast that announced the end of the war, Churchill emerged from Downing Street and walked into a phenomenal crowd thronging Whitehall – estimated by a Daily Mirror *reporter to be some 50,000 in strength. A little later, the royal family appeared on the 'crimson and gold draped' balcony of Buckingham Palace before uncountable masses in the Mall, and so too did Churchill – 'bare-headed' as the* Daily News *noted. There was 'no cigar, no V-Sign' and no speech. It was not the place. Instead, Churchill gave a 'deep, all-embracing bow'. Later he returned to Downing Street, and the crowds in the Mall and around St James's Park took up the cry: 'We want Winnie!'*

That evening, for the first time in six years, the city glowed with all the light that had been denied it in blackout. And as Big Ben was bathed in a luxuriant radiance, Churchill took to the balcony of the Ministry of Health overlooking Whitehall. The wide street was still packed solidly with civilians and soldiers. So too was Trafalgar Square, and Parliament Square. The more agile had clambered up on the lamp posts for a better view.

'My dear friends, this is your hour,' declared Churchill from that balcony. 'This is not victory of a party or of any class. It's a victory of the great British nation as a whole. We were the first, in this ancient island, to draw the sword against tyranny. After a while we were left all alone against the most tremendous military power that has been seen. We were all alone for a whole year. There we stood, alone. Did anyone want to give in?'

At this, there was a terrific mass shout of 'No!' – as though at the music hall or pantomime. Churchill then said: 'Were we down-hearted?' And again, he awaited the shouted response from the crowds: 'No!'

'The lights went out,' he said – and at that, there was a surprising wave of laughter from the crowd – for owing to a technical hitch, the lights on the ministry balcony had temporarily faltered. Churchill continued gamely, enjoying this engagement with all the people below.

The lights went out and the bombs came down. But every man, woman and child in the country had no thought of quitting the struggle. London can take it. So we came back after long months from the jaws of death, out of the mouth of hell, while all the world wondered. When shall the reputation and faith of this generation of English men and women fail?

I say that in the long years to come, not only will the people of this island but of the world, wherever the bird of freedom chirps in human hearts, look back to what we've done and they will say 'do not despair, do not yield to violence and tyranny, march straight forward and die if need be – unconquered'. Now we have emerged from one deadly struggle – a terrible foe has been cast on the ground and awaits our judgment and our mercy.

But there is another foe who occupies large portions of the British Empire, a foe stained with cruelty and greed – the Japanese.

With this – again as at a pantomime – there was a terrific wave of booing that echoed all the way back along White-hall. Churchill, clearly amused, acknowledged it. 'They would give us much worse than that,' he told the crowd. 'I rejoice we can all take a night off today and another day tomorrow,' he concluded. 'Tomorrow our great Russian allies will also be celebrating victory and after that we must begin the task of rebuilding our hearth and homes, doing our utmost to make this country a land in which all have a chance, in which all have a duty, and we must turn ourselves to fulfil our duty to our own countrymen, and to our gallant allies of the United States who were so foully and treacherously attacked by Japan. We will go hand in hand with them. Even if it is a hard struggle we will not be the ones who will fail.'

With this, he descended once more to his people; emerging from the ministry, in a homburg hat, dark suit and bow tie, he mingled with the jubilant crowd.

But the tides and currents of history can also turn with shocking speed. Churchill was not prepared for the extraordinary blow that lay ahead.

A Walk Through the Ruins

Berliners, July 1945

The gaunt people of Berlin – who had lived under tyranny for the past twelve years and who had in recent months endured bombing, mass rape and near-starvation – might have been among those to be startled by the news that the victor of the war could at any moment be deposed – democratically – by his celebrating citizens.

Just a day or so before the vast multi-power peace conference in the Berlin suburb of Potsdam got underway, Churchill wandered through the jagged, ruined, reeking centre of the city, with Field Marshal Alan Brooke and some token security. He wanted to see the Reich Chancellery, the centre of the web of evil. He wanted to see where Hitler and Eva Braun had met their end.

It was an impulse that was curiously courageous in its own way: given the horrors that they had been through, how could anyone guess how the civilians of Berlin would react to seeing the man they had been taught to view as a vicious war criminal walking among them?

'He looks good, the old man,' said one civilian reluctantly (within earshot of a *Manchester Guardian* reporter). Another said: 'So that is supposed to be a tyrant, is it?' It might be averred generally that Berlin was never really Hitler's city; its cynical, sceptical population had, on the whole, never wholly swallowed the Nazi faith. Apparently there were even some ragged cheers from those who spotted Churchill. Hitler's bones would have been spinning furiously on that blazing funeral pyre. 'My hate died with their surrender,' said Churchill of the Berliners, 'and I was much moved by their demonstrations and also by their haggard looks and threadbare clothes.'

'A Lot of Hooey'

Harry S. Truman, July 1945

*Just four weeks before the defeat of Nazi Germany and the sui-
cide of Hitler, President Roosevelt had been at his retreat in
Georgia, sitting for a portrait. 'I have a terrific headache,' he said,
before slumping forward unconscious. Hours later, he was pronounced dead.*

*By July 1945, with Berlin under the control of the Red Army (they
had yet to allow the American and British troops to take over their
own allocated zones of the city), Roosevelt's successor, Harry
Truman – the bespectacled, one-time proprietor of a haberdashery
store, who'd had very little preparation for this or indeed the atomic
future that lay ahead – attended Potsdam with Stalin and Churchill.
The conference was held at the Cecilienhof Palace, formerly the home
of the Kaiser's son.*

'He is a most charming and a very clever person,' wrote
Harry S. Truman of Churchill, having met him for the first
time. 'Meaning clever in the English not the Kentucky sense.
He gave me a lot of hooey about how great my country is
and how he loved Roosevelt and how he intended to love
me etc. etc. Well. I gave him as cordial a reception as I could –
being naturally (I hope) a polite and agreeable person. I am
sure we can get along if he doesn't try to give me too much
soft soap.'

There was no opportunity for soap, soft or otherwise
(though the two men would meet again shortly, as we shall
see). While Potsdam was Truman's uncertain debut on the

world stage, it was also Churchill's temporary farewell to it. As the conference progressed, the voters of Britain (including all the soldiers posted around the world) made their choice: Churchill the war leader had served his purpose. He was voted out in the general election. The future was now to be addressed by his Labour deputy, the austere Clement Attlee.

The war with Japan was to be ended weeks later with two atom bombs on Nagasaki and Hiroshima; and a new phase of undeclared war was to begin almost immediately, as the US and Soviet Russia assumed their roles as the world's newest superpowers. What mark could Churchill make upon a nuclear age?

The Unexpected Path

The Constituents of Woodford Green, 1945

'The Right Honourable Winston Churchill . . . had an audience of the King at 7 pm today and tendered his resignation as Prime Minister and First Lord of the Treasury and Minister of Defence, which His Majesty was pleased to accept.' This was the official announcement on 27 July 1945 of the fall of Churchill's government. Labour's victory in the election had given it a towering 145-seat majority. Churchill had won the war; but in peace, the majority of voters wanted a government that would prioritize the establishment of

universal social security, health care and housing. (In the 1946 war fantasy film A Matter of Life and Death, *even David Niven's upper-middle-class bomber pilot Peter Carter confided that his politics were 'Conservative by instinct, Labour by experience').*

Clement Attlee was driven through the gates of Buckingham Palace five minutes after Churchill left; he was reportedly little noticed by the waiting crowds. The car was driven by Mrs Attlee; the contrast to the grandeur that had gone before was stark. From this point, Attlee would pick up the baton of peace and continuing war in the East, as well as facing the daunting challenges of a bankrupted war-shocked nation.

For Churchill, the immediate shock of political loss was intense. Two years later, in 1947, he would make this philosophically witty observation: 'Many forms of Government have been tried, and will be tried in this world of sin and woe. No-one pretends that democracy is perfect or all-wise. Indeed it has been said that democracy is the worst form of Government except for all those other forms that have been tried from time to time.'

It might have been natural at that point of ejection in 1945 for a seventy-year-old man to accept pottering retirement. It was being urged upon him by Clementine. 'This might be a blessing in disguise,' she said. 'If so, it is very well disguised,' he replied.

What was not reported at the time was that the King had offered to create him a dukedom. This was no small matter; outside of the royal family the last time such an honour was created was in 1874 for Hugh Grosvenor, who became the Duke of Westminster (partly because this fantastically wealthy landowner was an old family friend of Queen Victoria, and partly due to the urging of Prime Minister William Gladstone). Churchill declined the honour of becoming Duke of Dover, however; it would have denied him a seat in the Commons. He was now Leader of the Opposition, and determined to win Downing Street back. And he was still the constituency MP for Woodford (after a boundary review of Epping created the new

*seat). At the very much humbler end of the scale for honours, his con-
stituency chairman, Sir James Hawkey, ensured that he received his
due from local voters in many ways. Not quite a dukedom, but a
touching honour none the less.*

'WANSTEAD FREEDOM FOR MR CHURCHILL. Mr Winston
Churchill and Mrs Churchill were given the honorary freedom of the borough of Wanstead and Woodford at an
impressive ceremony in the great hall of Bancroft's School,
Woodford,' reported the local press on 22 October 1945.
'The 700 people present accorded the ex-premier and his
wife an enthusiastic welcome.'

Bancroft's School (it is still there, amid the leafy heights
of Woodford Green) was originally set up in the eighteenth century for poor boys from the East End, and the
ethos was roughly the same in 1945 – many of its boarders
were still drawing on bursaries and from deprived areas
like Stepney and Bow. Sir James Hawkey was among those
presiding over the ceremonials, at which Churchill was
presented with a gilt mace and an illuminated scroll.
Churchill then rose to speak.

I freely avow to you, my friends, that it was not without a
pang that I found myself dismissed at the General Election from the honourable task of guiding our country.
I had hoped that the position I had gained in the world,
the experience and knowledge which I had acquired, and
the links which had been forged in the fires of war with
other lands and leaders might have been of service in this
critical time of transition, and in the fateful work of trying
to revive the life and glory of Europe within the circle of
assured world peace.

I shall not waste your time or my own with vain repin-
ings, but, on the contrary, you may be sure that I will
devote myself unwearyingly to whatever duties may come
my way . . .

There were, reportedly, cheers. And indeed, despite the wider
political earthquake, nothing had diminished Churchill's
intense popularity within his constituency, nor his enthusiasm for participating in its life. At around the same time he
was also made a patron of the Woodford Operatic and Dra-
matic Society – which, according to its business manager
Don Leach, left members understandably 'delighted and
thrilled'. Churchill's appearances at local events always caused
flurries of excitement; on one occasion, his car arrived near a
children's party and he briefly popped on a 'coloured party
hat'. How many present at the Bancroft's freedom ceremony
that day would have guessed at that point that this grand but
elderly statesman would have continued thus through to the
1960s?

House of Cards

Harry S. Truman, 1946

*A Universal Studios newsreel in January 1946 gave Churchill a
warm welcome to Miami, Florida, at the start of a 'six week vac-
ation' in the US. Naturally, one of his first acts – after having been
distracted by the beauty of local butterflies, of which he was a great*

aficionado – was to give a press conference. He counselled against any moves towards what the newsreel narrator described as 'world collectivism'.

With Clement Attlee's Labour government trying to reconstruct Britain – against a backdrop of the slow demobilization of soldiers, continued rationing and grey austerity – Churchill had decided upon this fresh US tour. It was leisurely in its progress; he made his way north starting from the Surf Club in Miami. It was in Washington, DC, that Churchill made rendezvous with President Truman – noticeably warmer towards him than at their previous encounter in Potsdam – and the two of them set off together on a thousand-mile train journey to Truman's home territory of Missouri.

En route, Truman – a dedicated poker player – inveigled Churchill into a number of games. But Churchill, it seemed, was not a natural at this particular discipline.

At one point, having almost been cleaned out by the president and several other White House players on board the train, Churchill excused himself to visit the bathroom. In his absence, Truman told his fellow players that they must allow Churchill to win, in order to get him back into the game.

It is always tempting to look for political symbolism: with post-war Europe in the dust and awaiting the rejuvenating injection of American money from the Marshall Plan, Truman may have seen something pitiable in both Churchill and the nation that he represented; he may have detected a sense of crushed pride. Just weeks beforehand, Clement Attlee had been invited to address the US Congress, and his declaration that the British government planned to start nationalizing key industries was met with a distinctly muted response. Might the US president also be allowing Churchill 'back into the game' because he recognized the importance of maintaining a steady friendship with a statesman who was more obviously attuned to the American enthusiasm for free markets?

And perhaps Truman went just a little further than he had intended in terms of giving Churchill a stage from which to project his message to the world. For one of Churchill's most famous speeches – a talk that came to shape an entire era – came about at Truman's prompting: an invitation during that 1946 US tour to Westminster College in Fulton, Missouri.

When the idea had presented itself to Truman, he had written to the former prime minister: 'This is a wonderful school in my home state. Hope you can do it. I'll introduce you.'

Back on the World Stage

Dean Acheson, 1946

Churchill's speech at Fulton is now best remembered for this sentence: 'From Stettin in the Baltic to Trieste in the Adriatic, an iron curtain has descended across the Continent.' The term 'iron curtain' (apparently coined by H. G. Wells several decades previously) gave it lasting historical resonance; some have argued the Cold War – the decades-long enmity between the West and the Soviet Union – started right there. But the speech – and its effect on its influential listeners at the time – was rather more subtle and wide-ranging than the headlines suggest. And it was Dean Acheson – Roosevelt's foreign policy chief overseeing aid to a Europe in ruins – who would be especially mesmerized by Churchill's rhetoric.

Dean Acheson, in later years, was happy to compare Churchill to Elizabeth I. 'Both Elizabeth and Churchill needed, and used, all their superb qualities of heart and brain, their indomitable courage, inexhaustible energy, their magnanimity and good sense, to bring their country through its two periods of darkest peril.'

Acheson – raptor-eyed, luxuriantly moustached and wide-smiling – was, as Secretary of State, one of those who found himself at that moment one of the supreme powers in this broken post-war world. He was there at the inception of the International Monetary Fund and the World Trade Organization; Churchill was alive to his relationship with President Truman. But immediately after Churchill's Fulton speech at Westminster College, Truman tried to keep them apart: Churchill had created a diplomatic blaze and Truman thought that a little distance in the immediate aftermath might be best. Churchill and Acheson thought otherwise.

Part of the problem was that Churchill had given Truman no advance notice of what he was going to say. The Fulton speech had begun innocuously enough: he joked that he seemed to have heard of 'Westminster' before. He was dressed in honorary academic robes, having never earned his own. And as well as the fine language and structure of the talk, Churchill seemed in no way diminished by his recent domestic political ejection. If anything, his personal stature and fame in the US seemed, in general, perhaps even more prominent than the influence of his home country itself.

But as the talk went on, so started the turbulence in US political circles. This was not just about the warning notes on the territorial ambitions of Stalin's Soviet Union. (Churchill also went out of his way to diplomatically state his 'strong admiration and regard for the valiant Russian people', and for his 'wartime comrade, Marshal Stalin' and to 'welcome Russia to her rightful place among the leading nations of the world'.)

No: this was also to do with diplomatic distaste. Churchill not only used the phrase 'iron curtain', but also – in talking of the US and Britain – 'special relationship':

Neither the sure prevention of war, nor the continuous rise of world organisation will be gained without what I have called the fraternal association of the English-speaking peoples. This means a special relationship between the British Commonwealth and Empire and the United States. Fraternal association requires not only the growing friendship and mutual understanding between our two vast but kindred Systems of society, but the continuance of the intimate relationship between our military advisers, leading to common study of potential dangers, the similarity of weapons and manuals of instructions, and to the interchange of officers and cadets at technical colleges. It should carry with it the continuance of the present facilities for mutual security by the joint use of all Naval and Air Force bases in the possession of either country all over the world . . . This would perhaps double the mobility of the American Navy and Air Force. It would greatly expand that of the British Empire Forces . . .

To a number of American politicians and commentators, here was an elderly imperialist calling for the US to become Britain's partner in Empire. The idea was, to many, repugnant – even though Churchill was perfectly correct in a sense to foresee US forces permanently based in Britain and across the world on various British-held islands and territories.

For the sake of a quieter life, President Truman instructed Dean Acheson that he was not to attend a special post-speech reception for Churchill in New York. But the two men did catch up in Washington, DC. And it was at a lunch there that Acheson and Churchill found neutral non-political territory upon which to enjoy each other's company. Acheson recalled the meeting in his memoir *Present at the Creation*:

> After Mr Churchill's Iron Curtain speech . . . my wife and I lunched with him and his daughter Sarah and Ambassador and Lady Franks at the British Embassy. My wife, who idolized Mr Churchill, anointed him with ample flattery, which he obviously enjoyed. When the talk turned to painting and he discovered that she had seen reproductions of his work and was herself a painter, he asked for a criticism of his. In doing so he passed from a field in which he was a world master to one in which she accorded him no superiority whatever. While she liked his work, she pointed out areas where improvement was possible. This was not what he expected or wanted; she did not yield an inch. He puffed harder on his cigar and fought back. Our hostess broke up the criticism by rising. He chuckled as we walked out of the dining room, and remarked to me that the critic had plenty of spirit – a quality of which we were already aware.

There was a pleasing postscript: 'In 1950, the Churchills entertained us at luncheon and my wife was shown the originals of the works she had criticized.'

Yet mixed in with this affection was a sense of some wonder at Churchill the war leader:

Here, raised to its highest, is the leadership which alone can call forth from a free people what cannot be commanded. Neither courage, nor right decisions, nor speaking good words is enough. Art, great art, transforms all these into something different and superlative. What Churchill did was great: how he did it was equally so. Neither action nor style could have accomplished the result alone. Both were needed.

Not only was the content of his speeches wise and right but they were prepared with that infinite capacity for taking pains which is said to be genius. So was his appearance; his attitudes and gestures, his use of all the artifices to get his way, from wooing and cajolery, through powerful advocacy to bluff bullying – all were carefully adjusted to the need. To call this acting is quite inadequate. Acting is a mode infinitely variable and adjustable. What we are speaking of is a transformation, a growth and a permanent change of personality.

Horses for Courses

Christopher Soames, 1947

'Horses were the greatest of my pleasures at Sandhurst,' wrote Churchill of his youthful years. 'We organised point-to-points and even a steeplechase in the park of a friendly grandee, and bucketed gaily about the countryside.' There was also his skill at polo; and as we have seen, the spectacle of Churchill on horseback in battle in Sudan.

The love for all matters equestrian never left him. Being in political opposition is traditionally dreary; amid the bomb-struck ruins of post-war Britain, horses were a vital form of escapism that brought vivid splashes of colour back into his – and many other – lives.

'At the start, he jumped off in front,' recalled Christopher (later Lord) Soames. 'There was a terrific cheer from the crowd when he won – and they all surged forward to see him come in and gave him a wonderful reception.' He was speaking of a big grey racehorse, named Colonist II, which he had persuaded Winston Churchill to buy. The beast and its races were to have a rejuvenating effect upon the former prime minister. But his son-in-law would go on to have an even more intriguing influence upon the memory of Churchill.

Soames was a twenty-seven-year-old officer in the Coldstream Guards when his romance with Churchill's youngest daughter, Mary, began. He had the look of a young Terry Thomas: slicked-back hair, wide grin. He was an assistant military attaché in Paris – the foundation of a deep European sensibility – at the time when the post of ambassador was held by Churchill's old friend Duff (there with wife

Lady Cooper). This made it rather easier for Churchill to accept his new prospective son-in-law (his other daughter Sarah's divorce from the comedian Vic Oliver had come through in 1945).

As newlyweds in 1947, Mary and Christopher moved into the farm next door to Chartwell that Churchill had purchased. They set about the matter of conceiving a large family without delay. And there was one vital factor, other than a love of the Kentish landscape (and a skill at playing gin rummy for money) that linked the young officer Soames to his father-in-law – his love for horses. Before long, with Chartwell Farm transformed by the countryman Soames into a thriving and lively concern (including, as we shall see a little later, one mad bull), he was ready to branch out a little.

A racing contact had alerted Soames to a lively colt, and in 1949 persuaded him – and his father-in-law – to buy this horse for £2,000. Colonist II would soon be hitting the headlines; even before the beast had raced, it had been noted in the racing press that the former prime minister had re-registered his late father's racing colours: bright pink, with chocolate sleeves and cap.

In the manner of a situation comedy, Clementine was apparently both horrified and indignant over the development. She was not quite alone. Some Tory parliamentary colleagues were nervous – in the face of a forthcoming election – of a Tory leader in this new technocratic age being seen to indulge in such shamelessly aristocratic pleasures.

But when Colonist II began winning races – to the uproarious delight of bookies and punters alike – other colleagues sensed there might be some political capital in an otherwise grey world. 'Conservatives and Colonist!' was one larkily suggested election campaign poster. 'Winnie wins!' was another.

Colonist II had a galloping run of thirteen wins, all of which helped the Churchill family finances considerably. And the shrewd Christopher – seeing both the material rewards but also the intense cheer that racing brought his elderly father-in-law – set about creating a stud farm (away from Chartwell). Sleek racehorses with names like Vienna and High Hat were trained there, and in a development that might not have been foreseen in the post-war years, Churchill was elected to the Jockey Club.

It is worth noting that Christopher Soames had a rather more substantial career afterwards – in politics, and then in diplomacy. There was a time, in the early 1950s, when he was constantly within Downing Street, aiding Churchill but also in some curious way becoming a family extension of him. As we shall see a little later, this role would expand startlingly when Churchill was forced for a time to withdraw following serious illness. Yet Soames's growing stature was also acquired independently, and he was to forge a distinguished career for himself.

Much later, in a speech in 1975 – two years after Britain had joined the Common Market – Lord Soames, now the ambassador to Paris, invoked his father-in-law and his dream of a united Europe. Soames was a fervent believer in this new European framework where sovereignty was pooled but nations could nonetheless retain their distinct identities. In his speech he quoted Churchill: 'Let Europe arise!' The question of whether Churchill would have welcomed – or rejected – an ever-closer relationship beyond the Common Market, and with what would later become the European Union, eventually became one of many sore points in the frazzle-tempered Brexit debates.

Whatever Churchill's deeper intentions regarding Britain's integration into a European super-structure, his adoration of the continent in purely aesthetic and sensual terms could at last be given free rein in the post-war years. He had an intense partiality for the south of France, for instance, and an especial fondness for the luxury of the Hôtel de Paris in Monte Carlo in the principality of Monaco. Even better than that, though, was the prospect of long hazy holidays in sumptuous villas that in essence cost him nothing.

'I Mustn't! I Promised Clemmie!'

Lord Beaverbrook, 1949

The house was on a rocky outcrop jutting into an ocean of richest blue, and surrounded with the intense pinks, violets and crimsons of bougainvillea. It was called La Capponcina, and it was situated on the French Riviera – at Cap d'Ail, close to Monte Carlo. It belonged to Lord Beaverbrook, former wartime minister for aircraft production, and proprietor of the then hugely popular Daily Express. *He and Churchill had known each other for some forty years.*

La Capponcina represented a form of continental luxury tha. many of Beaverbrook's readers would have regarded with wonder (ir 1948, the Powell and Pressburger film The Red Shoes *captivate. audiences not merely through its thunderous balletic melodrama, bu.*

also through its sumptuous Technicolor Riviera locations). Churchill was frequently invited to take holidays with Beaverbrook and – as was often the case with his rich friends – he never shied away from accepting this generosity. His old friend W. Somerset Maugham once described Monte Carlo as 'a sunny place for shady people', but Churchill was drawn helplessly to its glitz like a light-dazzled moth. One particular holiday in 1949 – when he was Leader of the Opposition – came as Attlee's government was struggling in the aftermath of the devaluation of the pound.

'From the moment [Churchill] arrived at the villa, it was clear that he was in a holiday mood,' wrote Michael Wardell, one of Beaverbrook's associates and a former brigadier in the army.

He insisted immediately on putting on a pair of blue bathing drawers and walking down to the sea, down a hundred steps through Beaverbrook's enchanted garden of bougainvilleas and orange trees and roses. Arriving at length where the Mediterranean laps the rocks at the foot of the garden, Churchill literally plunged into his holiday. He wallowed like a porpoise; he blew spouts of water like a whale, and he swam round and round like a schoolboy. He turned and he twisted, and he lost his baggy blue bathing drawers. It didn't matter, for there was no one there to see him but Beaverbrook and me and his own male retinue.

Clambering out, he was rubbed down by his manservant and wrapped in a towelled dressing gown. He started to climb the hundred steps home, stopping every little while to sit and rest and talk and refresh himself from a waiting decanter.

Wardell was fascinated by the way that Churchill appeared to have played a major role – through his evocation in speeches of a 'United States of Europe' – in setting in motion the post-war continental accord; the first steps towards a Common Market. Wardell observed that the newly formed Council of Europe had just been holding its first session in Strasbourg – and this he was happy to attribute to Churchill's encouragement of a 'recreation of the European family'. But Churchill was at Cap d'Ail purely in pursuit of pleasure. This would be the case for summers to come.

That first night, the three of us dined in the open air on the verandah. The outline of Monte Carlo was silhouetted against the evening sky, the shore lights reflected on the smooth surface of the sea, mingling with the mirrored beams from the small boats moving silently back and forth across the bay. Churchill gazed at the lights of Monte Carlo. 'How inviting it looks! How much I'd like to go there after dinner,' he said, and paused . . . 'But no. I mustn't. I promised Clemmie!' And he told how he had visited Monte Carlo when he was no longer Prime Minister. He cashed a cheque, quite forgetful of the foreign exchange restrictions that he himself had made. He had gambled and lost and enjoyed every minute of it, until afterwards he had suddenly remembered he had committed a heinous offence against the laws of Britain.

Incredibly, these ferocious exchange controls – you could not take more than a certain small sum of cash out of the country – were to remain in place until 1979.

On that same holiday, Churchill and Beaverbrook had a visit from the Minister of State for Monaco, who apparently disapproved of gambling and was keen instead for Monte Carlo to be recalibrated as a cultural destination. Churchill was apparently hugely amused by the prospect – agreeing with quiet irony that it would indeed be a beautiful place to listen to music. With this, he began to serenade the minister with one of his old music-hall favourites: 'As I walk along the Bois-Boolong / With an independent air / You can hear the girls declare / "He must be a millionaire!" / You can hear them sigh and wish to die / You can see them wink the other eye / At the man who broke the bank at Monte Carlo.'

The holiday in 1949 involved interludes on public beaches too; onlookers delighting at Churchill splashing around in the sea and crying out to him, 'Vive Churchill!' Wardell was also privy to a conversation between Churchill and Beaverbrook about his trademark V-sign.

'It's a very good thing, the V-sign,' [Churchill] said. 'Everybody feels it's a personal message to themselves. The Italians are particularly fond of it (with this he chuckled) . . . they must think they won the war. I'm going to Germany in the autumn,' Churchill continued. 'I have little doubt that the Germans will give me a very warm reception, and will not fail to make use of the V-sign.'

'I'll bet they won't,' said Beaverbrook. 'Of course the V-sign has many meanings in various parts of the world. It was originally supposed to represent the devil, with two horns. In Canada, when I was a boy, the sign had a very special significance.'

'Not only in Canada,' Churchill replied. 'In England too; and no doubt in other places. But I made it respectable.'

Yet it was on this holiday that Churchill also heard the clanging bell of mortality. One night, as he retired, he declared that he was feeling 'peculiar'. On the stairs, he suddenly declared to Wardell: 'The dagger is pointing at me. I pray it will not strike.'

He made it to his room, now being closely watched. The main symptom was a 'cramp'. Churchill took a sleeping pill. When he awoke the next morning, the cramp was still there and he found that he could not write so well. Beaverbrook arranged for Churchill's physician, Dr Moran, to fly out at once.

It appeared Churchill had had a mild stroke. His speech was apparently unaffected but his pen grip was weaker. There was no memory loss; he had been very fortunate. He rested for several days and, to the slight astonishment of those around him, rallied completely. It was noted that Churchill was unwaveringly focused on the proximity of the next general election.

Back in Britain, the exploits of his racehorse Colonist II had – like the newly respectable V-sign – likewise bestowed a curious respectability on the otherwise rackety business of horse racing (and Churchill told Beaverbrook and Wardell how proud he was of his winning horse). As it happened, Churchill's more traditionalist Tory Party colleagues might also have come to consider their earlier celebratory instincts re the widely publicized exploits of Colonist II and its owner to be correct. There was a general election in 1950: it reduced Attlee's majority from 145 to just 5. Though Attlee's government had achieved much in terms of social reform, the unyielding grind of austerity and continued rationing – years after the end of the conflict – meant that many exasperated voters were once more looking at the florid old-school traditionalists. Certain symbols of Tory pleasure-seeking – horse-flesh, loud tweed, studying the odds – were not wholly abhorrent to a wide swathe of the public. And Churchill, as Leader of the Opposition, would be looking on as fractures became fissures in the Labour Party.

Tears Before Bedtime

Aneurin Bevan, Jennie Lee and Harold Wilson, 1951

Just before the 1951 election – the fresh poll necessitated by that razor-thin majority the year before – Clement Attlee's Labour government was struggling against elements such as a continuing housing crisis. A combination of badly bombed cities plus a post-war shortage of the raw materials needed for a huge programme of mass rebuilding and construction meant that there were occasional outbreaks of civil disobedience, and civilian families had been squatting in now-disused military facilities. In addition, large numbers of families had to live in small prefabricated houses – like concrete kit assemblies – which were dotted around various suburbs, and which, since demolition, have latterly acquired immense retro appeal.

The party was also riven by a row over proposed prescription charges and defence spending. Aneurin Bevan, architect of the newly inaugurated NHS, objected to a rise in militarism, which he thought came at the cost of alleviating poverty and distress, and in 1951 he resigned from the government. He was followed by a junior minister of much intellectual promise called Harold Wilson. In this sense, both cast themselves into the cold. Churchill, as Leader of the Opposition, might have been justified in dancing a little jig of glee. But his actual response caused some surprise.

'So far as I am concerned,' said Bevan famously, 'they [the Tories] are lower than vermin.' Of all Churchill's political opponents, Aneurin Bevan had been the most consistently angry. In the early years of the war – and especially after the fall of Singapore in 1942 – it was Bevan who gave voice in the House to the idea that perhaps Churchill was not up to the job as Britain's war leader. His cutting line was that the prime minister 'wins debate after debate but loses battle after battle'. After the war, Churchill expressed equal distaste for the newly appointed Minister of Health, declaring that Bevan 'will be as great a curse to this country in time of peace as he was a squalid nuisance in time of war'.

Most strikingly, Bevan referenced Churchill elliptically in his 1948 speech where he described the premature death of his father and how 'no amount of cajolery, and no attempts at ethical and social seduction can eradicate from my heart a deep burning hatred for the Tory Party that inflicted those bitter experiences on me'. After the 'vermin' image, he added: 'They condemned millions of first-class people to semi-starvation.' Churchill afterwards made angry reference to the 'odium of the words' that would 'lie upon the Socialist Government'.

And yet in the spring of 1951, with Bevan walking out of Attlee's government, something chimed within Churchill's parliamentary instincts. Perhaps it was the memory of how he had found himself in the political cold after taking a stand against his own party. In this sense, while his opponents angered him, he was also capable of sympathizing with their moments of crisis.

It was reported that Churchill sought out Aneurin Bevan's wife, Jennie Lee – the fiery Scottish MP with whom he had across the years enjoyed occasional jousting encounters. He located her in the Commons Smoking Room, where she was having tea with Bevan. 'I see you are standing by your husband,' Churchill said lightly. Lee's response was equally light: 'Someone must put a bit of backbone into him.' At this, Churchill was suddenly serious. 'Do not underestimate your husband.'

And in the years to come, Bevan was to write of Churchill that it was 'hard for even his political opponents – in the House of Commons at any rate – to *dislike* him. I say in the House of Commons because people who remember the vigour with which he set about organizing the armed forces to be able, if necessary, to smash the strikers in 1926, regarded him as a monster.'

The memories of the General Strike had, even by the 1950s, reached almost folkloric status. For this, Churchill could never be redeemed. Yet Bevan was at pains to stress that Churchill the parliamentarian was quite a different animal; that 'in spite of the brutality with which he sometimes laid about him, it was impossible systematically to dislike him. His sulkiness and morose ill-temper were frequently almost forgivable, so childish were they, but nearly always his sulks would explode in a fit of rage, and after that he would forgive and forget with as much generosity as public life allows.'

Bevan's junior colleague Harold Wilson – who himself would rise to the office of prime minister in 1964 – found that Churchill went even further than forgiving on the occasion of his resignation from government in 1951. First, there was a little light joking – that Wilson had 'gone out with honour' but, Churchill added with 'a twinkle', he and his party would make the most of all the trouble he had caused Attlee. But then, later, there was an unexpected outbreak of sensitivity and emotion. Wilson gave the following account in his book *A Prime Minister on Prime Ministers*:

> That evening Brendan Bracken sought me out. He had been charged, he said, 'by the greatest living statesman, for that is what Mr. Churchill is', to give me a message to convey to my wife [Mary]. First, Mr Churchill wanted me to know, he had been 'presented' to my wife, otherwise he would not presume to send her a message. [Here, Churchill's inner Victorian appeared to be roaring through. But the message was a surprise to Wilson.] The message was that whereas I, as an experienced politician, had taken a step of which he felt free to take such party advantage as was appropriate, his concern was with my wife, an innocent party in these affairs, who would undoubtedly suffer in consequence.
>
> He recalled the number of occasions his wife had suffered as a result of his own political decisions. Would I therefore convey to her his personal sympathy and understanding? Thanking Bracken, I went home about 1 a.m. . . . and conveyed the message, which was greeted with gratitude and tears. I was enjoined to express her personal thanks. On leaving home the next morning I was again enjoined to see 'the old boy' and make sure I delivered the message.

In the early evening I saw Winston in the smoke-room and went up to him and told him I had a message from my wife . . . and expressed her thanks. Immediately – and with Winston this was not a rare event – tears flooded down his face, as he expatiated on the way that wives had to suffer for their husbands' political actions, going on to recall a number of instances over a long life.

When I reached home – it was 2 a.m., but she was awake – I was asked if I had seen the old boy and thanked him. I had, and recounted the interview. She burst into tears, and I was moved to say that whereas two days earlier I had been a Minister of the Crown, red box and all, now I was reduced to the position of a messenger between her and Winston Churchill, each of whom burst into tears on receipt of a message from the other. Of such is the essence of Parliament, or at least of bygone Parliaments, but this was the essential Winston Churchill.

Strictly Between Ourselves

Lord Beaverbrook, 1951

Throughout the course of his life, Churchill was a constant delight for journalists in the sense of providing such vividly colourful material for copy. Yet his long friendship with Lord Beaverbrook brought another element to press coverage – and that was unhelpful stories being sat upon. As we shall see a little later, a graver crisis in Churchill's health would result in a press blackout that would never conceivably

*be tolerated now. Even before that, though, seemingly lighter stories —
like this one recounted by 1950s Sunday Express show-business
correspondent Logan Gourlay — could be squashed.*

It starts in Rome. I'm there for the best part of a week to
report on the filming of *Quo Vadis* in which Peter Ustinov
is playing Nero. I have spent a good deal of time with
Ustinov and that means, of course, that I have also been
in the company of the wide-ranging cast of characters he
mimics so brilliantly. It includes not only all the other
leading actors and actresses in the film . . . but also prominent statesmen like Winston Churchill.

For reasons not unconnected with Ustinov's expansive
hospitality in Rome, I am late in returning to Fleet Street.
Instead of arriving on Friday morning to write up my *Quo
Vadis* piece so that my column can be locked away well in
advance of the eve-of-publication rush on Saturday,
I don't reach London till Friday evening. I creep into the
office from the airport around 11.00 p.m. At that hour,
the *Sunday Express* editorial floor, the fifth, is deserted.
I settle down at my typewriter and try to work. But the
words do not flow easily: part of my mind is still on the
Via Veneto.

The phone rings. When I pick it up, a voice asks me
to take a call from Winston Churchill. I assume I am
listening again to Peter Ustinov, phoning perhaps to
apologise for delaying me in Rome, but unable to resist
an opportunity to mimic. When what sounds like the
voice of Winston Churchill flows over the line, I say
unhesitatingly: 'Why don't you f*** off and let me get
on with my work? You know I should have been back
here sooner . . .'

It is 1951, and Churchill, as Opposition Leader without direct access to the news he was accustomed to making as Prime Minister, has formed the habit, on Saturday evenings after dinner, of phoning John Gordon, the *Sunday Express* editor [Express circulation then was about 4 million], who can tell him as he puts the paper to bed what's making the headlines.

And the result of his expletive?

There is a loud rumbling at the other end of the phone, and a gruff demand for an explanation that is unmistakeably Churchillian. The enormity of my mistake leaves me dumb for a moment, but when I recover the power of speech and offer profuse apologies, he accepts them with remarkably good grace in the circumstances and says he has obviously been put on to the wrong Scotsman: he wants to speak to John Gordon as he usually does on Saturday nights. I say somewhat tentatively that I think it is Friday night and I'm terribly sorry but I'm afraid that at this hour John Gordon will have gone home.

A pause, then Churchill declares: 'It is Saturday night. Get me Gordon.'

His voice has now taken on a harsh, commanding edge. I apologise again, and tell him I will find Gordon without delay. I must have got back from Rome even later than I thought. If Winston Churchill says it is Saturday night, it *is* Saturday night: it's indisputable. But when I rush round the corner of the office to Gordon's room, it is dark . . . I bump into a night watchman and I ask him for confirmation. Convinced no doubt that I've just staggered in from the Press Club, he looks at me pityingly, and states categorically that it is Friday night . . . I hurry back to my desk, wondering desperately after my four-letter insult if there is a diplomatic way of telling Winston Churchill he doesn't know what day it is. But when I get to the phone, Churchill has hung up . . .

Early next morning, I am summoned to Beaverbrook's presence . . . He says: 'I believe you had an interesting conversation on the phone with Winston Churchill?' I nod and he goes on: 'D'you agree with me that he is the greatest living Englishman?' I nod again. 'And that he will be back as Prime Minister?' Another nod. 'Now you wouldn't like it to be known that the greatest living Englishman, and our future Prime Minister, didn't know what day it was.' I nod yet again. 'He's got so much on his mind, it's easy even for a great man like him to make a small mistake like that – even if he hasn't had a bit too much brandy after dinner. It must be our state secret. Just between you and me. And Winston. You must give me your solemn promise that you will never dine out on this story.'

In fairness to Gourlay, he probably only told every single one of his colleagues in El Vino, the Fleet Street bar. And he waited a few years before publishing this account. But he also rather brilliantly provided this winning postscript: 'One of [Beaverbrook's] most loveable qualities was his self-deflating sense of humour. Churchill had it too. On one occasion when I met him in the company of Beaverbrook after the unfortunate telephone conversation, Churchill said: "Ah, yes, Gourlay. I remember you. Tell me, what day is it?"'

As it turned out, Churchill was not the 'future' prime minister for much longer. He was back, as Beaverbrook predicted, when the 1951 general election returned him to power. When he had first walked into Downing Street as prime minister in 1940, he had not done so as a result of a democratic vote, but rather the resignation of Chamberlain and his selection as successor. This time he had won on his own terms (albeit with a modest majority of 17). Life was restored to what seemed its proper axis: Downing Street, Chequers and Chartwell.

To Thine Own Self Be True

Laurence Olivier and Richard Burton, 1951–3

It is not unusual for great actors to have an armoury of witty theatrical anecdotes; what is unusual is for two toweringly brilliant actors to lay claim to the same anecdote. Churchill, who had long been fascinated by Vivien Leigh, wife of Laurence Olivier, would get to know her husband, a great cinematic Shakespearean, better. But this was also an age of fiery new naturalistic talent, and the young Welsh actor Richard Burton would also find his professional life entwining with that of Churchill. The anecdote – which Olivier and Burton each told without reference to the other – has a charm in both versions.

'The great excitement of 1951 for us was our meeting and acquaintanceship with our glorious Winston Churchill,' wrote Laurence Olivier, himself sounding like a star-struck fan, bouncing up and down outside the stage door.

The first time we realised he was honouring us was at a performance of *Caesar and Cleopatra* [the George Bernard Shaw play]. In the interval, I was hovering about in my dressing room, wondering what the great man was thinking of us, when the door opened and that immortal head with the wonderful blue eyes came around it. I was too much taken aback to say anything, but he said at once, 'Oh I'm so sorry, I was looking for a corner.' [By this he meant the lavatory.] Realising his need, I took him back through the outer office and indicated to him exactly where to go and how to get himself down the stairs again, where there would be someone waiting for him to take him back through the pass-door and into his seat.

He always allowed himself the minor extravagance of buying three seats, one for himself, one for his much-loved daughter Mary, and one for his hat and coat; I thought this one of the most sensible extravagances I had ever heard of. A little later Mary told me that, returning to his seat and sitting next to her, he had said: 'I was looking for a luloo, and who do you think I ran into? Juloo [Julius].'

And there was a subsequent curious theatrical encounter:

During *Richard III*, I had heard myself being gently accompanied from the third or fourth row. Reports came back to me afterwards that he had said every single line in unison with me. When I told him how envious I was of such a wonderful memory, he said: 'Oh, but you – so many myriads of words packed into your brain? It must be a great burden.' I had to admit honestly that three weeks after I had finished playing a part, I could not quote a word from it; but he managed with a batsman's skill to glance that to leg and turn it back into another sort of compliment, by courteously nodding in approval of my special gift and saying: 'Ah, that must be a great mercy to you.'

He was obviously most taken with Vivien, and when we went to Sunday lunch at [Chartwell], he gave her one of his paintings; we were assured that this was the only picture of his that he had been known to give away. After lunch poor Christopher Soames was condemned to take us over [to] the model farm with its proud breed of belted Galloways.

There was a highly valuable bull which was issuing the most distressing sound I have ever heard, a groan of agonised pain and grief; his head was pressed tight against the wall and his wild eyes rolling. Soames told us he was dangerously mad and had killed a man; and to clean his stall out, a cow in season had to be thrust into the next pen, the iron door between them opened, and only when he was about his amorous duties did it clang shut . . .

We returned to the house and found our host, having walked to the top of his garden to feed his fish, on his way upstairs for his afternoon nap . . . I spluttered, 'I say, sir, we're frightfully worried about your bull!' He waved this aside, saying, 'Oh, he's all right.' He took a step up; then, as if in forgiveness of my idiocy, he made me a present of a marvellous Churchillism, minted on the spur of that moment especially for me. He turned and, placing his hand in a beautiful gesture upon the newel-post of the balusters, he produced, 'And even if . . . he does lead a life of unparalleled dreariness, it is punctuated . . . by moments of intense excitement.'

Olivier's rather over-sugared enchantment with Churchill was brightened further by invitation to 'supper' at his London home in Hyde Park Gate, Kensington.

It was a very full menu for a supper, more like a dinner, necessitating the full complement of accompanying red and white wines, champagne and port. During the port, at a look from Clemmie the three ladies left the three men. As we three turned to seat ourselves again, I fancied I caught a glimpse of ancient Harrow days as he declared in a youthful enthusiasm his appreciation of Vivien: 'By Jove,' he said, 'by Jove, she's a clinker.' [This slang term, denoting attractiveness, apparently originates in Ireland.]

He pushed the whisky decanter towards me, and with a slight flutter of dismay at mixing drinks so much, I obediently helped myself: what the hell, I thought, we're *not* only young once. I pushed it on to Soames and reached for the water. Soames passed the decanter to Winston who helped himself, and as he reached for the soda syphon . . . impelled to that ghastly self-conscious banter, I said: 'Excuse me, sir, but have you ever tried plain water with it? I believe it to be the soda that crawls up the back of our necks the next morning.' 'Oh well,' he said with his usual polite interest, 'if you say so,' and poured the water meekly.

Time came for another round and he automatically reached for the soda and of course I had to remonstrate with him in that accursed would-be waggish tone: 'Oh sir, I think you're letting me down.' 'Oh, I'm sure you're quite right; but I think I prefer my little *prangle*!' [It is reasonable to assume that this was a slang neologism of Churchill's own devising, suggesting fizziness.]

By way of intense contrast, the young actor Richard Burton seemed allergic to this form of tweeness. Yet his own recollections of – and attitude towards – Churchill seemed to oscillate wildly across the years. Their first encounter – a night of Shakespeare – bore the most incredible resemblance to the story that Olivier had told. Or was it possible that it had happened to Burton first, and that Olivier had subsequently misremembered? It surely could not have happened to them both.

Burton claimed that when he was in his epic run as Hamlet at the Old Vic in 1953, he was told by the manager one night that 'the old man' was in. 'The Old Man in England could only mean one person,' remembered Burton. And indeed there Churchill was, sitting close to the front. Burton, like Olivier before him, was aware of a curious 'rumbling' noise as he delivered his lines; and he quickly ascertained that Churchill was speaking the part of Hamlet along with him.

In his version of the story, Burton tried to take evasive action. 'I went faster, I went slower, I went edgeways,' he recalled. 'But the Old Man always caught up.' It was accepted practice by then to shorten the prodigious running time of *Hamlet* by cutting chunks out. Burton became aware of when Churchill noticed, because there was a 'thunderous' noise from his seat declaiming the missing lines. The cuts had apparently infuriated him.

Then, at the end of one of the acts, Burton, looking through a spyhole, saw Churchill making as if to leave. 'That's it, we've lost the Old Man,' he thought. He repaired to his dressing room. And suddenly the door creaked open. Churchill was there and gave him the bow of 'an Elizabethan courtier', greeting him with the words 'my good lord Hamlet'. Then he asked to use the bathroom.

What is even more remarkable than the doubled incident is the idea that Churchill could carry entire Shakespeare tragedies in his head without consulting a text. Perhaps that is the unlikeliest element of all.

Later, when Burton was hired to narrate *The Valiant Years* – an American TV documentary series based on Churchill's memoirs, for which Burton was in part required to perform Churchill's voice – he learned from the network that Churchill himself had asked for the job to go to Burton. 'Get the boy from the Old Vic,' the Old Man was said to have commanded.

Some nine years after Churchill's death, Burton portrayed him in a lavish TV movie entitled *The Gathering Storm*, based upon Churchill's memoirs of the 1930s. In an article for the *New York Times*, all Burton's former good-humoured reticence about the former prime minister had for some reason curdled into the most intense loathing. 'Churchill and his kind . . . have stalked down the corridors of endless power all through history,' he wrote. 'Whether Sir Winston Churchill was a genius I don't know, but certainly he was one of the few people – two others were Picasso and Camus – who have frightened me almost to silence when we came face to face.'

He added elsewhere for good measure in the US magazine *TV Guide* that meeting Churchill 'was like a blow under the heart . . . my class and his hate each other to the seething point.' Thankfully this seething had not made him forbid Churchill from using his lavatory.

Keep It in the Family

Clarissa Spencer-Churchill, 1952

The romance came as a surprise to the world, and apparently to Churchill too. In 1952, the man that he had repeatedly promised his job to very suddenly announced that he was to marry Churchill's niece.

Anthony Eden had already been married – and divorced. His new wife-to-be Clarissa Spencer-Churchill, some years his junior, had forged an extraordinarily diverse career for herself (especially in an era when women were being urged out of the workplaces they had occupied during the war, and encouraged instead to be homemakers and housewives). The daughter of Churchill's brother Jack, Clarissa read philosophy at Oxford, where she caught the rapt attention of Isaiah Berlin and A. J. Ayer. In the 1930s, she was a frequent guest at Chartwell, where, as she later remembered, Churchill took on the air of a prophet, warning 'that we would all be gassed'. Throughout the war, she decoded telegrams in a basement near the Foreign Office. With some style, she lived in a room on one of the upper floors of the Dorchester (such rooms being rather less in demand throughout the Blitz).

Then, after the war, she worked in publishing alongside George Weidenfeld, and then in film with Churchill's old friend Alexander Korda. Part of a social set that included Lord Berners and Evelyn Waugh, she was the very picture of confident intelligent sophistication, as well as possessing a beauty that made her gold dust for the society pages.

Then a chance meeting with Anthony Eden – and what used to be termed a whirlwind romance – propelled her into a rather different cosmos; one that entailed her sacrificing some of the freewheeling intellectual independence that she had become accustomed to. The wife of a senior politician at that time was there as support and ornamentation: a supercharged version of that idealized 1950s housewife.

Churchill, having won the 1951 election, could feel Eden's breath on his neck; that understandable impatience for the prize so long promised. Yet here was a development that made the Tory succession seem almost dynastic in nature: the heir married to a Churchill; the family line continuing in Downing Street. The wedding, certainly, had a curious feel – in part because it had to be at a registry office because of Eden's divorce, but also because of the way that Downing Street, and the Churchill family, featured so largely in the proceedings.

As one report had it:

Downing Street, so often the venue of grave-faced statesmen in hours of national crisis, yesterday buzzed with happier activity, the preparations for the wedding today of Mr Anthony Eden and Miss Clarissa Spencer-Churchill, the niece of the Prime Minister.

Last night, the long vigil of the gay crowds of well-wishers who had waited all day in the brilliant sunshine, was over, for the bride-to-be drove up Downing Street in a green Morris Minor and parked at the end.

To clapping and cheering, she slowly walked back to the Prime Minister's house, posed at the door for photographers and waved to the happy crowds who heartily agreed that she looked 'nice, pretty and sweet'.

Those crowds – if the journalist's account can be taken as wholly reliable – seemed a rather surreal selection of young people. There were 'French girls in pretty frocks, boys in Tyrolean leather shorts, kilted Scottish scouts and young Americans in jeans'. Each one of these discrete groups raises questions to which there are no answers.

However, from them, 'there were cheers and claps for Mrs Winston Churchill when she drove up to number 10 in a black car, from which were taken baskets of flowers and fruits . . . The cake was ordered by Mrs Winston Churchill . . . The Prime Minister will be one of the principal witnesses at the event at Caxton Hall registry office in the same room where he acted in a similar capacity at the marriage of his son Randolph . . . After the ceremony, about 20 people will be received by the Prime Minister who will be accompanied by Mrs Churchill at a small family luncheon party at no 10 Downing Street.'

The curious point was that, quite by accident, the Churchill clan had once more somehow made it all about themselves, rather than the prime-minister-to-be and his happy bride. And dynastic competitiveness of a subterranean nature was also to infuse Churchill's complex relationship with the royal family.

The Queen and I

Elizabeth II, 1953

The early death of King George VI in February 1952 came as a shock to Churchill; and it became another reason why he could not imagine relinquishing the role of prime minister. As well as the desire to be there at the forefront of the coming coronation of Elizabeth II – who was then only twenty-five years old – there was also his sense that he had to pass a torch of continuity on to her.

'One saw this dirty commercial river as one came up,' recalled Her Majesty the Queen after sailing the still-industrial Thames with Churchill on her return from her 1954 Commonwealth tour. 'And he [Churchill] was describing it as the silver thread that runs through the history of Britain.' He saw things, she noted, 'in a very romantic and glittering way; perhaps one was looking at it in rather too mundane a way'.

Although Churchill's relationship with Elizabeth II has frequently been depicted across the years as a kind of royal *Pygmalion* – Churchill as Professor Higgins to Elizabeth's Eliza Doolittle, the old man tutoring the young woman in the myriad complexities of the British constitution – it also seems clear from the flashes we can see that she was always fractionally ahead of him, in terms of adapting ancient ways to modern purposes. Theirs appeared to be an association rich with humour but also with realpolitik.

They first met when the Queen was a toddler and Churchill was at Balmoral in September 1928. He wrote about it to Clementine, deliberately anticipating her future title, as if wondering what it would sound like when that time came. 'There is no one here at all except the family, the Household, & Queen Elizabeth – aged 2. The last is a character. She has an air of authority & reflectiveness astonishing in an infant.'

In the intervening years, the 1936 abdication crisis appeared to have smoothed out the more medieval edges of Churchill's belief in the inviolable traditions of the monarchy. He had come to understand, through Edward VIII, that it was not sufficient to defend the Crown; the head that wore the crown had to work to be a suitable figurehead for all those subjects around the world. Monarchy was not simply passed on through anointment and prayers in Westminster Abbey; it was an art, a craft, that had to be learned. Churchill's early encounters with Princess – and then Queen – Elizabeth are sometimes framed as a series of lectures. But as Churchill was watching her, she was watching him too.

There was a charming interlude in the summer of 1951 when Princess Elizabeth made a visit to Churchill's constituency. Together they met at the newly opened Grange Farm Centre in Chigwell. This was an event about youthfulness: the farm had been transformed into a kind of holiday camp for Boy Scouts and Girl Guides, with chalets and dormitories in that distinctive rectilinear 1950s style. The princess herself, in a long coat and cloche hat, curiously looked a little older than she later did upon ascending the throne. Churchill, meanwhile, hands clasped behind his back as he spoke, and in a bow tie and waistcoat, looked suffused with pleasure.

Yet when in 1952 news came through of George's death,

Churchill had a moment of self-doubt. He burst into tears and declared of Elizabeth: 'I hardly know her. And she is only a child.' He quickly pulled himself together, and he was there to greet the grieving daughter as she arrived back from Kenya. At the airport, he bowed deeply to the new Queen.

In those days – as now – it was the custom for the prime minister to have a weekly audience with the monarch at Buckingham Palace. According to Churchill's ever-faithful secretary Jock Colville, the Queen 'got more fun out of her audiences with Churchill than with any of his successors'. (But how can this really be quantified? Other accounts have suggested that in fact her favourite in terms of wit and laughter was Labour prime minister Harold Wilson – with his Labour successor James Callaghan also having been greatly appreciated for his company.) The Queen's private secretary Sir 'Tommy' Lascelles also averred that these audiences were punctuated with 'peals of laughter' and that Churchill emerged 'wiping his eyes'. Yet this is slightly beside the point: Churchill understood himself to be a mentor; the Queen, however, was perfectly adept at bringing herself up to speed. He was the grand old Victorian; she was the New Elizabethan.

Just before her coronation in 1953, she and Churchill and all the prime ministers of the Commonwealth were gathered for a special lunch within the ancient grey walls of Westminster Hall on the parliamentary estate. It was at this lunch that Churchill set forth his strikingly patriarchal views of the new era:

> In this hall of fame and antiquity, a long story has been unfolded of the conflicts of Crown versus Parliament . . . But those days are done. The vehement, passionate, moral

and intellectual forces that clashed in tragic violence three hundred years ago are now united. It is no longer a case of Crown versus Parliament, but of Crown *and* Parliament.

In our island by trial and error and by perseverance across the centuries, we have found out a very good plan. Here it is. 'The Queen can do no wrong.'

Yet even as he said these words, all present, including Her Majesty, would have been piercingly aware of the King who did go wrong a mere seventeen years beforehand. Churchill continued:

Bad advisers can be changed as often as the people like to use their rights for that purpose. A great battle is lost. Parliament turns out the Government. A great battle is won. Crowds cheer the Queen. We have found this a very commanding and durable doctrine. What goes wrong passes away with the politicians responsible. What goes right is laid on the altar of our united Commonwealth and Empire . . .

Of course some envious people say we want to have it all ways at once. That may well be true. We seek the best of all worlds and certainly we have got the pick of this one.

Yet it is worth wondering whether the Churchills – and Spencer-Churchills – as a clan regarded themselves as being even further rooted in the soil of English history than the relative newcomer Saxe-Coburgs? The question arises with Churchill's conclusion, as he told the Queen that 'it is because I have served Your Majesty's great-grandfather, grandfather, father, and now yourself, that I have been accorded the honour of expressing our thanks this afternoon to you, Madam, for your Royal presence here'.

This was a curious way of putting it: Churchill was actually there as a politician, not because he had 'served' generations of kings. Yet this rhetorical sleight of hand made it look as though all the monarchs he had 'served' were ephemeral, and that he was the solid spine of the constitution.

There is little doubt that – young though she was – Queen Elizabeth would have seen and understood all this; though little is known of her private thoughts on many matters, her adeptness at defending the stature and dignity and superiority of monarchy was consistently sharp and agile. Moreover, at the time of her coronation, her youth seemed to chime with a newly invigorated realm: this was an age of jet travel; of the discovery of the DNA double helix; of the conquest of Everest. In contrast, despite his extraordinary powers of physical endurance, Churchill was in his declining years – something that would soon become more glaringly obvious to his colleagues.

A Prescription of Sherry

Russell Brain, 1953–65

Seen through the kaleidoscopic prism of today's health anxieties – smoking, drinking, fatty food, lack of exercise – it now seems almost inconceivable that Churchill should have survived as long as he did. Nothing abated his enthusiastic inhalation of fourteen cigars a day, his consumption of Champagne, port and whisky also continued with gusto. His one concession to health food appeared to be an intense fondness for onion soup.

Throughout the war, Churchill's personal physician Lord Moran had always been in careful, discreet attendance: Churchill was then in his late sixties, and there were episodes of serious pneumonia, which in those days still carried a very high mortality rate. It was also assumed for many years that, during the war, Churchill had suffered a heart attack. This is now understood to be not necessarily the case; the symptoms that confined him to bed could have been side effects of respiratory complications. And his recovery was amazingly swift. But then came that 1949 stroke. By the 1950s, with Churchill in his late seventies, his health was understandably more precarious. One of the factors that perhaps kept him going was the continuing unwellness of his nominated successor, Anthony Eden, who was suffering bile-duct complications.

Then, with 1953, came the glories of the coronation: another of Churchill's reasons to have clung so tenaciously to the keys of Number 10. But days after, colleagues began to notice him slurring . . .

'I had a mysterious message from [Lord] Moran asking me to go and see Churchill with him at 10, Downing Street,' wrote Lord Russell Brain. 'He did not give any reason for this, and at the time, I was involved as Chairman of the Joint Consultants' Committee in negotiations with the Government about doctors' pay, which I had discussed on more than one occasion with Moran, who, of course had direct access to Churchill. I thought at first that he had found an opportunity to discuss this with the Prime Minister but when I got there, I found that Churchill had had a stroke. He had been feeling very tired lately on account of the coronation and of having to do the work of the Foreign Secretary as well as his own on account of Eden's illness.'

Dr Brain was an eminent neurologist; an expert on the

brain and all its vulnerabilities (as well as a living embodiment of nominative determinism). But that summer's day in 1953 was not the first time he had encountered Churchill; some four years previously, Lord Moran had inveigled him to pay a visit to Chartwell in the wake of Churchill having had a smaller, milder stroke. Brain's visit then had been absolutely top secret; no one was to know (partly for fear on Churchill's part that there would be calls for his retirement). On that occasion in 1949 Lord Brain had been bemused by the vigour of his new patient. Initially Churchill was in bed, wearing a silken bed jacket of oriental design, a decanter of whisky on the shelf beside him and a small white bucket on the floor by his bed. Thankfully, this appeared to be for cigar ash.

Possibly to impress this neurologist, Churchill hopped out of bed, legs bare. Brain recalled:

Moran had told him not to have his bath water too hot, and [Churchill] asked me about this. 'I have two baths a day. I enjoy my baths; they mean as much to me as my meals.' He was due to have one and it was supposed to be ready for him, he insisted on our going to feel the water, which, however, he had to admit, was not as hot as usual.

By this time, he was wandering around in his ridiculous little bed jacket and night shirt, bare from the middle thighs downwards. 'You must see me walk,' he said, and did a kind of goose-step, and then stood still with his eyes closed to show how steady he was. He insisted on our having a drink, though Moran was anxious to get away as the Duke and Duchess of Westminster were coming to dinner, and it was essential for political reasons that no one should know that I had seen Churchill.

However, he got his way. 'I diagnose that you would like some sherry!' We drank a hasty glass and left him splashing in his bath. The Duke and Duchess of Westminster arrived, and Moran and I had to hide in the Secretary's room.

In the intervening four years, Churchill had once more taken on the weight of office – and at a point when the new tensions of the Cold War were being felt across the world. There were British troops fighting in the Korean War; the city of Berlin, within the realm of Soviet-controlled East Germany, had not long since been blockaded by Stalin; and the Soviets had also detonated their own atomic bomb, by means of a test, in the vast roseate deserts of Kazakhstan. Churchill had always cultivated the knack of wearing responsibility lightly; but the world he had understood was fast becoming unknowable. He was at this point seventy-eight years old.

Of that June 1953 visit to Downing Street, Brain recalled:

The previous morning Moran had been to see him to pay a routine visit, and thought his speech was somewhat slurred. In the evening, [Churchill] had presided over a dinner for the Italian Premier, at the end of which he had made a speech, and again his speech was somewhat slurred, and he became unsteady on his legs, and had to be assisted out of the room.

He had a good night and on the morning of June 24th, Moran saw him again, and found his speech still slurred. [Churchill] presided over a Cabinet Meeting, however, which lasted two hours. He felt very tired, and his slurring speech was noticed by his colleagues. He slept in the afternoon and his secretary mentioned that she thought there was some drooping of the left side of his face. This was apparent when he spoke and also when he smiled, and his speech was at first somewhat slurred, but there was at no time any evidence of aphasia. There was slight weakness of the left lower face on voluntary and emotional movement, and his tongue deviated slightly to the left. There was no weakness of the limbs, and no change in sensation, but the left plantar reflex was extensor while the right was flexor.

He walked about the room with only a slight trace of unsteadiness. He said he had no headache but felt as though there was something in his head. He was put on a dose of trinitrin night and morning.

And yet even now – essentially incapacitated – Churchill could not quite bring himself to desist, treating his neurologist to a monologue on current geopolitics.

After my examination was finished, Churchill gave me an address on foreign policy. Since he had taken Eden's place as Foreign Secretary, he said, our influence in the world had increased. He didn't always agree with Eden but nine times out of ten, he did, but he had been firmer with Naguib [then Egyptian president] and Naguib saw we meant business. It should be possible to settle Egypt soon, but we couldn't afford to keep 80,000 men there. Egypt wasn't worth it: its strategic importance was much less. Then Korea – a terrible business. All was going well. 'I had stretched out a paw – privately – to the Russians and suggested that the time had come to lay off at Panmunjom [the Korean village where the Americans and Chinese were negotiating], and the Americans were being brought along, and then that bastard, Syngman Rhee [president of South Korea], deliberately and maliciously wrecked it all.'

In short: that iron determination to hold on to ultimate control was indomitable; but it was obviously impossible for Churchill to carry on as though nothing had happened. A stroke of that severe a nature – and for a man of that age – might reasonably have been expected to carry him to the grave.

What happened next still seems extraordinary: the voluntary agreement of a complete press blackout on the news of the prime minister's health. The arrangement is simply impossible to imagine now; the mirror of the most byzantine Kremlin manoeuvres.

Churchill was conveyed to Chartwell; it was there that his progress would be monitored. In the meantime, with Eden still ill as well, the everyday business of government would secretly be conducted by R. A. (Rab) Butler, plus Jock Colville and – rather arrestingly – Churchill's son-in-law Christopher Soames, who had recently been elected an MP. Churchill's dynastic instincts were every bit the equal of any royal household's.

The crisis continued, although Dr Brain found the endurance of his patient rather fascinating. On 26 June, three days after the stroke had hit, he travelled down to Kent to rendezvous with Lord Moran at Chartwell.

He had obviously deteriorated. His speech was more dysarthric and his left hand was becoming weaker and his gait more unsteady. At times he would choke and cough when swallowing. There was considerable clumsiness of the left hand, but his left grip was still fair and movements of the arm at the elbow and shoulder good. The main weakness was in the small muscles of the hand. Power was little diminished in the left lower limb, but he tended to stagger to the left when he walked. There was no impairment of appreciation of pin prick or postural sensibility. The tendon reflexes were brisker on the left side than on the right, and as before, the left plantar was extensor while the right was flexor.

Yet though the flesh was weak, the mind was still intensely alert.

[Churchill] has noticed loss of emotional control. He said that he was 'always rather blubbery' but now he was much worse. He wept if moved, for example, by poetry. He read me from *The Times* a passage saying that more attention had been paid to him in the Russian press than to Stalin, and this made him weep.

I have a vivid memory of him getting out of bed in his little night shirt, and striding up and down the room with his hemiplegic left arm and leg to show me what he could do, and he took me along to his tank of fish.

Then there was a fresh outbreak of international analysis — and a fascinating glimpse of a future which recalled his old optimism about technology:

In conversation [Churchill] said that if the tension between Russia and the Western Powers could be relaxed, by giving Russia guarantees against aggression, the production of the world could be doubled within a few years, and people could have what they needed more than anything else — leisure (he said this very emphatically). They could work hard for four days and have the other three to enjoy themselves.

The latter forward-thinking sentiment is startling; Churchill is the very last person in the recorded annals of humanity that anyone might associate with 'work/life balance' free-thinking and as a proponent of the four-day week.

As his recovery – and astonishingly fast recovery at that – began, meaning that he was up in Balmoral with the Queen by September and back at the cabinet table directly after that, Churchill still felt himself to be actively in the centre of the present. But the Britain he had once known was changing fast; was it really possible for the elderly imperialist not merely to adjust to but to embrace this new realm and a new generation?

The Old Man and the Monster

Prince Charles, Age Five, and Christopher Long, Age Five, 1953

There are many rather wonderful photographs of elderly (and convalescent) Winston Churchill with tiny children either staring up at him or indeed (in the case of his brilliant granddaughter Emma Soames) clutching on to him. Here are two brief instances of his encounters with infant minds – at moments when he was still recovering from that 1953 stroke – and how these encounters lodged in their memories.

*

There is a brief spool of colour film from the early 1950s; the celluloid tones of those days giving blues and reds an unusual intensity. It is of the royal family – the newly crowned Queen Elizabeth, her husband Prince Philip, the Queen Mother, and Winston and Clementine Churchill. They are on the Balmoral estate in the north-east of Scotland. The weather looks murderously cold, and dreich, as the Scots say; Churchill is swathed in a large grey overcoat and wearing a grey homburg. He is sitting by the shore of a loch – Clementine a little behind him, on a tussock – and the mighty surrounding mountains fill the sky. He is waving a piece of driftwood. And there is a fleeting shot of him being approached by a small boy wearing a blue sou'wester.

Churchill is smiling; but this is a silent film, so we hear no words. The boy was Prince – now King – Charles, and he recalled decades later what the seventy-eight-year-old prime minister was telling him. He was, he told the boy, 'waiting on the Loch Ness Monster'. But the striking thing is how much a part of the landscape of Queen Elizabeth's life Churchill was – the old man by the loch who had also been there when she was little. He seemed as fixed a part of that landscape as the surrounding mountains.

Back at Chartwell, Churchill's life was now festooned with grandchildren and their friends, and he seemed perfectly at ease with them all; the polar opposite of his own chilly father.

Christopher Long, who lived nearby, had this to say about his own childhood encounter with Churchill:

On a gloriously sunny afternoon in the early 1950s, not long after the coronation of Queen Elizabeth II, about a dozen of us were celebrating the fifth birthday of our friend Nicholas Soames at Chartwell Farm, where he and his sister Emma lived with their parents, Mary and Christopher Soames. The inevitable conjuror had been and gone. Now, on the lawn outside the French windows, the nannies were organising the obligatory sack races and egg-and-spoon races that preceded a ritual tea of birthday cake and jelly.

For some reason I refused to join the others in these games and instead spent the entire afternoon in the drawing room, clambering all over an accommodating old man in an armchair who seemed designed for the purpose. Though very ancient, he had several unusual attractions to recommend him, which included an interesting gold watch on a chain strung across his stomach and a cigar which needed to be cut with a cigar-cutter. Indeed, at my insistence, it needed to be re-cut quite frequently.

Less to his credit and rather disappointingly, this was a man who had never heard of *Thomas the Tank Engine*, which the Rev'd Awdry had specially written for 'Christopher' (which I assumed was me, since I didn't know he had a grandson Christopher). However, when I asked him to tell me a story about trains – the only subject of intense interest to me at the time – my ancient friend invented quite a good story about escaping from somewhere to somewhere else on a train in extremely dangerous circumstances.

After tea, the inevitable rowdy anarchy broke out as children and their exhausted nannies waited for mothers to collect them. By this time I had returned to my friend in the armchair, who was now nursing a glass of whisky. I remember my mother appearing with Mary Soames through the doorway on a raised dais at the end of the drawing room. She smiled brightly and, in that irritating way mothers have, told my elderly friend that she very much hoped I had not been a nuisance.

'Oh no, not at all,' Sir Winston Churchill assured her. 'Been here all afternoon. Funny little chap.'

The Open – and Closed – Heart

Churchill And Immigration, 1954

There is nothing controversial about applying the relatively modern term 'racist' to Churchill, even though it was not a term that was much in use in the 1950s. But it still raises questions. Was it really the case that he disliked and discriminated against people solely on the colour of their skin? His views on India and its people were apparently clear; yet did they also apply, for instance, to peoples across the nations of Africa too? In 1906, Churchill declared of southern Africa: 'We will endeavour . . . to advance the equal rights of civilised men irrespective of colour.' Balanced against this, however – as we shall see – were later, more general expressions of ugly prejudice.

In February 1954, immigration to Britain from Commonwealth countries was becoming more of an incendiary political issue. Cabinet papers released under the fifty-year rule reveal Churchill and his colleagues mulling the question of whether limits on numbers of migrants should be set. What makes the discussion unsettling is not so much the racist language, which we would expect, but more a sense of cynicism about the way that politicians, up to and including Church-ill, seemed to approach the issue.

According to those papers for 3 February 1954 – the notes of which are abbreviated – Churchill (as quoted by the Cabinet Secretary Sir Norman Brook) said: 'Problems wh[ich] will arise if many coloured people settle here. Are we to saddle ourselves with colour problems in UK? Attracted by Welfare State. Public opinion in UK won't tolerate it once it gets beyond certain limits.'

This led to an intervention from Florence Horsbrugh, the then Minister of Education and Conservative MP for Manchester Moss Side, who said: 'Already becoming serious in Manch[este]r.'

The Home Secretary David Maxwell-Fyfe quoted a figure of 40,000 immigrants compared to 7,000 before the Second World War, and it was he who raised the possibility of immigration control. He told the Cabinet: 'There is a case on merits for exclud[in]g riff-raff. But politically it w[oul]d be represented & discussed on basis of colour limitation. That w[oul]d offend the floating vote viz., the old Liberals. We sh[oul]d be reversing age-long trad[ition] th[a]t B[ritish] S[ubjects] have right of entry to mother-country of Empire. We sh[oul]d offend Liberals, also sentimentalists.'

He added: 'The col[onial] pop[ulations] are resented in L[iverpool], Paddington & other areas by those who come into contact with them. But those who don't are apt to take a more Liberal view.'

Churchill's further intervention is now haunting in its ambiguity. 'Question is,' he said, 'whether it is politically wise to allow public feeling to develop a little more before taking action.' But what precisely did he mean by this? Was it remotely possible he was anticipating that 'public feeling' would grow more relaxed over time? Or was there much likelier a darker meaning? By 'public feeling', did he mean outbreaks of racist rage that would develop into violence? The Notting Hill race riots were just a few years away; was he advocating for 'public feeling' to 'develop' more in this direction?

His additional comments don't offer reassurance – he said that it would be 'fatal' to let the situation develop too far. Again, we have to wonder: 'fatal' for whom? For the immigrants and their families suffering discrimination and abuse? Or 'fatal' for the politicians who risked angering white voters by consenting to immigration in the first place? He then concluded by saying that he 'w[oul]d l[i]ke to study possibility of quote no. not to be exceeded'.

In certain lights (which possibly may be a little too obscure for some), one small point might just favour Churchill: the fact that he did not seem to attach any real urgency to this 'study'. Not long afterwards, he was asked a question in Parliament by a Midlands Labour backbencher who wanted to know if there should be a special commission looking into immigration and its general impact on the workforce. Churchill on that occasion seemed very relaxed; he himself saw no need for any such commission. Nor in the end did he introduce any immigration quota numbers.

Yet there are a couple of further points: it was alleged by Harold Macmillan (in his diary) that, a little later, Churchill was 'thinking' of a shocking election slogan: 'Keep Britain White!' The abhorrence of such an idea is – and was then, as well – intense. The articulation of the phrase alone is heard as a call to violence – and that was as true in the 1950s as it is now. The fact that this slogan was, in the end never used by the party – or indeed mentioned again by any of Churchill's other colleagues – is not important. As well as the chilling sentiment, it once more suggests a certain malign electoral calculation.

But it is also slightly puzzling: for, just twelve years previously, at the height of the war, when it was reported to Churchill and the war cabinet that Black American troops stationed in England were being excluded from venues such as pubs and cinemas by their white American officers, the resolution of that cabinet meeting was that no Black Americans should have to suffer the 'segregation' or 'restrictions' that were in place back in the US.

So which Churchill was he?

Another knot of perplexity: the younger Churchill's response in 1904 (when he was a Liberal MP) to the then government's introduction of the 'Aliens bill' – the first measures to restrict immigration to Britain. Churchill was opposed to the bill; he thought then that it was wrong to restrict immigration. In a leaflet, he wrote: 'It does not appear . . . that there can be urgent or sufficient reasons, racial or social, for departing from the old tolerant and generous practice of free entry and asylum to which this country has so long adhered, and from which it has so often greatly gained.'

People change as they get older; compassion can calcify, and gradually turn into indifference or hostility. And nothing that Churchill said or thought as a younger man can excuse any outbreaks of malevolent racism in later decades. But when considering those 1954 deliberations on immigration quotas, an even more unattractive prospect is that of icy calculating cynicism.

In a curious way, it is better that Churchill be accused of naked Victorian imperialist racism than that.

'I Felt A Tap on My Shoulder'

Bessie Braddock, 1954

One of the less attractive Winston Churchill stories – an anecdote that was funny decades ago, and repeated on endless radio and TV panel shows – involved his encounter with a ferocious left-wing Liverpool MP called Bessie Braddock. She upbraided him after a Commons performance. 'Winston – you're drunk!' she exclaimed. 'Madam, you are disgustingly ugly – but I shall be sober in the morning,' he was said to have replied. He now sounds curdlingly misogynistic, as well as simply being thunderingly rude. It also gives the impression that this was all that their association amounted to. But curiously, this is very far from being the case; and indeed – despite the fervent clash of principles – Mrs Braddock and Churchill occasionally found moments of nectared harmony.

As Bessie Braddock wrote in her memoirs:

> I'm afraid politics is as full of people who say one thing and mean something else as any other activity. I know we can't do without a bit of humbug now and then, for life would be insufferable without it. Imagine your husband always having to tell you he couldn't stand the sight of your new hat!
>
> The House of Commons tried to do that for Sir Winston Churchill on his eightieth birthday, and I wouldn't join in. The idea was to give Sir Winston a Birthday Book in which each Member of the House had signed in a special place beside the name of his constituency. That was

fine. But in the front of the book there was a quotation from *Pilgrim's Progress*, slightly amended. It read:

'You have been so faithful and so loving to us, you have fought so stoutly for us, you have been so hearty in your counselling of us, that we shall never forget your favour towards us.'

I could not allow myself to be associated with such a reference to Sir Winston Churchill. There was a hell of a row about it, but I wouldn't sign his book. I simply didn't believe the words were true of him. No doubt those who signed were perfectly sincere but for me to sign would have made me a hypocrite.

I know Sir Winston is a great man. He has been called 'the greatest living Englishman' and I won't quarrel about this. But when the great capitalist offensive against the workers began in 1925, Winston Churchill was the Chancellor of the Exchequer who announced the return to the gold standard which forced down wages and living standards.

Mrs Braddock had made the headlines showing her contempt for Churchill a few years previously; one day, in his absence from the Commons chamber, she theatrically rose from the government benches, crossed the floor and sat in the position on the opposition bench that he usually occupied. As an offence, it seems mild; yet at the time it was considered unparliamentary and uncouth. She was wholly unabashed, however.

As to the story of his drunkenness, her rebuke, and his unkind reply: if it happened, she most certainly was not going to mention it in her memoirs. Instead, she wrote of a couple of instances where she and Churchill made an unlikely connection across the vast canyon of ideology.

Only twice have I spoken to Churchill. The first time was after the House of Commons had discussed setting up the Royal Commission on Mental Health. I had said I hoped it would be possible to have young people on it, because I thought that the typical approach of old people to these problems was not what was needed . . . Soon after this, I was standing at the bar of the House when I felt a tap on my shoulder. It was Churchill. He said: 'I'm announcing the composition of the Royal Commission on Mental Health today, and I shall be saying that you are one of the Members serving on it.'

This was revealed with some condescension so I retorted: 'Oh! Will you? Well, you ought to be very honoured indeed that I'm prepared to allow you to mention my name as one of *your* Royal Commission!'

Churchill roared with laughter. When he spoke my name that afternoon, he looked across at me and grinned . . .

The only other time I spoke to Churchill was when I brought Hogan 'Kid' Bassey, then world featherweight champion, into the House and he asked me to introduce him to Sir Winston, who behaved with his customary charm, seeming as delighted to meet the little Nigerian [sic!] as Bassey was thrilled to meet him.

There are few, if any, other accounts of Churchill meeting Black celebrities; on this occasion, he appeared, at least in the eyes of Mrs Braddock, to have made a good account of himself.

Peaches and Cream

Churchill's Resignation, 4 April 1955

'You must always know the impact you want to make at the
beginning and the impression that you want to leave at the
end,' Churchill told his Woodford Conservative colleagues
over a private dinner at the King's Head in Chigwell back
in 1947. 'The end,' he added, 'can be more important than
the beginning.'

And now, eight years later, the end had come. 'It all
seems settled,' wrote Harold Macmillan. 'Winston will
resign on 4 April.'

Macmillan wrote that in March 1955, apparently after
having observed a lunch between Churchill and Eden.
There had been other signs. Jock Colville had observed
that 'he was ageing month by month and was reluctant to
read any papers except the newspapers or to give his mind
to anything he did not find diverting'.

But it is easy for those of us who have never been
prime minister to dismiss just how physically and intellectually demanding the role is: from the first light of
dawn to the early hours, the constant need for razor-edge
thought and sharp alertness. Churchill was now eighty.
Colville acknowledged that on 'some days', the 'old gleam
would be there'. It was that gleam, that spark, that
Churchill himself sought to fan right to the end. He could
not bear the idea of leaving, and so that resignation date
was anything but settled in Churchill's mind. He suggested to his colleagues that, ultimately, it was a matter

for the Queen; and she might very well ask him to move the date. Perhaps he imagined that she would command him to stay.

No such requirement was issued from Buckingham Palace. 'Though she recognised your wisdom in taking the decision that you had,' her private secretary wrote smoothly of his notice of resignation, 'she felt the greatest personal regrets and that she would especially miss the weekly audiences which she has found so instructive and, if one can say so of State matters, so entertaining.'

And so, on the night of 4 April 1955, the London crowds gathered at the end of Downing Street (there were no gates back then; the public were free to walk up and down it in daylight hours). Some may have caught a glimpse of one of Churchill's more striking costumes: created a Knight of the Garter in 1953 (thus becoming Sir Winston), he was all set to receive the Queen and the Duke of Edinburgh at Number 10 for a farewell dinner. The costume consisted of white tie, a bright sash, and quite startling black stockings, emphasizing the little legs supporting a bulbous frame.

And the guest list was a form of homage: naturally his successor Anthony Eden and wife Clarissa were there; they were joined by former prime minister Clement Attlee, Field Marshals Montgomery and Alexander, the Duke of Norfolk, plus Churchill's ever-devoted friends Brendan Bracken and Lord Cherwell. On the menu that night: turtle soup; salmon; lamb; peaches and cream – as vivid an evocation of 1950s tastes as anything. Churchill's oratory reached a pitch of purest purple as he toasted Her Majesty: 'We thank God for the gifts He has bestowed upon us, and vow ourselves anew to the sacred causes and kindly way of life of which your Majesty is the young, gleaming champion.' He made her sound a little like a racehorse. This is not something that she would have minded in the least.

On the Pathé News reel shown in the cinema, the noises of appreciative crowds were dubbed over the silent film. The people amassed on Whitehall and outside Buckingham Palace looked more engaged and pensive than the noises would have suggested. The newsreel narrator referred to Churchill simply as 'the Great Englishman'. His resignation was more than a simple political event. It was the moment at which an age – an epoch – gave way to a new sensibility. Just weeks beforehand, the song 'Rock Around the Clock', performed by Bill Haley and His Comets, had hit the charts. The film in which it featured – a gritty US drama about teenage delinquents called *Blackboard Jungle* – was causing anguish in the office of the British film censorship board because of its unusually raw depictions of violence. The music had a thrumming aggression that went far beyond the slick sexy speed of swing. The young were finding a new voice. This was no longer Churchill's world.

Yet his parliamentary career was not over; he told his Woodford constituents he would continue to serve. And when his successor as prime minister, Anthony Eden, called a general election for later that spring, Churchill was back on the hustings in those east London suburbs, and seemingly grateful for being so. 'If I did not feel myself capable of representing your views in the House,' he told a meeting in Walthamstow, 'I would not intrude myself upon you.'

What a Grand Climax!

Harry S. Truman, June 1956

Truman, who had left the White House in January 1953, came to England for a ten-day visit with his wife, Bess, in 1956. One of his pressing engagements was to receive an honorary degree in civil law from Oxford. The Pathé News reel depicted him in his gowned pomp. Later there was dinner at Buckingham Palace with the Queen and Prince Philip. In Downing Street, Prime Minister Anthony Eden was but several short months away from the Suez Crisis: a conflict with Egypt's ruler Gamal Abdel Nasser over control of the Suez Canal. Britain was to send in troops – and thence to face humiliation that would demonstrate the icy nature of the 'special relationship' with President Eisenhower's US (Britain was told to desist). This would tip Eden from office in 1957. But before all that, in the sunshine before the storm, Truman concluded his British tour by paying a visit to a lushly appointed valley in Kent.

'Sir Winston and Lady Churchill met us at the door,' recalled Harry Truman of his valedictory visit to Chartwell. 'We stopped for pictures. Many of the neighbor people were at the gate. They gave a wave and a cheer as Mrs Truman & I entered.'

Though the event was discreet, there were nonetheless a few press photographers around who wished to record the meeting. And there is a sun-drenched picture of Churchill and Truman, together with wives (and indeed the by-then ubiquitous son-in-law Christopher Soames), at the front porch of Chartwell, all lined up in a linked-arm row. Churchill looks hale and hearty; the visit was a little more than mere diplomacy. There did appear to be something of a proper bond there.

It was reported that Churchill gave Truman the obligatory tour of the grounds, but as they walked, they also discussed the tumultuous events of the recent past, including their very first encounter at the Potsdam conference. Stalin was long dead; the world was now trying to fathom his emerging successor Nikita Khrushchev. As tradition demanded, Churchill stopped at the ponds to give the fish their food with an exclamation of 'Hike! Hike!' He also told Truman he should run for the presidency again, although Truman demurred.

Mr and Mrs Truman were not staying the weekend, or indeed the night. They were simply there for lunch. The president obligingly signed the Chartwell visitor book (which is still very much a visitor attraction at the house today). He wrote: 'What a grand climax to a great visit!' After his return to the US, Truman then wrote privately to Churchill: 'I do not know when I have enjoyed a visit more than ours at Chartwell.' He would also later write that 'as time goes on, my admiration for your great contribution to the winning of the war and the establishment to organization for the peace continues to grow'.

That visit to Chartwell was the last time that the two men would meet. Given the bumpy start to their association – Churchill being ejected from office by the electorate before they had formed a solid idea of one another – the warmth was gratifying. In the years to come, relations between US presidents and UK prime ministers would cool sometimes to the point of contempt (notably President Nixon and Prime Minister Edward Heath). But Churchill, with his part-American ancestry, always leaned strongly out across the Atlantic.

A Reunion with the Little Tramp

Charlie Chaplin, 1956

In the anti-communist hysteria that seized the US in the 1950s, Charlie Chaplin was among many Hollywood figures who fell victim to the witch hunts. In 1952, his comedy-drama Limelight, *in which he plays a faded comedian coming to the rescue of a young dancer (played by Claire Bloom), opened in London, and Chaplin travelled to England for the premiere. It was at this point that the US authorities rescinded his visa, citing his communist sympathies. The FBI, under Edgar Hoover, had denounced him as one of 'Hollywood's parlour Bolsheviks'. Though the British-born Chaplin denied being a communist, he was certainly an eager socialist. For this, in essence, he was exiled from his adopted land. He and his fourth wife, Oona, then moved to Switzerland. But there were return trips to London, including this occasion in 1956 when Churchill — out of office — was dining with Clementine at the Savoy. As with their previous encounters, it was as though Churchill and Chaplin consistently misunderstood one another. Was Churchill consistently wrong-footed by Chaplin's unwavering left-wingness?*

'Oona and I dined alone in the Grill at the Savoy,' wrote Chaplin in his autobiography.

In the middle of our dessert Sir Winston Churchill and Lady Churchill came in and stood before our table. I had not seen Sir Winston or heard from him since 1931. But after the opening of *Limelight* in London, I had received a message from United Artists, our distributors, asking permission to show Sir Winston the film at his house. Of course I had been only too pleased. A few days later he sent me a charming letter of thanks, telling me how much he had enjoyed it.

And now Sir Winston stood before our table, confronting us. 'Well!' he said.

There seemed to be a disapproving note in the 'Well!'

I quickly stood up, all smiling, and introduced Oona, who at that moment was about to retire.

After Oona had left I asked if I could join them for coffee, and went across to their table. Lady Churchill said she had read in the papers about my meeting with Khrushchev.' [Chaplin had been at a London diplomatic reception for the new Soviet premier.]

'I always got along well with Khrushchev,' said Sir Winston.

But all the time I could see that Sir Winston was nursing a grievance. Of course, much had happened since 1931. He had saved England with his indomitable courage and inspiring rhetoric; but I thought his 'iron curtain' Fulton speech had achieved nothing but an intensification of the cold war.

The conversation turned to my film *Limelight*. Eventually he said: 'I sent you a letter two years ago complimenting you on your film. Did you get it?'

'Oh yes,' I said enthusiastically.

'Then why didn't you answer it?'

'I didn't think it called for an answer,' I said apologetically.

But he was not to be cozened. 'Hmm,' he said disgruntledly. 'I thought it was some form of rebuke.'

'Oh no, of course not,' I answered.

'However,' he added, by way of dismissing me, 'I always enjoy your pictures.'

I was charmed by the great man's modesty in remembering that unanswered letter of two years ago.

But perhaps it was less about modesty and more about the sense that Churchill considered Chaplin to be colossally rude.

Carry on Cruising

Aristotle Onassis, 1958–63

By virtue of his colossal wealth, Aristotle Onassis, a Greek shipping magnate, was once one of the most famous men in the world. But wealth by itself is not always sufficient as a lasting memorial, and his name is now becoming obscure. By contrast, those with whom he sought to surround himself continue to burn bright. From Hollywood stars such as Cary Grant, Greta Garbo and Frank Sinatra, to statesmen such as John F. Kennedy (whose widow, Jacqueline, Aristotle would marry in 1968), Onassis offered untrammelled luxury on board a super-yacht called the Christina *(named after his daughter). And among the most glittering of the guests walking up its gangway were Winston and Clementine, plus occasionally daughter Diana and granddaughter Celia Sandys. In Churchill's latter years, he embarked upon eight sunshine-filled cruises on board this extraordinary craft, and had a raft of extra-ordinary encounters along the way.*

'We love you, we do, Sir Winston, we *looove* you,' sang the popular northern artiste Gracie Fields, apparently to the tune of the Dean Martin hit 'Volare'. 'God's teeth,' whispered Churchill as she continued her performance. 'How long is this going on for?'

They were in one of the extensively book-lined lounges on board *Christina*. Ms Fields, the Rochdale-born actress and singer who had been Britain's biggest star on film and stage in the 1930s, lived on the Mediterranean island of Capri, which is where the yacht had come to pick her up. Ms Fields (later Dame Gracie) had met Churchill before, in 1940, just days after he became prime minister, seeking his advice on how to avoid her Italian husband being interned as a potential enemy alien. She had then gone on to entertain troops with cheering songs. Now, as well as this extemporized on-board karaoke, she was to lighten Churchill's mood with a variety of his old Edwardian music-hall favourites, and the image now seems startling: a millionaire's yacht, under a wide, starry, velvet expanse of night, gliding through a calm, ink-black ocean; and from within its brightly lit interior, the raucous chorus of 'Daisy Bell' ('Give me your answer, do').

The *Christina* was a yacht on a Bond-villain scale of opulence. There were ten staterooms, marble bathtubs, a library and a salon, a cocktail bar featuring gold and silver ashtrays, a variety of lavishly appointed dens and corners, items of furniture from the reign of Louis XV, wood-burning fireplaces in the drawing rooms, and most spectacularly of all, a swimming pool with a minotaur theme. The theme, however, was not the spectacular part. Its real eye-popping feature was that it could be drained at the push of a button and transformed within minutes into a dance floor. If Onassis was feeling mischievous, the positions could quite easily be reversed at speed, with bewildered dancers finding their feet getting wet. Churchill's weakness for luxury would never be indulged elsewhere on such a scale. He was even permitted to take his pet budgerigar, Toby, on board.

Here was a life of ceaseless glamour; on one occasion, the famously elusive and retiring actress Greta Garbo dined with Churchill, and he begged her to return to the screen. On another, the great opera singer Maria Callas – who became Onassis's mistress – sat next to Churchill at lunch and attempted to feed him ice cream from her spoon, a display of coquetry which was observed with ill will by other members of the Churchill clan.

But there was one episode involving Callas that caused the same clan, including Celia Sandys, to whinny with laughter. The *Christina* had weighed anchor near the Greek city of Epidaurus, which boasts an astonishing ancient theatre. Maria Callas had once performed there under the open skies. Churchill's party arrived and found that the locals had been told in advance that he was coming. They had put up a vast floral V-sign in his honour. Callas instantly assumed the flowers were for her, and then became seethingly furious when she understood that they were not. She was later to remark (to the further delight of the Churchills): 'It's a pleasure to travel with Sir Winston. He removes from me some of the burden of my popularity.'

Once More to the Hustings

The General Election of 1959, Churchill's Last Battle

Harold Macmillan, successor to Anthony Eden and an early disciple of Churchill's, went to the polls in 1959 with the simple message that Britain's people had never had it so good. Labour leader Hugh Gaitskell begged to differ. Churchill was eighty-four by this time, and he was reselected in Woodford to fight one last election. The local posters were impressively stark: they simply featured the words 'Vote For' and then, below, a painted image of Churchill in an open-collared shirt. The idea was that he did not even have to be named. In a sense, this campaign would be an autumnal farewell tour, eventually culminating in his unveiling of a statue to himself – a living monument beside a bronze one. Even then, Churchill was still capable of surprise, as these newspaper reports from left-leaning newspapers throughout and after the election campaign illustrate.

'The words came haltingly last night, as from a tired old man,' reported Joyce Egginton in the *Daily News* on 30 September 1959. 'But the message was clear – a call for peaceful negotiations towards complete disarmament, coupled with the warning that western defence must not be based upon the deterrent power of the H-Bomb alone.'

This was a period of long marches and demonstrations staged by the Campaign for Nuclear Disarmament (CND), which was formed in 1958 following a call from the writer J. B. Priestley for unilateral disarmament: ranks of duffel coats, polo-neck sweaters and tortoiseshell glasses, misted in the rain. It is emphatically not a movement that anyone might have immediately associated Winston Churchill with. Just twelve years previously, he had told the Canadian prime minister Mackenzie King that it would be worth challenging Stalin's power over Eastern Europe by threatening to detonate an American atom bomb over Moscow. Yet in the intervening period, there had been a crucial change in his attitude: not only had Britain itself acquired nuclear weaponry, but both America and Britain had been testing the newest generation of mass destruction – the hydrogen bomb.

The Americans had tested their first in the Pacific; the result was 1,000 times more powerful than the bomb that had destroyed Hiroshima. It produced a light so intense that – with the eyes shut and covered – it was possible to see the bones in one's hand. The radiation fell like burning snow. This was a weapon that looked – to Churchill – like the end of the world. For a man educated in a system of cavalry charges and sabre-work – a man who had learned of war when the newly invented Maxim Gun was the deadliest weapon – the hydrogen bomb was in an entirely different philosophical realm. He would never be a unilateral disarmer, but he still had more in common with those young women and men of the CND than they might have thought.

In that Woodford election rally in 1959, journalist Egginton observed as 'Sir Winston reminded his audience – a crowded hall of several hundred, enthusiastic to the point of idolatry – of the Soviet Bloc's 'overwhelming superiority in guns, tanks, aircraft, submarines and sheer weight of manpower'.

Quietly and movingly he added: 'Against all this, western defence has been based upon the deterrent power of the nuclear bomb. Since no complete defence against the bomb has yet been found, any aggressor knows he would have to reckon upon retribution – swift, certain, and annihilating.

'From out of this deadlock there are no short-cuts. The only solution is disarmament applied to all kinds of weapons, freely accepted by all nations and guaranteed by effective international control.'

It was a great sign of hope, said Sir Winston, that the proposals which Mr Khrushchev – he pronounced it 'Krooshef' – put forward in New York were not essentially different from the plans which the British government had tabled to be examined by the new United Nations committee.

'But much remains to be done. We must above all resist any temptation to rush into agreements which do not provide a workable system of inspection and control. Not to be firm on this principle would be a great error.'

He began to speak slowly, sometimes faltering over his words. But they were words warmed by familiar Churchillian phrases . . .

Nuclear geopolitics aside, the voters that autumn gave Tory PM Harold Macmillan a thumping majority of 100 seats; the third election success in a row for the Conservatives. Churchill won once more in Woodford and Epping, a constituency that he had now served for thirty-five years. Various newspapers carried this pooled report of his reaction on election night: 'Sir Winston Churchill, in at Woodford with a slightly decreased majority, smoked a cigar as the result was declared – just after midnight. Wearing a white silk muffler under his black overcoat, Sir Winston shook hands with his Labour opponent, Arthur Latham, and said: "He will take away with him recollections of how very pleasant and agreeable an election in the Woodford constituency can be."'

A few days later came an event which might perhaps have felt to Churchill as though he were looking at his own monument or even tombstone. His constituents and local Conservatives had held fundraising events to have a statue of their great MP erected amid the chestnut trees of Woodford Green, a plush area that lay some way above the industrial pea-souper fogs of east London, some eight miles away. The special guest to preside over this ceremony was none other than Field Marshal Montgomery.

The event was covered by, among many others, a reporter from the *Sunday Dispatch* who especially relished the way that the old man stared up at his freshly unveiled graven image:

Sir Winston Churchill – in bronze – poses in a way everyone knows with his left hand pulling back the flap of his jacket as if reaching for his watch. And Sir Winston Churchill – the man – in black homburg, black overcoat, and white muffler, looks up at his eight ft tall sculptured self, towering on a five ft granite plinth.

He is pictured yesterday after Viscount Montgomery had unveiled the statue by David McFall on a hillock at Woodford Green in Sir Winston's constituency. Said Monty: 'He has been my friend, faithful and just to me. I can say, quite simply, that I love him and would do anything to prove the honour in which I hold him.'

Puppy-Kitten

Diana Churchill, October 1963

'Mrs Diana Churchill, eldest daughter of Sir Winston and Lady Churchill, and former wife of Mr (Duncan) Sandys... died suddenly at her home in Chester Row, Belgravia, it was announced last night', reported the *Daily Telegraph* on 21 October 1963. 'Lady Churchill, who is in Westminster Hospital for a rest, was not told the news by the hospital staff.'

Nor did the newspaper report on how the news was eventually conveyed to either Lady Churchill or to Sir Winston; or to whom this terrible task fell. Diana Churchill – who had been given the nickname 'Puppy-Kitten' as a baby – was just fifty-four years old; she had died of an overdose. In earlier years, she had suffered a breakdown – but it can't be known if this had a bearing on this tragedy. She left three grown-up children – Julian, Edwina and Celia.

A few weeks later, there was a memorial service at St Stephen Walbrook, a church in the City of London. Sir Winston and Lady Churchill were there, as was the wider family. The rector, the Reverend Chad Varah, presided. He was also the pioneering director of the Samaritans – an organization for which Diana Churchill had volunteered and which at that point was based in the precincts of the church.

'Most of us here knew Diana Churchill either as members of her family or as colleagues in the work of the Samaritans,' Varah said. 'It was in the room in that corner where she was accustomed to work, humbly and without publicity, in an office job regularly Mondays to Fridays, from nine to five or six ... We knew her as a loyal and friendly concerned person, warm and impulsive. Not all human beings are impulsive and those who are have advantages and disadvantages. Often they do and say things that more reserved people hesitate to do and say and those others are the losers because there are so many kind impulsive things that one can do and say.'

It is fruitless to try to imagine the grief: a second child lost. It is just possible that Churchill, now increasingly adrift in his own gathering infirmities, did not fully register it – or at least, not all of the time. The sadness for the rest of the family must have been illimitable. Diana's youngest daughter, Celia, already devoted to Churchill, now drew ever closer to him.

Down at the Old Bull and Bush

Ninety Years On, September 1964

A novel blend of harsh guitar dissonance and sweet, unbearably catchy melodies was filling the nation's air. This was the autumn of The Beatles' A Hard Day's Night, *an album which remained at number one for what seemed an eternity. They – and so many other bands – were also now being seen regularly on television via ITV's* Ready Steady Go! *and the BBC's recent inception of* Top of the Pops. *But they did not have overall command of the airwaves: light entertainment – as embodied by the Cliff Adams Singers, who performed everything from 1920s flapper favourites to covers of Elvis Presley – pleased those who were older than teenagers.*

Sir Winston Churchill – who had never taken to the medium of television, either to appear on it or simply to watch it – was to be honoured on the occasion of his ninetieth birthday: a lavish BBC show that would heavily feature the music of his own youth, when artistes like Florrie Forde, who had dressed and sung like a man, got music-hall audiences singing along.

'I heard that the Great Man fell asleep during the show and missed most of it,' recalled a BBC camera technician who had worked on *Ninety Years On*, broadcast in November 1964. 'I now know how he felt.'

Yet perhaps this is not quite fair. Churchill adored the old music-hall tunes. Just a few years previously, there had been a gala night in his constituency at the Wanstead Community Hall. Performing was a group called The Aspidistras, who had appeared on the BBC: their act was about music-hall nostalgia and Churchill was on stage with them, sitting on a form of dais, singing along lustily.

Ninety Years On was a rather more polished on-screen affair. Basically taking the form of a live variety show, it had lured in quite an astonishing array of talent. The script was by playwright Terence Rattigan, with extra contributions and music from Noël Coward. Among the performers was the ballet dancer Margot Fonteyn. Yet the core of it was still music and comedy from a different time, calculated to appeal to Churchill. Thus, the popular singer Kathy Kirby impersonated the music-hall star Marie Lloyd, to give ringing performances of 'My Old Man' and 'Down at the Old Bull and Bush'. There was comedy from the bespectacled Arthur Askey and from

younger Goon Harry Secombe; turns from Wilfrid Bram-
bell and Ian Carmichael; honeyed harmonies from the
Cliff Adams Singers (their radio show *Sing Something Simple*
was in terms of audience size every bit as popular as The
Beatles). And there were further songs from the Harrow
School Boys' Choir.

The essential point is that this was akin to a Royal Command Performance; it is difficult to imagine any other
politician being honoured with their own birthday show,
which would then be subsequently sold around the world.
Unlike the Royal Command, however, this was not performed in a theatre, but rather within the soundproofed
studios of the BBC Television Centre in White City.
Churchill was very old and very frail; he watched from his
home in Kensington.

He had made a fleeting public appearance that day to
acknowledge his ninetieth birthday. He was behind
a French window, supported by Clementine. Harold
Wilson – the new Labour prime minister – told the press
he had spoken to Sir Winston. Did they discuss modern
politics, asked one reporter. 'No,' replied Wilson, 'we talked
about forty years ago.'

An odd response: had they been discussing the General
Strike? Whatever the case, that slightly ghostly glimpse at
the window would be the last that the wider world would
see of Churchill.

Black Velvet

Russell Brain, January 1965

In an era when average life expectancy was barely seventy for both women and men, Churchill's ninetieth birthday had been a form of achievement in itself. But the curtain was drawing around his life. In January 1965, under the auspices of Dr Moran, Churchill was confined to a bed in the drawing room of his London home at Hyde Park Gate, an impossibly grand street mostly composed of tall stucco-fronted mansions (his was red-brick). Word of his failing health had reached the newspapers, and now Moran was issuing daily bulletins, largely assuring the public that Churchill was sleeping most of the time. But as these bulletins progressed, small crowds began to gather nearby at the railings of Kensington Gardens; the grieving had begun in advance of his surcease.

Churchill, though never renouncing his vague ideas of religion, confided to Dr Moran that he could not quite envisage heaven; what he saw instead was an expanse of 'black velvet' in which he would sleep. Moran also called upon his colleague, the neurologist Russell Brain, who observed Churchill's final hours as his children and wider family paid their daily visits in anticipation of the end.

'Charles Moran telephoned to say that Winston was not well and asked me to go and see him,' Brain later wrote in a short memoir. This was on 11 January 1965.

> I went between tea and dinner, picking up Moran on the way. As we drove there, he said that Winston was going down-hill and the last few days he had been increasingly

drowsy. We went straight to his room. His nurse said that he had deteriorated during the last few days. He could no longer stand unsupported . . .

He lay in bed with both eyes closed, peacefully. One could get a little response to questions – a grunt only, and he would not put out his tongue for me. He was like someone in a deep sleep. I could not detect any evidence of a fresh cerebral lesion, and both his plantars were flexor. I told Charles Moran I thought this was an episode of cerebral ischaemia and it was terminal. We went in to see Lady Churchill in the sitting room. She said he had been deteriorating recently. He could no longer feed himself, which had been embarrassing, and it meant he had had to have meals in his own room. I said he was seriously ill. I did not see him again but continued to discuss his case with Moran on the telephone.

On January 12th, I advised nasal feeding and an antibiotic – Achromycin. On January 13th Moran rang up and said that he now had weakness of the left arm and leg. How long would he live – two days? I said it might well be a week . . . January 15th: Moran said Churchill was worse and a bulletin would have to be issued. We agreed on terms. I had asked Moran on January 11th how much Winston took in about his birthday. Moran said it was hard to know. There had been a music hall broadcast in the evening [that is, *Ninety Years On*] and they thought he had appreciated some of it.

Lady Churchill said it had been very depressing that he had been so unhappy recently.

That unhappiness was soon to cease. Churchill died on 24 January.

Afterword

The State Funeral – The World's Final Meeting

As death approaches, the fears of the powerful and of the humble converge sharply and become the same. Yet in those final darkening hours, there was a hint of solace. Churchill was never alone; and he was loved. Amid all the sadness that he carried in that old heart, he was surrounded with warmth.

'At about 8 o clock in the morning my grandfather died,' wrote Celia Sandys. 'I was at his bedside with my aunts Sarah and Mary, my uncle Randolph and his son Winston. Ten days before he had suffered a serious stroke . . . we visited him every day. We would find him sleeping peacefully with his faithful marmalade cat snuggled up beside him . . . As he got older, it was clear that he was growing tired of life and frail. There were moments when he perked up but a lot of the time he would sit in silence staring at the fire while he puffed at his cigar.'

Celia Sandys's own mother, Diana Churchill, had passed away so tragically just over a year previously. It is not unreasonable to imagine that when Churchill sat by that fire, he thought of her, and also of his two-year-old daughter Marigold, both in their graves. Even amid the dense fogs of illness and age, the grief must still have been as keen as a blade. Though there was no cause for self-recrimination – just simple, terrible, bitter sadness – to have buried his own children must have haunted him to the end.

He knew his own grave awaited. He knew that his own

state funeral had been planned meticulously – even if (uncharacteristically) he had declined to become too involved. Partly this was because Her Majesty the Queen had been consulted heavily. And it is also possible to imagine (in the days before he needed round-the-clock nurses) that as Churchill sat and stared at those flames, he evaluated – in the manner of a true historian – his own position and influence upon the tide of affairs. He had suggested to aides in latter years that he felt that there was more that he could have done; that his vast experience might have helped in an unstable world. We can envisage him gazing into that fire and thinking of the intensity and the horrors not just of World War Two, but also of the charnel-house conflict of the Great War before it. Did he think back to Sudan, and to India, and to even more distant days when a man might be said to turn the course of a battle?

Yet there he was, beside that fire with his cigar, in the company of an affectionate marmalade cat. There were worse places to be. One curious fact: Churchill had always foretold to his wife that he would die on the very day that his father had died: 24 January. And so it proved.

The news of his death brought a public reaction that suggested a wider public that somehow knew him personally, or at least had an extremely strong emotional connection. They felt they had met him, even if they had not. The responses were led by Her Majesty the Queen, whose message was addressed to Lady Churchill. 'The news of Sir Winston's death caused inexpressible grief to me and my husband,' she said. 'We send our deepest sympathy to you and your family. The whole world is poorer by the loss of his many-sided genius while the survival of this country and the sister nations of the Commonwealth, in the face of the greatest danger that has ever threatened them, will be a perpetual memorial to his leadership, his vision and his indomitable courage.'

Other tributes from leading politicians were equally moving. 'It was Sir Winston, above all others, with his passionate hatred of evil, who rallied the nation against tyranny,' said Sir Alec Douglas-Home, former PM and Tory Leader of the Opposition, 'and who, by his will-power and courage, swung the balance of war from defeat to victory.'

Prime Minister Harold Wilson showed a shrewder, more intelligent appreciation of Churchill as a landmark. 'Sir Winston will be mourned all over the world by all who owe so much to him. He is now at peace after a life in which he created history and which will be remembered as long as history is read.'

There were other powerful words, from old comrades around the world. Former US President Truman, as well as praising Churchill's 'intrepid spirit' in 'defeating the forces of evil and darkness', added more poignantly: 'He was my very good friend.' In France, President de Gaulle, who had argued so bitterly with Churchill throughout the war, declared that 'for all in my country, and for myself, Sir Winston . . . contributed powerfully to the salvation of the French people and to the liberty of the world. In the great drama, he was the greatest.' But he also sent a separate, more emotional message to Lady Churchill. 'I see disappear in the person of so great a man, my wartime companion and my friend,' he told her.

The great man would first lie in state at Westminster Hall, giving the public a chance to view his catafalque and pay their own respects. As we have all seen recently following the death of Her Majesty Queen Elizabeth II, there is an elemental power about the stark, centuries-old surroundings of the Hall, dominated by the coffin raised on a dais and framed with candles. But more than this: it was also one of those rare historical moments when – away from the noise and drama of newspapers and television and radio and popular entertainment – another side of the public was revealed.

In the intervening twenty years since the war, many of those who had fought in it – in all those different theatres of conflict around the world – had kept silence on their return; they had tried to bury trauma and grief for the sake of reconstructing their families. War was not spoken of at home. But days such as these, when the nation was suspended in remembrance, made a wider form of grieving possible too.

On Wednesday 27 January, after the prime minister and senior politicians had paid homage at the catafalque, other groups composed of former soldiers joined the line. 'War-blinded and disabled [sic], wearing their medals, went to Westminster Hall today,' reported the *Coventry Evening Telegraph*. 'It was a touching scene as some in wheelchairs were pushed by friends. Other disabled moved past the black-draped catafalque on crutches or with the aid of walking sticks. The blind filed through the Hall, touching the shoulder of a friend.'

For those three days of Churchill lying in state, the Hall remained open throughout the nights. 'Soon after 4 am,' ran another report, 'charladies, on their way to work, were among the first of the new crowds at the Hall.' This was Swinging London, 1965, yet the vast majority of those in this groovy city were living lives that would have been recognizable a hundred years previously. 'They came in small groups, wearing their coloured headscarves – for once, their gay morning chatter silenced – to file past the catafalque.' Churchill, in death, had transcended the old hostilities of class.

'It was like a stage set,' said Colin Frewin, who was taken to see Churchill's coffin as a small boy. The queue to get into the Hall stretched right back across to the south side of the Thames. It was 'dark and cold and very solemn – an amazing experience for a child'. Some 320,000 people came to see the coffin in those three days.

That January cold deepened on the day of the funeral itself. The iron chimes of Big Ben vibrated through the frozen white-misted air at 9.45 a.m., Saturday 30 January. There was a ninety-gun salute in Hyde Park. Churchill's coffin was borne out by the 2nd Battalion Grenadier Guards, placed upon a gun carriage and draped in a Union flag. In front of that gun carriage were ninety-eight sailors; they would be pulling through the streets eastward, with forty sailors behind, the rhythm of their pace held by a Royal Navy drummer. Behind the sailors walked Churchill's son Randolph, his grandson Winston and other male members of the Churchill clan. His widow, his daughters and granddaughters were in horse-drawn carriages.

An hour later, the carriage and the cortege drew up Ludgate Hill to St Paul's Cathedral, where the coffin was met by the pallbearers. There were honorary pallbearers too, walking ahead of the coffin: among them were Anthony Eden, Harold Macmillan and – extraordinarily, given his own great age of eighty-two – former prime minister Clement Attlee (now Earl Attlee, having been raised to the House of Lords).

In Attlee's case, the bond stretched back decades; he was among those who had fought in the Gallipoli campaign of 1915, and unlike many, he had never blamed Churchill for its failure. And Churchill and Attlee had worked side by side in the war against Hitler; the gulf between their political beliefs had always been bridged by outbreaks of genuine warmth. Now, on the steps of St Paul's, Attlee sank under the effort. He temporarily buckled and stumbled backwards, which threatened to unbalance the pallbearers behind; two soldiers jumped up to steady him, and the casket, and restore balance. But Attlee had been very insistent on performing this honorary duty – a final gesture of respect and friendship.

'From where we stood,' wrote former Royal Marine Michael Kernan, who had surveyed the wider scene outside the cathedral, 'I could see the Argyll and Sutherland Highlanders and all I could think was: "They must be frozen in their kilts." Because it was the coldest day ever. It was bitter, even in my uniform, with long trousers and greatcoat.'

Churchill, it has been observed, would have adored the choice of hymns – they were his favourites. Among them were 'He Who Would Valiant Be' and 'O God, Our Help in Ages Past'. It was also noted that the Queen broke protocol on this day; in every other circumstance, the monarch is the last to arrive, taking ultimate precedence. On this occasion, she was among the first. In addition, she and other royals did not leave first, as royal protocol normally demands. Instead, Lady Churchill and the family led the procession, with the Queen following.

On leaving the cathedral, the coffin was then carried by the Grenadier Guards through the soot-blackened streets of the City, down to Tower Hill and the River Thames, that 'silver thread that runs through history', where a launch called MV *Havengore* was waiting. The coffin was piped aboard by naval ratings; and as it set sail up the still-working Thames, riverside crane operators in what was then the Pool of London (roughly where Hay's Galleria is now) lowered those cranes as a gesture of respect that had not been anticipated by the authorities. Some years later, it was claimed that these dock workers – who were not usually there on Saturday afternoons – had been bribed (presumably by officials in the Port of London Authority) to man and lower the cranes; but there were those among them who were adamant that this had been a spontaneous gesture on their parts.

As the launch progressed upstream through the dirty, freezing waters, the skies above roared with a fly-past – sixteen RAF 'Electric Lightning' fighter jets: silvery, stubby, dart-like. These were the one futuristic element in a day otherwise steeped in visual tradition. The coffin made the shore at Festival Pier, near the Royal Festival Hall, and was carried thence to Waterloo station, where a specially commissioned train awaited. Here again was one of those curious signs of an epoch in transition. The steam engine that was to convey Churchill's coffin took a form that would have been familiar to Charles Dickens – and indeed to the youthful Churchill. A similar steam locomotive, running at midnight, would have carried him down to Camberley, in time to sneak back into his Sandhurst barracks. But many trains were now being pulled by diesel locomotives; the electrification of railways was mooted. In 1965, steam engines were starting to be phased out; by 1968, they would be gone completely. By the 1970s, they would look like the very quaintest antiques. This steam engine was bound for Hanborough railway station in Oxfordshire.

And from there, Churchill was carried to the graveyard of St Martin's Church in Bladon, just minutes' walk from his birthplace of Blenheim Palace, and the last resting place of generations of Spencer-Churchills. Bladon itself is a pretty prospect of Cotswold stone, deep sunsets giving it an amber glow.

And Churchill's gravestone – flat, rectangular, grey Portland stone, modern yet carved with an eye to tradition – was a final dash of nonconformity. He had been guaranteed a final resting place among kings in Westminster Abbey, as befitted a leader of his unusual stature; yet he was determined in death that he should be returned to the bosom of his family in Oxfordshire. Twelve years later, in 1977, his widow Clementine followed him on the longest journey. She was buried with him. The grave remains an almost too-popular site of secular pilgrimage today; and it is tended by the family.

The mourning was not universal, however: just seventy-two hours after Churchill died, Evelyn Waugh wrote to his friend Ann Fleming, wife of 007 creator Ian: 'He was not a man for whom I ever had esteem. Always in the wrong, always surrounded by crooks, a most unsuccessful father – simply a "Radio Personality" who outlived his prime. "Rallied the nation" indeed! I was a serving soldier in 1940. How we despised his orations.'

Waugh had missed the point, though (and rather snobbishly too, since he was assuming only he was clever enough not to be taken in). No one ever looked at Churchill and imagined that he was perfect. Not even the most devoted of his Woodford constituents would have thought that he was a paragon of selflessness. That was not what they – or indeed a nation under the storm clouds of war – were looking for.

Churchill was admired and loved because he *galvanized*. He took his own extraordinary energy, his astonishing language, and aimed it like an electrifying thunderbolt. It wasn't moral high-mindedness that many people were looking for; it was confidence. He had the preternatural ability to communicate a kind of good-cheered strength (even if he personally was suffering crises of self-doubt).

And the proof that Waugh had misjudged his fellow citizens can be traced right the way through Churchill's life. Whether those who met him loved him or despised him, they each saw some kind of an essence that he never sought to disguise.

However, Waugh might be forgiven – being too close to events – for not realizing that Churchill the historian had already burnished himself into that history by the time of his death, and not merely through the five weighty volumes of his own account and study of World War Two. When Churchill was informed in 1953 that he had won the Nobel Prize, he was transfigured with happiness – until it was pointed out to him that it was for literature; he had wanted the Nobel Peace Prize, for that was how he fundamentally understood himself – the man who achieved peace, rather than the man who waged war.

In the gathering twilight of his life, Churchill had continued to imagine that he might have helped in brokering some form of understanding between West and East. Waugh might have snorted at this. But Churchill's image in history was always going to have greater depth and range than war alone. If anything, it was Dean Acheson who had summed up what would become the central historical fascination: Churchill's weirdly charismatic power of leadership.

In historical terms, it is now very old-fashioned, if not downright reactionary and sinister, to believe in a 'Great Man' theory: that one individual through sheer force of hypnotic personality can mould the days to come. Historians examine huge numbers of other factors – ranging from economic to social to geographic – when seeking to analyse and explain the past. History in this sense is akin to meteorology: there are thousands upon thousands of different factors and events and pressure points to be weighed and taken into consideration when examining anything as complex as conflict – especially a conflict on the extraordinary scale of World War Two. In this sense, Churchill ought – and does – take his place amid explorations of dissolving empires, of modern industrialization and economic insecurity, of nationalism and global trade. Yet somehow that endlessly energetic – even eccentric – persona always contrarily appears, by some mischievous illusion, to transcend such concerns. It shouldn't, but it does. Even in today's ringing denunciations of Churchill's seething racism, there is some sense of exceptionalism. Many of his colleagues on both sides of the House held identically abhorrent views, but Churchill is seen as uniquely culpable.

And in that sense, the continuing fascination on all sides can't really be described as 'hero worship'. Whether through repulsion or – equally frequently – through laughter, his is simply a personality that always seems to invite, to demand, further analysis. Even if compared to characters from Shakespeare, he is both colourfully present and always somehow elusive. Sometimes he is Henry V; other times he is Sir Toby Belch. But unlike Iago, who declared 'I am not what I am', Churchill always was what he was.

This was articulated best by one of his last secretaries, Jane Portal (later Lady Williams of Elvel) who described him thus: 'He had warmth and humour and there was no pretence about him. When he was mad, you knew it. When he was sad, he wept. When he was gay, he laughed like a child.

'In a word, he was all truth.'

Acknowledgements

My initial thanks are extended not to a person, but to an institution: the London Library, the stacks of which are a source of illimitable wonder, and which one could spend a lifetime exploring.

Deep gratitude is due to Viking editorial director Connor Brown, who set the hare running and then also – with fine judgement and ingenuity – ensured that it stayed on the right course.

Also huge thanks at Viking for the brilliance of Daniel Crewe (publishing director), Olivia Mead (publicity), Emma Brown (editorial management), Annie Underwood (production), Jane Delaney (inventory management) and a particular tribute to Kyla Dean (sales). Huge appreciation also to Gemma Wain, whose copy-editing is wise, precise, witty, knowledgeable and elegant. And, as ever, a very deep bow to my brilliant agent Anna Power, who made it all happen.

And Where Did We First Meet . . . ?

A Selected Bibliography

References and sources by encounter – in order of appearance.

Overture, 1914: Margot Asquith, *Margot Asquith's Great War Diary 1914–16: The View from Downing Street*, edited by Michael and Eleanor Brock (Oxford University Press 2014).

Elizabeth Everest, 1879–89: Winston Churchill, *My Early Life* (Thornton Butterworth, 1930).

Leo Amery, 1886: Leo Amery, *My Political Life*, Volume 1: *England before the Storm, 1896–1914* (Hutchinson, 1953).

Ian Hamilton, 1896: Ian Hamilton, *Listening for the Drums* (Faber, 1944).

Pamela Plowden, 1896: Churchill's correspondence; John Colville, *The Churchillians* (Weidenfeld and Nicolson, 1981).

Herbert Kitchener, 1898: Churchill, *My Early Life*.

John Robert Clynes, 1900: J. R. Clynes, *The Rt. Hon. J. R. Clynes: Memoirs, 1869–1924* (Hutchinson, 1937).

Sidney and Beatrice Webb, 1903–1908: Lisanne Radice, *Beatrice and Sidney Webb: Fabian Socialists* (Macmillan, 1984).

Violet Asquith, 1906: Violet Bonham Carter, *Lantern Slides: The Diaries and Letters of Violet Bonham Carter 1904–1914*, edited by Mark Pottle (Weidenfeld and Nicolson, 1996).

Mahatma Gandhi, 1906: The British Newspaper Archive; Amery, *My Political Life*.

Ethel Barrymore, 1906: This, and other romances, are detailed in Michael Shelden, *Young Titan: The Making of Winston Churchill* (Simon and Schuster, 2013), which, possibly to his surprise, was serialized with maximum salaciousness by the *Daily Mail*.

Edward Marsh, 1907 onwards: Edward Marsh, *A Number of People: A Book of Reminiscences* (William Heinemann, 1939).

Clementine Hozier, 1908: Of whom Sonia Purnell has written movingly in *First Lady: The Life and Wars of Clementine Churchill* (Aurum Press, 2016).

Violet Asquith, 1908: Bonham Carter, *Lantern Slides*.

The Siege of Sidney Street, 1911: Articles from contemporary popular newspapers *Reynold's, News* and the *Daily Mirror*.

Ottoline Morrell, 1911: Miranda Seymour, *Ottoline Morrell: A Life on the Grand Scale* (Hodder and Stoughton, 1992).

W. Somerset Maugham, 1912: W. Somerset Maugham, *The Partial View: Containing 'The Summing Up' and 'A Writer's Notebook'* (Heinemann, 1954).

David Lloyd George, 1914: Asquith, *Margot Asquith's Great War Diary 1914–16*.

H. G. Wells, 1915: H. G. Wells, *Experiment in Autobiography: Discoveries and Conclusions of a Very Ordinary Brain (since 1866)* (Victor Gollancz, 1934).

H. H. Asquith, 1914: Asquith, *Margot Asquith's Great War Diary 1914–16*.

Rupert Brooke, 1915: Nigel Jones, *Rupert Brooke: Life, Death and Myth* (Richard Cohen, 1999).

Lady Gwendoline Churchill and Company, 1915: Asquith, *Margot Asquith's Great War Diary 1914–16*.

Ivor Novello, 1917: James Harding, *Ivor Novello* (Welsh Academic Press, 1997).

Clare Sheridan, 1920: Clare Sheridan, *My Crowded Sanctuary* (Methuen, 1945).

Marigold Churchill, 1921: The terrible sadness is conveyed in *Speaking for Themselves: The Personal Letters of Winston and Clementine Churchill*, edited by Mary Soames (Black Swan, 1999).

Edwin Lutyens, 1921: Mary Lutyens, *Edwin Lutyens by His Daughter Mary Lutyens* (John Murray, 1980).

T. E. Lawrence, 1922: T. E. Lawrence, *The Letters of T. E. Lawrence*, edited by David Garnett (Jonathan Cape, 1938).

The People of Epping, 1924: The British Newspaper Archive.

Barbara Cartland, 1924: Barbara Cartland, *We Danced All Night* (Hutchinson, 1970).

John Maynard Keynes, 1925: Robert Skidelsky, *John Maynard Keynes: A Biography*, Volume 2 (Macmillan, 1992).

The General Strike, 1926: The British Newspaper Archive.

John Reith, 1926: John Charles Walsham Reith, *The Reith Diaries*, edited by Charles Stuart (Collins, 1975).

Walter Sickert, 1927: Marjorie Lilly, *Sickert: The Painter and His Circle* (Elek, 1971).

Jennie Lee, 1929: Jennie Lee, *This Great Journey: A Volume of Autobiography 1904–45* (MacGibbon and Kee, 1963); *My Life with Nye* (Jonathan Cape, 1980).

P. G. Wodehouse, 1929: Robert McCrum, *Wodehouse: A Life* (Viking, 2004).

Charlie Chaplin, 1929: Charles Chaplin, *My Autobiography* (The Bodley Head, 1964).

Brendan Bracken, 1929: Andrew Doyle, *Poor, Dear Brendan: The Quest for Brendan Bracken* (Hutchinson, 1974).

Maurice Ashley, 1929: 'As I Knew Him: Churchill in the Wilderness', a lecture delivered on 19 August 1989 by Dr Maurice Ashley CBE, Proceedings of the International Churchill Societies.

Frederick Lindemann, 1931: Adrian Fort, *Prof: The Life of Frederick Lindemann* (Jonathan Cape, 2003).

New York City, 1931: Winston Churchill, *The Gathering Storm* (Cassell and Company, 1948).

Ernst Hanfstaengl, 1932: Ibid.

Albert Einstein, 1933: Andrew Robinson, *Einstein on the Run* (Yale University Press, 2019).

Alexander Korda, 1934: Charles Drazin, *Korda: Britain's Only Movie Mogul* (Sidgwick and Jackson, 2002).

The Grand Opening of the Woodford Majestic, 1934: The British Newspaper Archive.

Vic Oliver, 1936: Vic Oliver, *Mr Showbusiness: The Autobiography of Vic Oliver* (George G. Harrap, 1954).

Edward VIII, 1936: Philip Ziegler, *King Edward VIII: The Official Biography* (Collins, 1990).

George VI, 1937: His letter is reproduced in Churchill, *The Gathering Storm*.

Ivan Maisky, 1937: Ivan Maisky, *The Complete Maisky Diaries*, edited by Gabriel Gorodetsky (Yale University Press, 2017); Churchill, *The Gathering Storm*.

Harold Macmillan, 1938: Harold Macmillan, *The Blast of War, 1939–45* (Macmillan, 1967).

Colin Thornton-Kemsley, 1939: David A. Thomas, *Churchill: The Member for Woodford* (Frank Cass, 1995).

Noël Coward, 1939: Noël Coward, *Future Indefinite* (Heinemann, 1954).

Vic Oliver's Flat, 1939: Oliver, *Mr Showbusiness*.

Charles de Gaulle, 1940: Among others, Jonathan Fenby, *The General: Charles de Gaulle and the France He Saved* (Simon and Schuster, 2010).

Bernard Montgomery, 1940: Bernard Law Montgomery, *The Memoirs of Field Marshal Montgomery* (Collins, 1958).

Reginald Victor Jones, 1940: Among others, R. V. Jones, *Most Secret War* (Hamish Hamilton, 1978).

Cosmo Gordon Lang, 1940: J. G. Lockhart, *Cosmo Gordon Lang* (Hodder and Stoughton, 1949).

Ivan Maisky, 1940: Maisky, *The Complete Maisky Diaries*.

Vivien Leigh, 1940: Hugo Vickers, *Vivien Leigh* (Hamish Hamilton, 1988).

John Reith, 1940: Reith, *The Reith Diaries*.

Cecil Beaton, 1940: Hugo Vickers, *Cecil Beaton: The Authorised Biography* (Weidenfeld and Nicolson, 1985).

Lady Diana Cooper, 1941: Diana Cooper, *Darling Monster: The Letters of Lady Diana Cooper to Her Son John Julius Norwich*, edited by Viscount John Julius Norwich (Chatto and Windus, 2013).

Nancy Astor, 1941: Christopher Sykes, *Nancy: The Life of Lady Astor* (Collins, 1972).

Franklin D. Roosevelt, 1941: Among others, Ted Morgan, *FDR: A Biography* (Simon and Schuster, 1985).

The Bletchley Park Codebreakers: Gordon Welchman, *The Hut Six Story: Breaking the Enigma Codes* (Allen Lane, 1982); John Herivel, *Herivelismus and the German Military Enigma* (M. and M. Baldwin, 2008).

Evelyn Duncan, 1941: The British Newspaper Archive.

Eric Ambler, 1941: Eric Ambler, *Here Lies: An Autobiography* (Weidenfeld and Nicolson, 1985).

James Chuter-Ede, 1942: James Chuter-Ede, *Labour and the Wartime Coalition: From the Diary of James Chuter-Ede, 1941–1945*, edited by K. Jeffreys (The Historians' Press, 1987).

Dwight D. Eisenhower, 1942: Piers Brendon, *Ike: The Life and Times of Dwight D. Eisenhower* (Secker and Warburg, 1987).

Joseph Stalin, 1942: Among others, Donald Gillies, *Radical Diplomat: The Life of Archibald Clark Kerr, Lord Inverchapel, 1882–1951* (I. B. Tauris, 1999).

Stanley Baldwin, 1943: H. Montgomery Hyde, *Baldwin: The Unexpected Prime Minister* (Hart-Davis MacGibbon, 1973).

Henry Wallace, 1943: Of whom there is a full biography: John Culver, *American Dreamer: The Life and Times of Henry Wallace* (W. W. Norton, 2000).

Anthony Eden, 1943: Pathé News.

Lady Diana Cooper, 1944: Cooper, *Darling Monster*.

Niels Bohr, 1944: Ruth Moore, *Niels Bohr: The Man and the Scientist* (Hodder and Stoughton, 1967).

Alan Brooke, 1944: Field Marshal Lord Alanbrooke, *War Diaries 1939–45*, edited by A. Danchev and D. Todman (Weidenfeld and Nicolson, 2001).

The London Crowds, 1945: The British Newspaper Archive.

Berliners, 1945: The *Manchester Guardian*.

Harry S. Truman, 1945: Among others, Robert Ferrell, *Harry S. Truman: A Life* (University of Missouri, 1994).

The Constituents of Woodford Green, 1945: The British Newspaper Archive.

Harry S. Truman, 1946: Ferrell, *Harry S. Truman*.

Dean Acheson, 1946: Among others, Dean Acheson, *Present at the Creation: My Years in the State Department* (Hamish Hamilton, 1970).

Christopher Soames, 1947: Among others, Brough Scott, *Churchill at the Gallop: Winston's Life in the Saddle* (Racing Post Books, 2017)

Lord Beaverbrook, 1949: Michael Wardell, 'Churchill's Dagger: A Memoir of Capponcina', published in Canadian general interest magazine *The Atlantic Advocate*, 1965.

Anuerin Bevan, Jennie Lee and Harold Wilson, 1951: Lee, *My Life with Nye*; Harold Wilson, *A Prime Minister on Prime Ministers* (Weidenfeld and Nicolson, 1977).

Lord Beaverbrook, 1951: Logan Gourlay (editor), *The Beaverbrook I Knew* (Quartet Books, 1980).

Laurence Olivier and Richard Burton, 1951–3: Laurence Olivier, *Confessions of an Actor* (Weidenfeld and Nicolson, 1982); BBC archives; the British Newspaper Archive.

Clarissa Spencer-Churchill, 1952: The British Newspaper Archive.

Elizabeth II, 1953: The British Newspaper Archive.

Russell Brain, 1953–65: Brain's account, published by his son Michael in *Medical History*, vol. 44 (2000) under the title 'Encounters with Winston Churchill'.

Prince Charles and Christopher Long, 1953: Prince Charles, speaking at a 2013 BAFTA event when the recovered Balmoral film footage was screened; Christopher Long, various articles written for *Finest Hour: Journal of the Churchill Centre and Societies*.

Churchill and Immigration, 1954: Immigration and cabinet papers, drawn from national newspaper reports in 2005.

Bessie Braddock, 1954: Jack Braddock and Bessie Bamber Braddock, *The Braddocks* (Macdonald, 1963).

Churchill's Resignation, 1955: Among others, Colville, *The Churchillians*; the British Newspaper Archive.

Harry S. Truman, 1956: Pathé News; the British Newspaper Archive; Chartwell, National Trust.

Charlie Chaplin, 1956: Chaplin, *My Autobiography*.

Aristotle Onassis, 1958–63: The British Newspaper Archive.

The General Election of 1959: The British Newspaper Archive.

Diana Churchill, 1963: The British Newspaper Archive.

Ninety Years On, 1964: The British Film Institute; the British Newspaper Archive; BBC archives.

Russell Brain, 1965: Brain, 'Encounters with Winston Churchill'.

Index

WSC indicates Winston Spencer Churchill.

BERLIN
SINCLAIR MCKAY

Throughout the twentieth century, Berlin stood at the centre of a convulsing world. This history is often viewed as separate acts: the suffering of the First World War; the cosmopolitan city of science, culture and sexual freedom Berlin became; steep economic plunges; the rise of the Nazis; the destruction of the Second World War; the psychosis of genocide; and a city rent in two by competing ideologies. But people do not live their lives in fixed eras. An epoch ends, yet the people continue – or try to continue – much as they did before. Berlin tells the story of the city as seen through the eyes not of its rulers, but of those who walked its streets.

How did those ideologies – fascism and communism – come to flower so fully here? And how did their repercussions continue to be felt throughout Europe and the West right up until that extraordinary night in the autumn of 1989 when the Wall – that final expression of totalitarian oppression – was at last breached? You cannot understand the twentieth century without understanding Berlin; and you cannot understand Berlin without understanding the experiences of its people. Drawing on a staggering breadth of culture – from art to film, opera to literature, science to architecture – McKay's latest masterpiece shows us this hypnotic city as never before.

> 'A masterful account of a city marked by infamy . . . If there is a book that must be read this year, this is it'
>
> Amanda Foreman

> 'Stunning . . . It's eye-opening, enlightening and wonderfully told'
>
> Norman Ohler, author of *Blitzed*

> 'An electrifying new account of Berlin'
>
> Julia Boyd, author of *Travellers in the Third Reich*

WWW.PENGUIN.CO.UK

DRESDEN
SINCLAIR MCKAY

The *Sunday Times* bestseller

In February 1945 the Allies obliterated Dresden, the 'Florence of the Elbe'. Bombs weighing over 1,000 lbs fell every seven and a half seconds and an estimated 25,000 people were killed. Was Dresden a legitimate military target or was the bombing a last act of atavistic mass murder in a war already won?

From the history of the city to the attack itself, conveyed in a minute-by-minute account from the first of the flares to the flames reaching almost a mile high – the wind so searingly hot that the lungs of those in its path were instantly scorched – through the eerie period of reconstruction, bestselling author Sinclair McKay creates a vast canvas and brings it alive with touching human detail.

Impeccably researched and deeply moving, McKay uses never-before-seen sources to relate the untold stories of civilians and vividly conveys the texture of contemporary life. Writing with warmth and colour about morality in war, the instinct for survival, the gravity of mass destruction and the importance of memory, this is a master historian at work.

'Powerful . . . grips by its passion and originality'

Max Hastings, *Sunday Times*

'Beautifully crafted, elegiac, compelling . . . a masterpiece of its genre'

Damien Lewis, author of *Zero Six Bravo*

'He makes Dresden come alive, before, during, and after the infernal 13th'

John Lewis-Stempel, *Daily Express*

WWW.PENGUIN.CO.UK